DONALD S. ZAGORIA is an Associate Professor of Government at Hunter College, The City University of New York, and Director of its Research Institute on Modern Asia. Formerly an analyst with the RAND Corporation, Dr. Zagoria has traveled widely in Asia and is currently a member of the National Committee on U.S.–China relations. He recently testified before the Senate Foreign Relations Committee hearings on China.

Dr. Zagoria has contributed widely to professional journals on the subject of Communism; his publications include articles for *The China Quarterly, Foreign Affairs,* and *Asian Survey.* His book, *Sino-Soviet Conflict,* has been translated into six languages. He is currently working on a book on Indian Communism.

VIETNAM TRIANGLE

Moscow, Peking, Hanoi

BY DONALD S. ZAGORIA

PEGASUS NEW YORK

The author wishes to acknowledge
the support he received
in the course of the preparation
of this study from the
Research Institute on Communist Affairs,
Columbia University.

CONTENTS

ACKNOWLEDGMENTS

It is with sincere gratitude that I wish to acknowledge at this time the support given to me in my continuing work on Asian communism by friendly institutions and individuals, of which this study is just a small part. The Rockefeller Foundation sponsored my trip to Asia in 1963 to assess the impact of the Sino-Soviet dispute on the Asian Communist parties. The Contemporary China Committee of Columbia University, headed by Professor A. Doak Barnett, has generously provided me with research and typing assistance. The staff of the Research Institute on Communist Affairs has been unfailingly helpful; my particular thanks go to Christine Dodson. Marian Kirsch, my research assistant, prepared a preliminary draft of Chapter Two. Chapter Three was originally written for a conference on Chinese foreign policy sponsored by The Center for Policy Study at the University of Chicago, and I want to express my thanks to the Center for allowing me to publish it here in somewhat modified form.

The constructive comment and criticism of several of my colleagues at Columbia University have been most helpful, and I am especially indebted to Seweryn Bialer, Zbigniew Brzezinski, Alexander Dallin, Kevin Devlin, and Joseph Starobin, as well as to a long-standing friend, H. S. Ruhe of New York. My appreciation goes to Victor Zorza, who has provided in his *Manchester Guardian* articles some of the best continuing commentaries on relations among the Communist parties. Thanks is due also to my wife Janet, whose acute suggestions have sharpened this book and who has patiently borne the burdens it has involved.

Let me finally express my keen sense of loss at the tragic and premature death of Bernard Fall. It was my privilege to know him and to benefit from his unrivaled knowledge of Vietnam and its war.

PREFACE

As THE discussion of the Vietnam war has warmed both here and abroad, one glaring gap, among others, has become increasingly apparent. This concerns our inability or refusal to come to grips with the complex interactions among the different Communist protagonists directly involved in the struggle. Each one of these protagonists—North Vietnam, Communist China, the Soviet Union, and, last but not least, the People's Revolutionary Party, which leads the National Liberation Front of South Vietnam—has its own particular interests and points of view, and these, while ostensibly geared to the common goal of ultimate triumph in South Vietnam, do not necessarily coincide. Indeed, they often conflict. In order to accommodate one another's goals, the four Communist parties are forced to compromise in ways substantially affecting their policies in Vietnam. Therefore, the divergencies among them cannot be safely ignored. In fact, an assessment of their differences is crucial to any appreciation of Communist strategies in Vietnam.

As one whose professional interests over the past fifteen years have been the study of politics within the international Communist movement, I am keenly aware of the handicaps that are suffered when access to the decision-making process is denied. There is one—and only one—research technique that can be used to compensate for this handicap. That is the one popularly known as Kremlinology, a technique poorly understood by laymen and academic specialists alike. For reasons that I cannot explore here, but which any student of medieval theology would readily understand, a close and systematic reading of the pronouncements of any Communist party or leader—when compared to the pronouncements of other Communists parties and/or leaders within the same party—yields important and indispensable clues to the strategic and tactical debates taking place within the Communist world. The increasing pluralism of the Communist world and the growing tendency of smaller Communist parties and states to act on their divergent interests have made this technique more fruitful than ever.

In this context, it seems to me that Kremlinology—properly used—can provide us with invaluable insights into Communist policies in Vietnam. It is no accident that the two earliest and most valuable analyses of Peking–Hanoi differences over the way to fight the war in Vietnam were written by analysts who employed this technique—Victor Zorza of the *Manchester Guardian* and David Mozingo and Tom Robinson of The RAND Corporation. Zorza was also the first journalist to uncover the early clues of conflict between Moscow and Peking almost a decade ago.

While I have employed this technique in assessing Communist policies in Vietnam, I am also keenly aware of its limitations. The clues and insights into the Communist decision-making process it offers are necessary—but not sufficient—to understand Communist policies and politics. For such understanding, it is necessary to fit the information available from a variety of sources and techniques into a larger framework of analysis. The larger framework I employ here is the global relationship of the three major powers, the Soviet Union, Communist China, and the United States. Apart from the forces which Vietnam has generated on its own, the present situation there cannot really be assessed except in the framework of the big-power conflict. For example, this conflict explains why, contrary to the expectations of some analysts, the Vietnam war has not only failed to heal the Sino-Soviet rift but has indeed driven these two powers farther apart.

Unfortunately, I have not been able to devote as much time to examination of the voluminous Communist source material on the Vietnam war as the subject warrants, I have only scratched this rich vein. I have taken time off from longer-range work in order to do it because I think there is a definite need for close and continuing analysis of the Communist side of the war to further discussion and thinking on this critical subject.

As an individual involved with his society and his time I have some very definite personal views on the war in Vietnam; I have studiously attempted to put these views to one side in writing this analysis. I have done this in the belief that my professional background imposes on me the obligation to scrutinize as impartially as I can all the facts and their consequences.

However, I believe that any author writing on Vietnam today has an obligation to his readers to state his position. It seems to me that, frustrated by the military and political complexities of the civil war in the South, we have mistakenly centered our attack on the North instead of seeking to develop a viable Southern strategy. We have increasingly become prisoners of our own rhetoric which insists on the half-truth that the main problem is Northern aggression. A viable Southern strategy would concentrate on political and social reform in the South, particularly on land reform, and would develop a more sophisticated, low-level war strategy to meet the military challenge in the South. The fact that such a strategy has not been developed raises serious doubts in my mind whether we as a nation have the wisdom, the skills and the manpower to cope with civil wars.

In moral terms, the issue is much more complex than either the Administration or its critics have brought out. I cannot resolve the issue easily. However, I am increasingly disturbed by the fact that as the war has escalated we have more and more had recourse to the Communist rationalization that the end justifies the means; that is, we have increasingly justified the human costs of our strategy in terms of keeping the options open for a democratic society. As a democratic society we have an obligation—that the Communists do not—to see that we employ means appropriate to our desired ends. Unlike some critics of the Administration I feel that our ends in Vietnam are honorable. But I am not at all confident that the means we are now employing are promoting those ends.

I do not favor withdrawal from Asia; nor do I regard the situation there with pessimism. I am convinced that it is necessary to bring about a balance of power in Asia that will enable small nations to develop independently of an expansionist China and that the only nation now capable of doing that is the United States. I am also convinced that most of the leaders of the smaller nations of Asia want to see a continuing American presence in that continent.

In retrospect, I think a good case could have been made prior to 1965 for cutting our losses in South Vietnam while increasing our commitments in Laos and Thailand. The view that such a setback would have been followed by the fall of all the other "dominoes" in Southeast Asia seems to me grossly oversimplified. Much would have depended on our own policy. If we had acted as though we were writing off Southeast Asia, we would have made the prophecy self-fulfilling. If, on the other hand, we had given increased proof of our resolve to defend those governments which had strong support among their own people, we might have localized the political effects of a Communist victory in South Vietnam. As the political elites of Southeast Asia recognize, the strength of Communism in South Vietnam testifies less to the weakness of American resolve than to the failure of the South Vietnamese political leadership. What happens elsewhere in Southeast Asia will depend more on indigenous conditions, the caliber of local leadership and on American policy in Asia generally than on what happens in South Vietnam.

Under present circumstances, however, given the sizable American investment in blood, treasure and prestige, I think we must remain in Vietnam. At the same time, I think we can make much more vigorous efforts than the Administration has yet made to bring about a settlement of the war. An end to the bombing of North Vietnam is an essential first step. It is, in my opinion, a dangerous illusion to think that North Vietnam can be bombed into surrendering its support of the NLF. If, for whatever reason, stronger efforts to end the war on a mutually tolerable basis were to prove unsuccessful, I would favor a long-term, defensive military holding operation in South Vietnam which would aim at consolidating the Saigon government's position in the cities and in limited areas of the countryside, combined with the most strenuous moves to revive and to reorganize non-Communist political life in the country.

VIETNAM TRIANGLE

CHAPTER ONE

The Triangle

IT IS difficult to comprehend any important aspect of the international relations of recent years without taking into account the triangular relationship among three countries: Russia, China, and the United States. For the past decade, these three great powers have engaged most of their energies in worldwide competition and conflict with one another. Their policies in particular parts of the world have often been decisively influenced not by local considerations but by the dynamics of this triangular rivalry.

Each of the three powers now quite clearly fears that a drawing together—or even a lessening of enmity—between the other two would be inimical to its own interests. Washington has, of course, feared a rapprochement of the two Communist powers from almost the first moment it acknowledged the Sino-Soviet conflict—and this acknowledgment came some time after the conflict emerged. Peking, ever since the late 1950's, has been convinced—not without reason—that a Soviet-American détente could be achieved only at China's expense because it would lead to the withdrawal of Soviet military support for Chinese objectives in Asia. Much of Peking's global strategy in recent years has been aimed at sabotaging the détente. In the past year, the most interesting and significant new development has been Moscow's increasingly obvious concern at any improvement of Sino-American relations. Peking and Washington are in fact a long way from a normalization of relations; but so long as Mao, because of domestic opposition to him and because of the way he views the future of the Chinese revolution, regards "revisionism" as a greater danger than "imperialism," Moscow has cause for concern. In short, each of the three countries is anxious to keep the other two apart.

THE BIPOLAR WORLD

It is worth making some general observations about the origins and nature of this relationship. From the beginning of the Cold War in the 1940's until the emergence of the Sino-Soviet split in the late 1950's, the great-power relationship was a bipolar rather than a triangular one. Each of the two superpowers—Russia and the United States—was almost exclusively concerned, if not obsessed, with the other. Each saw international relations as a zero-sum game— that is, as a situation in which a gain for one was a loss for the other. Each was painfully aware that the other was the only power in the world which represented a mortal danger to it. Each constructed alliance systems and sought influence in third areas largely to offset the power and influence of the other. That is why each mistrusted neutral nations.

In this bipolar world, any real ally of a superpower could be only a junior partner in the sense that its interests and priorities had to play second fiddle to those of the greater powers. Neutrals, for their part, were for many years judged by each side to be serving the cause of the other. Such were the terms of bipolarity.

It was in this bipolar world that the Sino-Soviet alliance developed in 1950, shortly after the Chinese Communists conquered the mainland. From the beginning, it was evident that Russia considered China a junior partner. China reluctantly accepted her role. The treaty Mao signed with Stalin in February, 1950, has been accurately described as the last of the "unequal treaties" that China signed with European powers. The Sino-Soviet treaty granted Russia rights to the principal railways in Manchuria and to joint use of the naval base at Port Arthur until 1954; later agreements called for establishment of several joint-stock companies to operate primarily in China's borderlands, where the Russians had long claimed special privileges. These agreements, as Khrushchev subsequently revealed, were bitterly resented by the Chinese.

Mao, however, was prepared to accept a junior partnership in order to strengthen his hand against the country he considered to be China's main enemy—the United States. The Sino-Soviet treaty, which specified that if either partner were attacked by Japan or any state allied with it the other partner would immediately "render military and other assistance by all means at its disposal," was clearly aimed at the United States.

Mao viewed the United States as the main enemy both for ideological and political reasons. He "leaned to one side" well before the start of the Chinese civil war in which Washington supported his enemies. This ideological stance was then reinforced by an important political factor: American support for Chiang Kai-shek during the civil war. Furthermore, within a year after the Communists took power in China, they found themselves at war with the United States in Korea.

The fact that Russia at that time shared China's hostility toward the American "imperialist" enemy was decisive in cementing the Sino-Soviet alliance and in making China dependent upon Russia in the first decade of the Cold War. Both Russia and China aimed at weakening the enemy's grip on Europe and Asia and at protecting themselves against American attack. Despite Mao's misgivings about Stalin's "unequal treaty," he saw in the Soviet alliance—and in an international Communist movement led by Russia—an instrument by which to compensate for China's own national weakness, as well as an instrument through which to redress the grievances of Western domination and regain for China its great-power status. So long as the Russians fought the "imperialists," Mao was prepared to support them on almost every crucial political and ideological issue. Thus, Mao backed Stalin against Tito in 1948, in spite of the obvious implications of this attack on "national Communism" for China. Mao did not, furthermore, hesitate to support Khrushchev against the Hungarian Communist rebels in 1956 when they threatened to weaken the Socialist camp by withdrawing from the Warsaw Pact. Mao took these actions in behalf of his own interests, not those of the Soviet Union. If the Communist bloc was to be used against China's national enemies—and particularly the United States—it had to be strong and monolithic. For this reason, Mao supported every step the Russians took to unify and discipline the bloc. When Mao intervened in Eastern Europe in 1956 to help restore Soviet hegemony in the bloc, it was not because he desired a European sphere of influence, but because he genuinely wanted to help revitalize waning Soviet authority. It was for this reason, too, that Mao insisted at the international Communist meeting in Moscow in November, 1957, that the Communist bloc must have a head and that the Soviet Union must be that head.

Because the Sino-Soviet alliance was directed against the United States, and because the Communist bloc was monolithic in this bipolar period, it was only natural that the United States should see the enemy not only in Russia and China but also in Communism as an ideological force. Any Communist victory in the bipolar world threatened the United States because such a victory represented an extension of Soviet power. What has subsequently come to be regarded in some circles as an American anti-Communist obsession in this period was based on the very real connection between Soviet national power and the spread of international Communism. In retrospect, it is easy to see that the Communist bloc contained within it the seeds of pluralism. But there were few if any observers who, on the eve of Stalin's death in 1953, accurately foresaw the rapid and sweeping changes that would occur in the international Communist movement in the decade to follow.

These changes were the product of four interrelated developments: the death of Stalin, the denunciation of Stalin by Khrushchev, the clash of national interests within the Communist bloc, and the Sino-Soviet conflict. Stalin's death was critical because none of his successors had sufficient authority, prestige, or power to continue ruling the Communist bloc as he had done. Any successor would have had to make concessions to the conflicting interests and views of other Communist states, for Stalin's death deprived the movement of its main force for unity. Stalin's successors were quick to appreciate that they could not reign in Stalin's manner. In 1954 Khrushchev and Bulganin traveled to Peking to put Soviet relations with China on a new and more equal basis, and in 1955 Molotov was already talking of Soviet and Chinese co-leadership of the Communist bloc. By 1956 the Russians were speaking of creating a "Socialist commonwealth." All of this was a reflection of their realization that the relations between Communist states and parties would have to undergo profound changes in the post-Stalin era. Of course, the changes that occurred went further than the Russians had expected or were willing to sanction.

If Stalin's prestige had remained untarnished after his death, it is possible that the decline of Russian authority in international Communism would not have been so swift. Within three years of his death, Khrushchev revealed a harrowing list of crimes, plots, and terroristic acts the late dictator had initiated in the course of his rule. Khrushchev not only destroyed the myth of Stalin's infallibility but the myth of Soviet infallibility as well. If Communist parties throughout the world had been following the lead of a murderer and a paranoid, how could a local Communist leader ever again justify subordinating the interests of his own party or country to *any* Soviet leader? This consideration became especially significant in view of the lack of institutional guarantees within the Communist system against another Soviet leader following in Stalin's footsteps. Italian Communist leader Palmiro Togliatti emphasized the lack of such guarantees. The de-Stalinization campaign, launched by Khrushchev for internal reasons, thus had enormous—and unforeseen—consequences within the world Communist movement. It damaged beyond repair the prestige of the Soviet Union as the leader of world Communism, and it gave rise to a host of competing pressures within the international Communist movement.

A number of these pressures centered on the increasing clash of divergent national interests. A number of Communist regimes appeared after World War II. Some of them—notably the Yugoslav and Chinese—had seized power independent of Soviet advice and assistance and therefore without strong allegiance to the Soviet Union. Such regimes proved troublesome for the Russians even while Stalin lived, as the Soviet-Yugoslav break in 1948 illustrated. By the mid-1950's, even some of the Communist regimes installed by Soviet troops at the end of the Second World War began searching for greater independence from Moscow in an effort to gain popular support in their own countries. These pressures for emancipation from Soviet imperial authority were greatly enhanced by the Sino-Soviet rift, which accelerated the disintegration of Soviet authority in world Communism. On the Western side of the Cold War line, there was also a loosening of ties within NATO as the specter of a Russian invasion of Western Europe faded. As a result, the bipolar relationship gradually yielded to a multilateral one. But within this multilateral world, the triangular relationship among Russia, China, and the United States was crucial.

THE TRIANGLE EMERGES

The principal reason why China began taking a separate path from Russia was its fear of a Soviet-American accommodation at its expense. As tension between Russia and the United States attenuated in the late 1950's, the main factor cementing the Sino-Soviet alliance gradually disappeared. While China sought to pursue an even more active anti-American policy than it had conducted earlier, Russia began gradually to seek ways of reducing tensions with the United States, tensions that might lead to nuclear war. As a result, Moscow found itself caught between China and the United States. Any militant Soviet actions increased tension with the United States; any moderate Soviet moves intensified problems with Peking. While Washington accused Russia of giving too much support to Communist parties elsewhere, Peking accused it of giving too little. While Washington wanted Moscow to become less "ideological," Peking wanted it to be more so. It was no accident that the Chinese opened public fire on Russia shortly after Khrushchev and Eisenhower met at Camp David in the fall of 1959 and took the first cautious steps toward a Soviet-American détente.

I therefore consider it incorrect to view the Sino-Soviet split as a product of a "pure" contest for power and influence within the international Communist movement, or of Mao's personal desire to replace Stalin at the head of the movement. What was at issue was Soviet *policy*—particularly its policy toward the United States. Peking did not seriously begin to challenge Soviet *authority* within the Communist movement until Moscow, for reasons of its own, began to move closer to Washington.

The reasons for Peking's bitter disappointment with Soviet moves toward Washington, and the factors that produced them, can best be seen by contrasting the Chinese and Soviet national relationships to the United States. They differ substantially.

Peking has a much more deeply rooted hostility toward the United States than Russia. Among the many changing and contradictory elements in Peking's foreign policy from 1958 to 1967, one theme remains consistent: the United States is the main enemy of all "peace-loving" forces throughout the world and a worldwide united front must be formed against it. All other elements in Peking's global strategy can be deduced from this anti-American posture. Peking first sought to use Soviet power against the United States on behalf of Chinese objectives in Asia. When Peking discovered that the Soviet Union would not take necessary risks to support these objectives, it increasingly began to regard the Russians as "objective" allies of the Americans in Asia—as well as in the entire third world—and it sought to isolate both Russia and the United States from the third world. An important element in the third-world strategy was an effort to foment violence. Too weak alone to bring about American withdrawal from Asia and unable to rely upon Soviet support, Peking sponsored and sought to foment "liberation wars," hoping they would force the United States to disperse its power throughout the under-developed areas.

But China did not indiscriminately advocate "liberation wars," nor did it seek to push all local Communists onto a violent path to power. It did so almost exclusively in countries where the national leadership was tied to an American alliance or was reluctant to pursue an actively anti-American policy. Where national leaders met China's anti-American requirements, the Chinese were perfectly prepared to abandon local Communists. Thus, when Chou En-lai visited Morocco in 1964, he hailed King Hassan as a "progressive" at the very time Moroccan Communists were going on trial for their lives. In Burma, where local Communists have been fighting the Ne Win regime for many years, the Chinese followed a middle course between limited aid to their comrades and support of the neutralist regime.

Two possible exceptions can be made: India and Indonesia. In the first case, Peking did attack an Asian country that was pursuing a policy of nonalignment. In the second, it lent support to an attempt by local Communists to take over an anti-American regime. However, in both cases China's policy can be explained in terms of its hostility toward the United States. Peking's objection to Indian policy was that it was too neutral. After 1957, Peking wanted "neutrals" to be actively anti-American. About the same time Nehru began to emphasize peaceful coexistence rather than anti-imperialism; that is, neutralism rather than anti-Westernism. If this policy were to be widely accepted in the Afro-Asian world, it would wreck Peking's strategic mobilization of the third world against the United States. Moreover, India, by courting both Russia and the United States, and by receiving aid from both in return for such moderate policies, was setting an example that went contrary to Peking's efforts to isolate Russia and the United States from the third world.

In the case of Indonesia, there is considerable evidence to indi-cate that the abortive coup supported by Indonesian Communists also had the tacit or active support of President Sukarno and that it was directed against anti-Sukarno and anti-Communist elements in the army. Peking thus did not seek the removal of the anti-imperialist Sukarno—whose policies in fact suited China better than those of any other Afro-Asian leader—but rather sought to bolster Sukarno's position against his domestic opposition.

AMERICA'S ROLE IN THE TRIANGLE

Chinese hostility toward the United States grows out of a number of factors. The main one is that the United States supports and protects an alternative Chinese regime which is a scant ninety miles off the coast of China and which proclaims its intentions to reconquer the mainland. Despite United States denials of support to a Nationalist invasion, the Chinese continue to fear such an invasion. Indeed, there are clearly some circumstances in which American support for such a Nationalist effort would have to be considered. This would jeopardize the very existence of the Chinese Communist regime. But even short of such a development, an alternative regime so close to the mainland catalyzes dissent there, and dissidence—as is now unmistakably clear—has markedly increased on the mainland in recent years. Moreover, there is the fear that United States policy is now or will soon be committed to a "two-Chinas" solution and that the Taiwan regime will thus gain permanent status. Meanwhile, there is considerable harassment of the mainland from Taiwan, with overflights by reconnaissance planes and U-2's.

Without American military and political support, the Chiang Kai-shek regime would not survive very long in its present form, and the chances of Peking's "liberating" Taiwan would substantially increase. At the very least, then, as Communist China sees it, the United States blocks its claim to legitimacy and prevents the culmination of a civil war begun more than three decades ago. At most, the United States and its Nationalist allies hold a dagger at Peking's heart. Imagine an American government-in-exile in Havana, supported by the Russians and Chinese, periodically raiding the Florida coast and proclaiming its intentions to conquer the entire country.

There are other reasons for China's intense hostility toward the United States. In Southeast Asian areas which China has traditionally regarded as part of its sphere of influence, American power prevents the expansion of Chinese influence. The United States props up a faltering anti-Communist government in South Vietnam, is active in Laos, and supports a vigorously anti-Communist government in Thailand.

Moreover, the United States supports India and Japan, China's two principal rivals for leadership in Asia. On the political front, the United States blocks China's diplomatic recognition by many states and Chinese admission into the United Nations. While a seat in the Security Council is not one of Peking's highest priorities, it is a symbol of great-power status. Economically, it is partially the result of U.S. policy that China cannot obtain badly needed long-range credits from non-Communist countries.

Meanwhile, in the military sphere, the United States maintains sizable military forces in South Korea, Okinawa, and numerous islands in the Western Pacific within easy striking distance of the Chinese mainland. While the Soviet Union can state with some justification that it is difficult to say who is encircling whom, the same statement cannot and has not been made by the Chinese Communists. There is no doubt in the Pacific of who is encircling whom.

Add to this the Korean war, in which the United States was a bitterly hated opponent, and the United States at once represents to China what the interventionist powers in 1918–1920, the Nazi German invader, and the United States in the Cold War period together represented to the Soviet Union.

By contrast, U.S.-Soviet relations, while still characterized by ideological conflict and the natural hostility of two great superpowers, are quite friendly. The Soviet Union is, distinctly more than China, a satisfied power. It has no irredenta analogous to Taiwan, it is recognized by the world community, it has a substantial buffer zone in Eastern Europe under its military domination, it is economically more viable than China and therefore less sensitive to economic sanctions, and its enormous military power reduces the threat of "imperialism." For all of these reasons, the degree of hostility the Soviets feel toward the United States is mitigated. The conflict of interests between Russia and the United States is less direct, less complete, and less confining to Russia than the China–United States conflict is to China.

Moreover, there are a variety of internal and external considerations that dictate a Soviet interest in limited accommodation with the United States. One of these is the Soviet Union's strategic inferiority to the United States, an inferiority which the Russians know cannot be quickly overcome and which compels caution. Another is the Soviet leaders' realization that third parties might want—in some cases—to drag them into war against their will. At home, industry and especially agriculture are showing disappointing results. There are competing demands on scarce resources, and the Soviet public has come to expect improvements in the standard of living. Such considerations have recommended a cautious foreign policy to Russian leaders and a relationship with the United States which can best be described as an adversary relationship—that is, one in which there are overlapping interests as well as elements of conflict.

During the decade in which the triangular relationship replaced the bipolar, the United States was slow to appreciate its own role in the triangle. Top American officials recognized the existence of the Sino-Soviet dispute only belatedly, then were extremely cautious about acknowledging it, and were always at a loss to know whether or how to exacerbate it.

It is true that at the lower levels of government—in the State Department and in the intelligence community—as well as in Congress, there were a few observers who recognized the earliest symptoms of conflict between Russia and China. But so deeply ingrained was the ideological orientation of those who had coped with bipolar politics, it took a long time for this analysis to be taken very seriously at the top levels of government. As late as April, 1960, the late Secretary of State Christian Herter publicly announced that it was too early to judge the reality or significance of the differences between Moscow and Peking. Many high-ranking American leaders—not to mention journalists and academic specialists—offered the view that regardless of differences within the Communist family, the two Communist powers were united in wanting to "bury" the United States. As late as in 1962, one of the assumptions behind the American support of the Geneva settlement on Laos was that the Russians were capable of restraining China in southeast Asia.

As the rift widened, particularly after the signing of the test-ban agreement in 1963, American officials began to explore ways to exploit the differences between Russia and China and to adjust America's strategic posture in accordance with the rift. More and more, American officials spoke of the separate policies and interests of Russia and China. They suggested that an American war with China need not mean war with Russia; it seems quite likely that American strategic forces—which in the 1950's were programmed to strike simultaneously at both Communist states—were separated into distinct striking forces some time in this period. At the same time, Washington began to actively pursue better relations with Russia and Eastern Europe while it continued to isolate China and her Asian Communist allies.

As time went on, the United States gave other signs that it favored the Russians over China. For example, when the United States rejected China's admission to the United Nations in 1966, it argued that any change in American policy would embarrass Moscow. And more and more some Washington officials began to speak of China as the main international danger while they minimized the points of Soviet-American friction.

THE TRIANGLE AND VIETNAM

Russia has never cared very much about the people or the local Communists in Vietnam unless what happened there influenced developments in Europe, or in Russia's relations with the United States or China. Despite the fact that the Vietminh was the only Communist party in the world to lead a national independence movement immediately after World War II (from 1945 to 1948) the Russians treated them with cool reserve, failed to champion their cause internationally and left the French Communists to guide them. The French Communists gave them very little support and, for a period, even supported the government's war effort against them.

The reasons for this Soviet policy are clear. In 1945, Stalin's armies were in physical control of all of Eastern Europe, Austria, and the eastern part of Germany. An even bigger prize loomed on the horizon—Communist governments in France and Italy. For Stalin a Communist or Communist-influenced France was a much more important prize than a Communist Vietnam. Naturally, he assumed the Vietminh would not do anything to undermine the French Communists, who were at the time—in Churchillian fashion—assuring the French electorate that they had no intention of presiding over the dissolution of the French empire.

Moscow and the French Communist party did not begin to support the Vietminh struggle until after the Communists had been ousted from the coalition government in Paris in the spring of 1947. Russia did not become really interested in Vietnam until the start of the Korean war in 1950. At that time Ho's struggle against France assumed increasing importance as a second front to weaken the Western powers. Yet when the first opportunity to strike a deal with France at the expense of Ho Chi Minh presented itself, Moscow did not hesitate. In 1954, the Russians, under new leadership, arranged a deal with French Premier Mendès-France to reject the European Defense Community in exchange for Soviet help in obtaining a Vietnam settlement that Ho almost certainly regarded as unsatisfactory.

In more recent years, the Soviet attitude on Indochina has been influenced by two conflicting interests: a desire to reach a détente with the United States, and an interest in gaining Hanoi's support in Moscow's struggle with Peking. The first interest required urging moderation on Ho, the latter required giving him enough support to prevent his going over to Peking. These conflicting pressures explain the persistent ambivalence in Soviet policy in Indochina in recent years. In 1964 Khrushchev sought to resolve the dilemma by disengaging the Soviet Union from Indochina altogether. But the new Soviet leaders have—with some success so far—sought to have it both ways. On the one hand they provide Hanoi with increasing amounts of defensive weapons, on the other they seek to continue the détente with the United States.

The Soviet Union's position on Vietnam may well be more uncomfortable and awkward than that of either of the other two major participants, China and the United States. Being in the middle, Moscow faces problems from both directions. The Chinese and spokesmen for the European left like Jean Paul Sartre who think like them, accuse Moscow of immobilism and appeasement for not taking a much stronger stand against American "imperialist" attacks on a fraternal Socialist state. On the other extreme, there are American congressmen and journalists who argue that Moscow will remain the real enemy in Vietnam so long as it supplies Hanoi at all. By acting too timidly, Moscow consequently loses prestige in the Communist and radical world. By acting too strongly, it risks a Cuban-type confrontation with the United States. Part of the reason for Moscow's increasing interest in a negotiated settlement of the war is that it would like to escape from this dilemma.

China's policy in Vietnam after 1949 cannot be understood out of the context of its goals vis-à-vis Russia and the United States—goals to which the aspirations of Ho Chi Minh have always been secondary and often in conflict. Although they sometimes overlap,

China's interests and those of North Vietnam have never been—and are not now—identical. This is because China has always looked on Vietnam in terms of its worldwide competition with the two superpowers. China has consistently sought to use the war less to reunify Vietnam under Ho—a prospect about which the Chinese may have mixed feelings—than to embarrass the Soviet Union, to weaken the United States, and to prevent expansion of the Soviet-American détente. China has sought to avoid both an enlarged war, extending to China itself, and negotiations. Instead, it has promoted a prolonged war of attrition.

Peking's concern to prevent escalation is evident from the fact that the Chinese have avoided provocative actions of their own; they have warned North Vietnam against military adventurism; and they have indicated quite clearly—beginning in early 1966—that they will not intervene in Vietnam unless the United States attacks China or invades North Vietnam; Peking has at the same time persistently opposed negotiations. Its public line on peace talks has been much less flexible than that of Hanoi, as evidenced most recently by a warning to Hanoi that American cessation of bombing of North Vietnam is not sufficient grounds for talks. Peking seeks to keep the war going by urging Hanoi to insist on a precondition for negotiation unacceptable to the United States: complete withdrawal from Vietnam. As we shall see, China's interests clash at some points with those of Hanoi, causing a strain between the two.

For the Americans—as for the Russians and Chinese—Vietnam has been a pawn in a global ideological and power struggle. For all our pretensions at the end of World War II to be the champions of national independence and anticolonialism, we supported the French colonialists in Vietnam against the patent aspirations of the Vietnamese people. We did this because after 1948 France became our NATO ally in Europe. We were so anxious to insure French support against Russia in the bipolar world that we avoided pressing France to give genuine independence to Vietnam.

Had the United States the foresight to come to terms with Ho after 1954, when we replaced France as the dominant Western power in Indochina, the present tragedy might have been averted. But we were intent—particularly after the Korean war—on drawing a Cold War line in Asia.

I intend to analyze, in separate chapters, the policies of Russia, China, and North Vietnam in the Vietnamese war. In the bipolar world, it was sufficient to know the Soviet policy in any given situation because Russia could speak for the entire Communist world. Even then, Soviet policy was not widely understood in the United States. Today in the triangular world, we face an infinitely more complex problem. It is necessary to understand the factors making up Soviet and Chinese policy as well as the policies of other Communist parties in the world. In the specific case of Vietnam, there are four Communist parties involved: the Russian, the Chinese, the North Vietnamese, and the South Vietnamese. Any sound American policy or informed opinion must take into account the complexities and subtleties of this relationship.

CHAPTER TWO *

The Soviet Quandary

SOME analysts of Soviet affairs consider the Vietnamese conflict the decisive factor shaping Soviet foreign policy—perhaps even domestic policy—in the post-Khrushchev era. Opponents of the war say that American policy in Vietnam has forced the Russians to adopt a harder line and that the war has strengthened Soviet society's most reactionary forces. The defenders of the Administration contend, on the contrary, that Washington's policy has intensified the Sino-Soviet dispute. Optimists say that when the war ends, we can look forward to resuming a very close relationship with the Russians; pessimists hold that the war has taught the Russians an unforgettable lesson, one that will leave a scar on the consciousness of the Soviet leaders so lasting that it will inhibit a close Soviet-American relationship in the foreseeable future.

This writer is not at all convinced that the war in Vietnam has thus far had such profound, long-lasting effects on Soviet policies, nor that it has been central to Soviet foreign-policy considerations. Naturally, the war colors Soviet foreign policy, influences the selection of particular methods of action, introduces certain constraints as well as opportunities, and influences tactical moves in one or another direction. Surely, for example, the Soviet desire for better relations with the United States would be more pronounced if there were no war. At the same time, although the war has afforded

---

* A preliminary draft of this chapter was written by Marian Kirsch in consultation with the author. This draft was of considerable help to me in preparing the final version.

new opportunities, the Soviet effort to capitalize on Western disunity would still constitute a major thrust of its policy in Western Europe.)

Whether the Vietnamese war will continue to be a peripheral consideration in Soviet foreign policy is not certain. But as of this writing it is an unwanted obstacle in the way of what Soviet leaders consider the main objects of their international activities. They neither use the war—to the extent they could—to press forward on American political flanks, nor do they close the "business-as-usual" door on relations with the United States and its allies. They stand as they do on so many issues—squarely in the middle. Clearly, the war in Vietnam is not considered by the Soviet leaders, as it is by the Chinese and by some Americans, as the Communist Armageddon.

Russia stands today at multiple crossroads. In its internal development, it must reconcile the survival of a rigid political system with the urgent needs of modernization and dynamic economic development that the system inhibits. Too, Russia seeks to integrate its society without resorting to mass mobilization and campaigns of the Stalin or Khrushchev type. In the international arena, Russia needs to discover how to use its newly and dearly won great-power status without entangling itself in risky ventures, and, at the same time, without retiring from active ambitions on the international scene. Here it faces the dilemma of keeping both the Chinese and American adversaries at bay when whatever it does will help one of the two.

Because the war in Vietnam *reflects* all the major Soviet dilemmas, it is an important episode in Soviet history. In other words, the quandary in which Soviet leaders find themselves fifty years after the October Revolution is far broader than the problem posed by Vietnam. This chapter describes the historical evolution of Soviet policy toward Vietnam. The reader, however, should keep in mind the larger problems of Soviet development lurking in the background.

PURSUIT OF NEGATIVE GOALS

In recent discussions of the kinds of future evolution that are likely in the Soviet Union, eminent specialists on Soviet affairs seem to agree on at least one point: the all-powerful party bureaucracy now ruling Russia is likely to prove unfit to meet the challenges of its own rapidly changing society as well as those encountered in the world outside. As Zbigniew Brzezinski put it:

It is doubtful that any organization can long remain vital if it is so structured that in its personnel policy it becomes, almost unknowingly, inimical to talent and hostile to political innovation.[1]

Or, in the words of an eminent Italian scholar:

. . . Soviet Russia is nearing [a] stage of paralysis. The recent 23rd CPSU Congress exposed to public view a political class that is standing still. Few leaders addressed the Congress. China was barely mentioned. The names of Stalin and Khrushchev were not to be heard at all. Those who were instrumental in bringing about the downfall of Khrushchev did not even dare to claim credit for it, referring to the event in bureaucratic terms as "the Central Committee's decisions of October 1964." This peculiar attitude of silence indicates the extent of immobility that has taken hold of the all-powerful bureaucracy of the Soviet Union: it has lost not only the ability to act, but also the ability to speak.[2]

Or, as a British specialist wrote:

. . . the present situation is one in which there is a seepage of the grey goo of doctrinaire bureaucracy into the top political levels, which were hitherto partially exempt. If the final crisis of the Communist regime is to begin under the present leaders, I would expect it to come not as the result of any of their specific policies, but rather through unforeseen catastrophes with which their methods, and indeed their personalities, are not fitted to cope. . . .

The current regime has learned one lesson from Khrushchev—that random reforms within the system have not done any good. But the immobilism to which they have instead retreated equally provides no solution.[3]

The picture of immobilism, stagnation, hostility to change, and inertia drawn by the specialists may be surprising to the general reader. But, by the absence of any clearly articulated immediate or long-range goals, and with a foreign policy that has as its chief characteristic the avoidance of any radical moves, Soviet policy in no way contradicts this image. Aware that the extension of Communist power in underdeveloped countries is no longer automatically in their interests, frustrated by the failure of the third world to move in ideologically preordained patterns of development, and challenged even within their own imperial domain by "satellite" states with whom they must bargain rather than coerce, the Soviet leaders show signs of confusion as to the proper and feasible aims of foreign policy. While ideology remains a factor influencing and shaping decision-making, it is no longer even remotely a suitable guide to action. Soviet policy is determined by what the Soviet leaders want to avoid rather than by what they want to gain. They want to avoid local conflicts, confrontations with the United States, and domination of other areas by hostile powers. As a result, rather than leap-frogging into Africa, Latin America, and the Far East, Soviet policy more steadily concentrates on traditional areas of influence or on contiguous areas in the Middle East.

Indeed, both the Italian scholar previously cited and Mao Tse-tung seem to have come to similar conclusions about the overriding purpose of Soviet leadership. In Galli's words, the bureaucracy's "only purpose is to enjoy its privileges in peace" without being forced to "face the problems of a world that is undergoing a process of rapid evolution." Less charitably said in a Chinese Government statement, the Soviet leaders allegedly

> . . . seek only to preserve themselves and would let other people sink or swim. They have repeatedly said that so long as they themselves survive and develop, the people of the world will be saved. The fact is they are selling out the fundamental interests of the people of the world in order to seek their momentary ease.[4]

Moscow's recent policy in Vietnam, like its policies elsewhere, seems best defined by what it seeks to avoid rather than what it seeks to gain. It seeks to avoid both a Chinese "victory"—that is, an outcome which would greatly enhance Mao's "liberation war" thesis and leave China with dominant influence in North Vietnam—and an American victory, which would greatly undermine Soviet prestige. In pursuit of these negative goals, Moscow provides North Vietnam with just enough defensive weaponry to make American bombing costly while it supports those leaders in Hanoi who think in terms of a political rather than a military victory in South Vietnam.

To be sure, the Soviet Union has made some gains as a result of the war. But these gains stem from the actions of China and the United States rather than from any Soviet grand design. China's refusal to join in common action with Russia over Vietnam has enabled Moscow to portray itself as "defender of Communist unity" and thereby to increase its influence among the smaller Asian Communist parties once loyal to Peking. American preoccupation with Vietnam has given Moscow an opportunity to fish in NATO's troubled waters. Once the Vietnam war is brought to a close, however, it seems doubtful that the Kremlin will be able to convert such opportunities into lasting gains.

SOVIET POLICY IN VIETNAM PRIOR TO 1965

Historically, Southeast Asia has never been an area of vital national security concern to the Soviet Union. The Russians have treated Indochina primarily as a pawn in their relations with other powers— a pawn to be sacrificed when necessary to Soviet interests in Europe, Soviet-American worldwide competition, and, more recently, Sino-Soviet rivalry within the international Communist movement.

It is not surprising, then, that prior to World War II, the Soviet Union had little success in promoting Communism there. The Soviet Union was far more interested in preventing China from falling under the sway of Japanese imperialism. The major efforts of the Comintern in Asia were therefore concentrated on China rather than on the Communist parties of Southeast Asia, which were weak and, in any case, had only a limited nuisance value in helping to weaken the European colonial powers.

WORLD WAR II

World War II was a watershed in many of the Southeast Asian countries because it provided the nationalist and Communist leaders the opportunity to mobilize peasants against Japanese invaders. Communism in Vietnam, like a bodyless head before the war, gained shape and form from the upsurge of nationalist sentiment as a result of the Japanese invasion. It is sufficient indication of Ho Chi Minh's success that the Chinese Nationalists saw fit to let him out of jail in 1943 because they wanted intelligence on the Japanese that only Ho's Communist cells in the Vietnamese countryside could provide. The Vietminh (League for the Independence of Vietnam), a coalition of nationalist revolutionary groups including the Indochinese Communist Party, spearheaded Vietnamese wartime resistance to the Japanese invaders and consequently established a mass base. This was to grow enormously during the struggle against the French, who returned to Vietnam after the war, determined to pick up the reins of colonial power.

Little contact existed between the Russians and the Asian Communists during World War II. In fact, from the time of its disastrous setback in China in 1927, the Comintern had virtually disengaged itself from Asia. From then until the end of World War II, not a single Asian Communist party figured in any important way in Soviet foreign policy. Even after Ho Chi Minh proclaimed Vietnam's independence in 1945, thus becoming the first Asian Communist leader to wage a successful national independence campaign, Moscow paid scant attention. Stalin was preoccupied with reasserting his rule at home and with advancing Soviet objectives in Europe.

In the immediate postwar period Stalin—insofar as he looked abroad at all—faced West. Several factors account for this Westward orientation. First, as I have indicated, prior to World War II the Comintern had met with disastrous defeats in Asia. Not only were these events traumatic for Stalin personally, but they also gave him reason to discount Asian Communist parties as important vehicles for pursuing his goals. Then, Stalin probably underestimated the strength of the Vietminh, just as he did the Chinese Communists. In addition, Stalin's subsequent attitude toward Tito suggests that he was reluctant to see the triumph of independent Communist parties in areas outside the range of Soviet artillery.

The most important consideration in Stalin's decision to ignore Southeast Asia undoubtedly lay in the rich opportunity for a Soviet political harvest in Europe. Russian armies occupied all of eastern Europe, Austria, and eastern Germany, while powerful, prestigious Communist parties existed in France and Italy at the end of World War II. Stalin's goal was to establish "people's democracies" or puppet Communist regimes in all eastern European areas under Soviet occupation. He hoped to see Communist parties, especially the French and Italian, win power in Western Europe. Because European "capitalism" seemed exhausted by the war, the United States appeared ready to return to its prewar isolationism, and because European communism—in the wake of its fight against fascism—stood at the height of its prestige and influence, Stalin's goal seemed realistic at the time.

The fact that the Cominform limited membership to European Communist parties symbolized Stalin's strong focus on European affairs in the immediate post-war period. Moreover, the "Eastern" or colonial question was almost totally ignored at the Cominform's opening session in 1947—as it was in speeches of top Soviet leaders and in the Soviet press. Even the substantial achievements of Asian Communist parties were soft-pedaled. Thus the military triumphs of the Chinese Communists against Chiang Kai-shek's forces after 1946 never received the attention they deserved, and the fact that the Vietminh had been the world's only Communist organization to lead a national independence movement was given only passing notice.

As he minimized the achievement of Asian Communists, Stalin worked to insure that Asian Communist aspirations would not conflict with the bright prospects of the West European Communist parties. He therefore assigned control of the Asian Communists to the Communist parties in the respective colonial countries. This arrangement gave the French Communists a guiding hand in Indochina, the British Communists in India, and the Dutch Communists in Indonesia.

From 1945 to 1947, Soviet policy in Indochina was dictated almost exclusively by Stalin's desire to see the French Communist Party (PCF) take power in Paris and to subsequently align France and Russia in a Soviet-dominated Europe. The PCF participated in a coalition government and from November, 1945, to the spring of 1947 held numerous cabinet posts. Receiving more than five million votes, it was the largest single party in France. Because France sought above all to restore its wounded dignity and to retain its colonies in the French Union, the PCF was compelled to pursue a strong nationalist line in order to outbid other French political parties. The PCF, consequently, failed to champion Vietnamese efforts for independence. After the collapse of negotiations for independence in 1947, the French Communists went so far as to support France's military campaign against Ho Chi Minh. In March, 1947, PCF chief Maurice Thorez, then Vice-Minister of France, countersigned the order for military action against the Communist-led Republic of Vietnam. In the same year, Jacques Duclos, number two man in the PCF, stated that "We are for the presence of France in the Far East, contrary to what is asserted by . . . *Le Monde.*" [5] The PCF's general policy during this period has perhaps best been described by Ellen Hammer:

> The French Communists characteristically pursued a ruthless policy of *Realpolitik.* They were key members of the government which appointed and supported Admiral d'Argenlieu, which permitted the failure of the Fontainebleau Conference and the attack at Haiphong, and which refused to negotiate with Ho Chi Minh after December 19, 1946. Although then the largest party in France, the Communists did not lift a hand in defense of Vietnamese independence, which they were later, in their weakness, to champion so vociferously; and when they left the government in 1947, it was on a domestic issue unconnected with the Vietnamese question.[6]

The Soviet Union, meanwhile, sought to avoid offending the French government. Not only did the Soviet press consistently play down the importance of the Vietminh, but Moscow refused recognition of the new Hanoi and Saigon government established by Ho Chi Minh in September, 1945.[7] Moreover, two days after a French military coup seized Saigon from the Vietminh, French Communists in the city issued a document advising their Vietnamese comrades to be sure that their struggle "meets the requirements of Soviet policy." The document warned that any "premature adventures" might "not be in line with Soviet perspectives."[8] At the U.N. General Assembly session in London in 1946, the Russians—wary about embarrassing their prospective French allies—failed to mention the question of Vietnam, and Soviet delegate Manuilsky made it clear that Moscow was not directly interested in the matter.[9]

The Russians were bound, by such tactics, to reap a bitter harvest in Vietnam. "The Annamite Communists I met," wrote Harold Isaacs, in commenting on this not-too-glorious era of "proletarian internationalism," were "men bitten deeply by the bitterness of having been abandoned by their ideological comrades overseas."[10]

Only after the ouster of the French Communist Party from the coalition government in the spring of 1947, the launching of the Truman Doctrine in March and the Marshall Plan in June of that year, and the beginning of the Cold War, did the Russians and French Communists gradually express verbal support for the Vietminh war effort and adopt a clearly anti-French government line.

HARDENING OF SOVIET LINE

By the fall of 1947, American aid to Greece and Turkey, the European Recovery Program, and the halt to American military demobilization, combined with the failure of the West European Communist parties to gain success with policies of national collaboration, led Stalin to a major reassessment. He considered the Marshall Plan a threat to his tenuous grip on Eastern Europe and the beginning of an American effort to secure hegemony in Western Europe. His reaction was to tighten his ideological and political controls in Eastern Europe and to urge West European Communist parties to wage more forceful struggles against their governments. This was the essence of Andrei Zhdanov's famous "two-camp" speech at the opening meeting of the Cominform in Poland in September, 1947. At this meeting the earlier national-front strategies of the West European Communist parties were condemned as "opportunist" and

Stalin began to insist on the kind of orthodoxy in Eastern Europe that was to lead to the expulsion of Yugoslavia from the Cominform a year later.

Throughout this period of mounting tension in Europe, which reached its height during the Soviet blockade of Berlin in mid-1948, the Russians' central concerns were with Europe, the increasing American presence there, and the growing dangers of World War III.[11]

To the limited extent that Stalin looked east at this time, it was to undermine what he perceived to be the growing threat from the United States and its European allies. Whether the Asian Communists were directed to move to the offensive at this point or whether they simply interpreted the new wind from Moscow as a license for such offensive, in 1948 they sparked a series of rebellions in India, Burma, Malaya, and Indonesia. The Vietminh struggle continued against the French.

The new militant attitude Moscow adopted toward the West signified little to Ho Chi Minh, beyond assuring him the full support of his French Communist comrades in his efforts to weaken the French government. However, neither they nor the Russians were in a position to send him much military or economic aid.

The situation changed significantly only when Chinese Communist armies reached the borders of Vietnam in late 1949. From then on, the Chinese Communists were able to supply Ho with military aid that was to prove decisive in the war against the French. Only at this point did Moscow, in January, 1950, extend diplomatic recognition to Ho Chi Minh's government. Coverage of the war in the Soviet and Cominform press greatly increased—a result, no doubt, of a new Soviet awareness of the importance of the Asian Communists.

\Soviet interest in Vietnam quickened appreciably after the beginning of the Korean war; Soviet press coverage of the Vietminh struggle then became continuous and extensive.\ Throughout the Korean war, the Soviet Union showed considerable interest in the Vietminh struggle for independence against the French. It was persistently linked to the Korean conflict to exemplify anti-imperialist struggles resulting from American aggression. This was undoubtedly because the conflict in Indochina presented a useful second front. Even though discredited elsewhere in Southeast Asia, the Russians continued to endorse a militant course for the Vietminh as long as the Korean war raged. However, no announcements of Soviet aid to Ho Chi Minh's forces were made, and on May 9, 1953, *Pravda* expressly denied a report of a Sino-Soviet–North Vietnamese aid agreement. Not until after Geneva did the Soviet press discuss formal cultural and other agreements between Moscow and Hanoi.[12]

Russian interest in negotiation of a settlement of both the Korean and the Indochina wars developed after Stalin's death in March, 1953. The Korean armistice was finally concluded in June, 1953. By the end of that year, Ho Chi Minh was expressing a desire for peace talks in which the Russians were to play a key role.

Moscow had two good reasons for wanting to end the Vietnamese war at this time. First, U.S. Secretary of State John Foster Dulles had unveiled the "massive retaliation" doctrine in January, 1954, and then flown to Europe, where he publicly sought "united action" against communism in Indochina. If negotiations at Geneva had failed, the Americans and a new right-wing French government might have joined in a massive assault against Ho Chi Minh that would have necessitated either Russian involvement or acquiescence— neither of which presented attractive prospects for the Kremlin. Therefore, when Mendès-France came to power and pledged to settle the war within thirty days or resign, Moscow recognized that only by persuading Ho to strike a deal with the French could a wider war be avoided.

The second reason for Moscow's desiring a negotiated settlement lay in the French Assembly debate, early in 1954, over French membership in the European Defense Community. According to one source, during the Berlin Foreign Ministers Conference to discuss Germany's future, Molotov suggested to French Foreign Minister Bidault that the Soviet Union would help arrange a cease-fire in Indochina in exchange for French abandonment of EDC.[13] Bidault apparently rejected the deal, but circumstantial evidence suggests that Mendès-France, whose government came to power on June 20, pledged to "peace within a month," did have such an understanding with Moscow. Molotov's efforts were in fact crucial in achieving a Geneva settlement, and Mendès-France did little to prevent the French Assembly from vetoing the EDC.

In any case, there seems to be widespread agreement among those who have investigated the background of the Geneva Conference that the Russians exerted considerable pressure on Ho Chi Minh to accept a partition of Vietnam on terms that must have been greatly disappointing to the Northern, and particularly to the Southern, Communists. The country's division at the 17th parallel left the non-Communist Southern government in control of about half the population and area of Vietnam, as well as the traditional "rice bowl" of Southeast Asia. The military position of the Vietminh on the eve of the Geneva agreement must have seemed to local Communists worthy of a much better settlement.

Moreover, as Bernard Fall, Jean Lacouture, and Philippe Devillers have all pointed out, the Communists accepted a document of extremely dubious legal force to end the war. The only accords actually signed at Geneva were military cease-fire agreements. The final declaration calling for elections was unsigned. As Devillers and Lacouture observe:

> The Geneva Conference will thus have invented a new form of peaceful coexistence—that which results from the tacit consent of the negotiators—as well as a new form of legal obligation between states: the unsigned treaty.[14]

It is not entirely clear why the Vietminh accepted a partition on such terms or why they accepted a document that was legally weak. Some believe it was a result of Soviet pressure. Others assert that the Vietminh expected South Vietnam to fall into northern hands within two years as a result of political instability. Formal provisions for reunification were therefore unimportant. A third explanation is that the Vietnamese Communists feared a continuing war with possible American intervention. Perhaps it was a combination of all three. What is certain is that the settlement left a residue of bitterness among the southern Communists, against both their northern comrades and the Russians, which has continued to this day.[15]

The July, 1956, deadline for elections in Vietnam passed without a ballot and without an incident. There is some reason to believe that whatever the Hanoi leaders thought, both the Russians and Americans at Geneva tacitly recognized that the partition of Vietnam would continue indefinitely—one more casualty of the Cold War. It is difficult to imagine that the Russians, or for that matter the North Vietnamese themselves, believed Saigon and Washington would peacefully relinquish to North Vietnam what it could not gain on the battlefield between 1946 and 1954. The Saigon government explicitly stated that it did not consider itself bound by the unsigned Geneva accords, and Dulles, by forming SEATO right on the heels of Geneva, served notice that he considered South Vietnam to be on the Cold War line.

Moreover, Moscow did little to advance Hanoi's cause; it scarcely uttered a protest in the United Nations when the 1956 Vietnamese elections were canceled. An unimpeachable authority, closely connected with the International Control Commission (ICC) at that time, told me that Hanoi was extremely annoyed over this Soviet attitude. Indeed, in early 1957, Moscow proposed the admittance to the United Nations of both North and South Vietnam, thus tacitly accepting the partition.

By early 1957 Hanoi itself seemed reconciled to the indefinite partition of Vietnam, and its statements began to speak of reunification as a long-term process which would have to await the economic development of the North. In line with this new perspective, Hanoi turned increasingly to Russia—not China—as the principal suppliers of aid.[16] In return for this assistance, Hanoi embraced the Soviet concept of peaceful coexistence. Although Communist-led guerrilla activity occurred in South Vietnam between 1957 and 1960, Hanoi's principal efforts were directed not at subverting the South but at consolidating the North.

FROM 1960 TO 1965

Since 1960, Soviet policy in Indochina has been dictated by two conflicting but equally important considerations: a desire to reach a détente with the United States, which has supported the South Vietnamese government against the Vietcong and North Vietnam; and a need to maintain Russian influence in the international Communist movement—and especially its Asian sector—in the face of increasing rivalry with China. The first consideration has required minimizing Hanoi's growing conflict with South Vietnam; the second has required support of it.

Khrushchev's inability to resolve the conflict between these two policy interests made his behavior in Indochina erratic but not ambivalent. In December, 1960, Russia intervened in Laos to support the neutralist army of Kong Le at some risk of a confrontation with the United States, which then supported General Phoumi Nosavan. Soviet aircraft flew 184 missions into Laos in the last two weeks of December.[17] Yet four years later, the Khrushchev who had intervened in behalf of the Vietminh-dominated Pathet Lao was prepared to resign Soviet cochairmanship of the permanent body of the ICC and to disengage from all of Indochina. *Pravda*, when proposing an international conference on Laos for August observed:

> A negative attitude on the part of other states toward this proposal
> . . . would place the Soviet government in a position in which it will
> feel compelled to review the question in general of whether the Soviet
> Union can carry out its functions as cochairman, since, in conditions
> of crude and systematic violations of the Geneva agreements by certain
> states, the role of cochairman loses any useful significance and becomes
> a fiction.[18]

While a number of factors undoubtedly influenced Khrushchev's deposition, the most important concerned Hanoi's role in the Sino-Soviet conflict. The bumptious Soviet leader was never given to the ambivalant course his successors have followed. He took the unusual risk of intervening in distant Laos largely in order to retain Hanoi's allegiance in the developing quarrel with Peking. In August, 1960, he had tried to bribe North Vietnam away from China with large credits to finance ambitious industrial expansion. The air-lift to Laos four months later was intended to demonstrate to the Vietminh and its Pathet Lao allies that Moscow could be relied upon in a crisis with the "imperialists."(By 1964, however, Hanoi had moved so close to Peking—a position from which it subsequently withdrew—that Khrushchev no longer believed the game was worth the candle. Soviet economic aid to Ho Chi Minh's government dwindled significantly in the last two years of Khrushchev's rule as he moved increasingly toward a détente with the United States.)

Hanoi's drift toward Peking, which began in the spring of 1963 and accelerated during much of 1964, halted suddenly in the latter part of that year. Evidence accumulated at that time to suggest that Hanoi and the Vietcong, probably motivated by United States military escalation in the aftermath of the Tonkin Gulf incidents of August 2 and 4, 1964, sought stronger links to, and support from, Moscow. As the Tonkin Gulf events and subsequent American reprisal raids on North Vietnamese PT-boat bases exposed North Vietnam's vulnerability to U.S. military power and posed the danger of a wider war, the Russians faced still new dilemmas. Moscow's anxiety over the possibility of an enlarged war that could lead to a Soviet-American confrontation was reflected in *Pravda's* nervous reaction to the Tonkin Gulf affair.[19]

In short, the Tonkin Gulf events intensified Russia's dilemma over how much aid and support it could give North Vietnam without wrecking the Soviet-American détente. This was one reason why the Russians began to evince considerable interest in a negotiated settlement of the war at this point. Another reason lay in the rapidly deteriorating military and political situation of the post-Diem government in South Vietnam. By the fall of 1964, South Vietnam was on the verge of collapse. The Vietcong was threatening to cut the country in half, and the South Vietnamese army and civil administration were shattered. Under these circumstances, negotiations that would in time almost certainly have led to a Communist-dominated South Vietnam must have seemed attractive in Moscow. During the emergency Security Council meeting convened at Washington's request after Tonkin, the Soviet delegate did in fact suggest that Hanoi send a representative to the Council to discuss the situation. This action provoked the ire of several Asian Communist parties, including the Chinese and Japanese, and was probably not well received in Hanoi itself, where the Security Council invitation was rejected.[20] The Japanese Communists probably reflected the sentiments of many Asian parties when they charged:

> In the face of . . . open armed aggression by U.S. imperialism against a socialist country, you . . . lent it a helping hand by trying to use the U.N. Security Council to legalize its crimes of aggression. By doing so, you in fact played the role of an accomplice.[21]

However, since a confrontation with Washington seemed on the horizon, Hanoi still indicated a desire to move closer to Moscow. In August, Secretary-General of the Lao Dong (North Vietnamese Communist Party), Le Duan, visited the Soviet capital and expressed an interest in increased Soviet aid. The following month, a conference in Hanoi paid court to pro-Soviet front organizations.

Most important, however, was that the period just before Khrushchev's ouster saw the Soviet Union actively involved in an attempt to negotiate an end to the Vietnamese war. Just after the Tonkin Gulf incident, Hanoi, with apparent Soviet encouragement, relayed a message to Washington through U.N. Secretary-General U Thant, who, in turn, dispatched it to Washington through Adlai Stevenson, then U.S. Ambassador to the U.N. The message contained Ho Chi Minh's response to U Thant's suggestion of a private meeting with U.S. envoys. Thant, after hearing from Ho, arranged for such a meeting at an estate outside Rangoon. Washington, however, refused to participate and reportedly also rebuffed a second invitation to meet with Ho.[22]

It seems likely, therefore, that the North Vietnamese at this point were interested in sounding out the possibility of negotiations, and particularly in determining what price the Americans were prepared to pay for a settlement. They apparently authorized Moscow to act as intermediary with U Thant and Washington for this purpose. The main reason that Hanoi was interested in negotiations at this point was probably its confidence that the military balance of power was in its favor. A year later, after the United States sent ground troops to Vietnam, Hanoi's position on negotiations hardened.

THE COLLECTIVE LEADERSHIP TAKES CHARGE

After Khrushchev's ouster in October, 1964, the new Kremlin leadership began immediately to back away from the radical departures Khrushchev had taken in both domestic and foreign policy. Instinctively the gray bureaucrats who took charge in the Kremlin groped for the safe middle of the road. Simultaneously, they sought to achieve the impossible: to stabilize their relations with both China and the United States.

As the new Kremlin leaders surveyed the situation in Vietnam at the end of 1964 and early 1965, they must have concluded that South Vietnam was on the verge of collapse and that America would accept a Communist victory there. Encouraged by signs that Hanoi was susceptible to Soviet wooing, and sensing a growing coolness between Peking and the smaller Asian Communist parties, the new Soviet leaders began to make a more active effort to re-establish Soviet influence in the international Communist movement, and particularly its Asian sector. Thus, Soviet Premier Kosygin led a strong delegation to North Vietnam and to North Korea in February, 1965, stopping in Peking en route.

The composition of the delegation[23] indicates that the Russians came equipped with substantial bait—in the form of potential military and economic aid—to help lure Hanoi away from Peking and closer to Moscow. The Soviet–North Vietnamese Joint Statement of February 11, 1965, contained the first known offer of Russian military aid to Hanoi. The purpose Moscow stated was to "strengthen the defense capacity of the Democratic Republic of Vietnam (DRV),"[24] but more immediate, probably, was the desire to lure

Hanoi to a crucial interparty meeting in Moscow scheduled for March 1st.

On the very day of Kosygin's arrival in Hanoi, the Vietcong attacked the U.S. base at Pleiku in South Vietnam, provoking the first American air strikes against North Vietnam. Some observers speculate that the Pleiku attack was organized by hard-line elements in Hanoi and the National Liberation Front (NLF) who sought to nip any Soviet initiative to begin peace talks.[25] This speculation, in turn, raises the question of whether Kosygin did in fact go to Hanoi to persuade the North Vietnamese to make peace.

To answer this question it is necessary to recall the immediate circumstances. Although the onset of the bombing took the Russians by surprise, there is reason to believe that they regarded it as a futile, last-ditch effort by Washington to strengthen its bargaining position in a forthcoming peace conference. At that time, the Communists were eagerly seizing statements by prominent American Senators, columnists, and newspapers which advocated negotiations, and rumors were circulating that the Administration itself favored peace talks. In fact, a counselor and close friend of President Johnson went to Paris to sound out possibilities for a "neutralist" solution to the war, while William Bundy, Assistant Secretary of State for Far Eastern Affairs, voiced the possibility of a return to the Geneva agreements.[26] Moreover, the military situation in early 1965 probably led Moscow to believe that Washington would soon seek a peace conference in order to avoid total defeat.

The South Vietnamese army, having been badly mauled by the Vietcong during the preceding year, was on the verge of collapse early in 1965. From the Communist side, it thus appeared that the final and decisive stage of the war was approaching.[27] In Hanoi the major issue was probably whether to force United States capitulation by delivering a *coup de grace* in the form of an American Dienbienphu, or to help Washington find a face-saving way out of Vietnam. Apparently, an important group of North Vietnamese leaders favored the latter approach as did the Russians. The Joint Statement issued on Kosygin's departure advocated the convening, "without delay and preconditions," of an international conference on Laos—a conference which many observers felt could provide a back door to negotiations in Vietnam.

Although it would be wrong to assume that he sought to pull American chestnuts out of the fire, Kosygin had several reasons for wanting a peaceful settlement. While he may have viewed the bombing of North Vietnam as a manifestation of U.S. imperialism's death throes rather than as the prelude to new escalation, he did fear the possibility of an enlarged war.[28]

Still another factor motivating Kosygin to seek peace talks in Vietnam lay in Moscow's desire to maintain the Soviet-American détente. A further contributing factor was the unstable political situation in the Soviet Union, where the new leadership was anxious to consolidate its position and to resolve pressing domestic problems rather than plunge into foreign adventures from which it had little to gain.

Kosygin's statements in Hanoi—and on his way home—evidence Russia's intent to initiate negotiations in Vietnam. His most important statement committed the Soviet Union for the first time to support a Geneva conference on all Indochina. Speaking at a Hanoi rally, the Soviet Premier not only called for an international conference on Laos "without any preliminary conditions," but also expressed support for a new international conference on Indochina as proposed by the Cairo Conference of Nonaligned Nations held in October, 1964.[29] The Joint Statement issued at the end of Kosygin's visit also indicated that Moscow was willing to resume the responsibilities of its ICC cochairmanship with Vietnam.[30] Furthermore, Kosygin implied that a quick end to the war would directly benefit Hanoi. Praising North Vietnam's economic achievements to date, the Soviet Premier added:

> We are firmly convinced that the Vietnamese people would have recorded still greater successes in their peaceful labor if they did not have to build socialism in the conditions of constant threat of provocations by the imperialists.[31]

There were other signs that the new Kremlin leadership wanted to bring the war to an end. On February 12th, both Brezhnev and Gromyko reportedly told the Indian Minister of Information—then visiting Moscow—that "the Soviet Union is extremely anxious to avoid an extension of the fighting in Vietnam," and that calling a conference would be "a step in the right direction."[32] On the same day, according to official sources in London, Deputy Soviet Foreign Minister Lapin informed the British Ambassador in Moscow that the Soviet Union would cooperate with Britain as Geneva cochairman. He reportedly said, "When the fire breaks out, firemen do not argue about their duties." Similar diplomatic efforts were made in Paris, where the Soviet Ambassador secured French government agreement to press jointly for an international conference on Vietnam.[33]

Further evidence that Moscow sought ways to end the war at this time comes from Chinese accusations published during 1965 as the Sino-Soviet dispute intensified. According to a lengthy article in *Peking Review*,[34] Kosygin had—in January—relayed to Hanoi an American message asking the Soviet Union to use its influence to persuade North Vietnam to accept two conditions for peace talks: stop giving military aid to the Vietcong and halt attacks on South Vietnamese cities. The following month, when Kosygin stopped in Peking en route to Hanoi, he reportedly stressed the need to help the United States "find a way out of Vietnam." Peking charged that on February 16 (the day after Kosygin's return home) Moscow officially put before North Vietnam and China a proposal for a new international conference on Indochina without prior conditions—a proposal, said Peking, tantamount to advocating "unconditional negotiations."

It thus appears that as of early 1965, Moscow was anxious to bring about negotiations, Peking was trying to forestall them, and the Hanoi leadership was somewhere in the middle—ready to listen to American proposals, but internally divided on whether to continue applying military pressure on the South or to negotiate.

NEW PHASE OF WAR, MID-1965

A new phase of the Vietnamese war began in early 1965 with the American bombing of the North and with the introduction of more than 100,000 U.S. ground troops. In the face of these developments, Hanoi's position began to harden and the Russians became increasingly sensitive to Chinese criticism that they were anxious to make a deal with the United States to end the war on terms disadvantageous to Hanoi. Moreover, after the National Liberation Front and Hanoi put forward their respective five- and four-point proposals on March 22 and April 8, 1965, Moscow had little choice but to endorse them. Not to have done so would not only have assured Hanoi's defection to Peking, but it would have enabled Peking and Hanoi to rally an anti-Soviet Communist coalition in Asia.

As the war entered a new phase, then, the Russians moved to the diplomatic sidelines, letting initiatives pass to North Vietnam and the NLF. During a visit to London at the end of March, Gromyko insisted that only the United States and North Vietnam were directly involved in the war and therefore should settle it between themselves.[35] Moreover, on April 24, 1965, the Russians allowed the NLF to establish a six-member permanent mission in Moscow with the equivalent of diplomatic status. At the same time, Moscow gave increasingly firm support to Hanoi's position. An eighteen-party meeting in Moscow in March fully endorsed the Four Points and demanded American withdrawal as a prerequisite for a settlement.[36]

By repeatedly stressing its intention to provide Hanoi with all necessary aid, and giving it full diplomatic support at this time, Moscow probably hoped to accomplish three goals. First, because it could supply sophisticated military equipment that China could not match, Moscow hoped to underline Hanoi's dependence on Russia, to increase Russian influence in Hanoi, and thus to draw North Vietnam farther away from Peking. Second, the Russians wished to demonstrate clearly to the world Communist movement that Moscow, and not Peking, was working most actively to protect North Vietnam and to secure an NLF victory. Finally, the Russians probably hoped to be able to use the leverage gained in Hanoi to draw North Vietnam to the conference table when the time was propitious.

Almost from the moment American bombs began to drop on North Vietnam, the Sino-Soviet dispute intensified. The antagonisms between the two Communist rivals were so deep that not even an attack on one of their common allies could bring them together. The depth of these mutual suspicions is reflected in the dispute over Soviet arms shipments that has raged since Kosygin visited Hanoi in February, 1965.

Peking has accused the Russians of neglecting to fulfill their pledges of assistance to Hanoi, of sending obsolete and damaged weapons to Hanoi, and of using this equipment to gain dominance in Hanoi for the purpose of arranging a "deal" with the United States to end the war.[37] Moscow has retorted that the Chinese themselves have been responsible for delays in weapons shipments moved through Chinese territory by their erection of bureaucratic obstacles.

Some time after Kosygin's visit to Hanoi, Moscow asked Peking for an air corridor over China to allow Soviet planes to supply North Vietnam, and for one or two air bases in southern China where, presumably, Soviet planes and pilots would be stationed to help deter American air attacks on North Vietnam. The Chinese rebuffed this proposal because "we have every reason to think that you have ulterior motives in offering such assistance."[38]

CLOSER HANOI–MOSCOW TIES

Hanoi may have shared Peking's suspicions about Moscow's motives, but it was not willing to rely solely on China for help in its war effort. On April 10, Le Duan and General Vo Nguyen Giap headed a North Vietnamese delegation to Moscow where they warmly thanked the Russians for "great fraternal and internationalist support and assistance."[39] They reportedly also endorsed a Russian proposal for a Sino-Soviet–North Vietnamese summit conference to coordinate weapons shipments to Hanoi. The Chinese rejected this idea, as they did any subsequent plans involving cooperation with Moscow.[40] The great differences between Hanoi and Peking on Moscow's role in the war at this time prohibited a joint communiqué when Le Duan's delegation stopped in China en route home.[41]

Another North Vietnamese delegation, this one headed by economic specialist and Deputy Premier Le Thanh Nghi, arrived in Moscow in July, 1965. The resulting agreements provided for economic and military aid beyond that already granted to North Vietnam by the Soviet Union under previously concluded agreements. This delegation, too, traveled on to Peking. The thanks it expressed for Chinese aid was noticeably less warm than that extended for Soviet assistance.[42]

Throughout the fall and winter of 1965, Hanoi drew closer to Moscow. Disregarding increased Chinese invective over Russian treachery, Hanoi continued to express warm gratitude for Soviet aid—most notably during a Moscow visit by a North Vietnamese National Assembly delegation in August, 1965.[43] The following month, Ho Chi Minh gave the Soviet Union favored place in expressing "heartfelt gratitude to the fraternal Socialist countries" for their aid.[44] In December, Le Thanh Nghi led a second delegation to Moscow, where new economic and technical agreements were signed. As Soviet–North Vietnamese relations warmed, China stepped up its warnings to Hanoi. In salvos obviously aimed at Hanoi, then Chinese Communist Party General Secretary Teng Hsiao-ping denounced revolutionaries who took an "opportunist" attitude in the Sino-Soviet ideological quarrel. Other Chinese spokesmen began to stress that Soviet revisionism must first be defeated before victory over imperialism was possible.[45] The Chinese thus implied that North Vietnam could not defeat the United States unless it first adopted a strict anti-Soviet line.

It should not, however, be assumed that Soviet military or economic aid to Hanoi was very great as of the end of 1965. The Soviet military aid to North Vietnam in 1965 was equivalent to about half a billion U.S. dollars, a meager amount compared to American aid to the South. It is small even when compared to Soviet aid to such non-Communist countries as the UAR and Indonesia in recent years.

An increased Soviet commitment of both military and economic aid seems to have been one of the major results of the visit by a high-ranking Russian delegation to Hanoi in January, 1966—the first such visit since Kosygin's a year earlier. This delegation, led by Alexander Shelepin and including Col. General V. F. Tolubko, Deputy Commander of the Soviet strategic missile force, arrived in Hanoi on January 7, 1966, having stopped in Peking en route.

Subsequent developments indicate that Shelepin promised Hanoi a substantial increase in both military and economic aid. *Komsomolskaya Pravda*, on January 23, 1966, mentioned Soviet delivery to Vietnam of ground-to-air missiles, "complex" antiaircraft guns with radar guidance systems, and antiaircraft automatic guns of "large caliber." By March, 1966, North Vietnam was reported to have twelve Soviet MIG-21 fighters and in early April it was reported that forty more had arrived. There were also reports that North Vietnamese were being sent to Russia in large numbers to train as fighter pilots and there were persistent reports that Soviet military personnel were in North Vietnam to serve as advisers on surface-to-air missile sites.[46]

The total cost of Soviet exports to North Vietnam in 1966 is not yet available, but there is reason to believe that the figure exceeded that of 1965, 67.4 million rubles—which was the highest amount in six years. Moscow was sending North Vietnam such items as road-building equipment, complete plants, tractors and agricultural machinery, automobiles, medicine, and radio sets.[47] It seemed likely that Moscow was giving Hanoi long-term credits for the purchase of this equipment.

The main *quid pro quo* exacted by Shelepin for the new aid was probably that Hanoi send a delegation to the 23rd Party Congress meeting in Moscow in March, 1966—a Congress which the Chinese and their few remaining Communist allies boycotted. Hanoi did in fact send a delegation; this prompted Peking to warn them "to draw a clear line" between themselves and Soviet revisionism or face the consequences.[48]

While Hanoi was willing to risk Peking's displeasure by sending representatives to Moscow's Party Congress, it was not willing to agree to Shelepin's proposal for a summit meeting of the ruling Communist parties in Europe and Asia for the purpose of discussing aid to Vietnam. The Albanians later charged that Shelepin's visit was designed largely to pressure Hanoi into attending such a conference.[49] Obviously such a conference would have been another step in Moscow's campaign to isolate China on the pretext of helping Hanoi. China would not have attended the conference and Moscow was well aware of that fact. If Shelepin had been able to persuade Hanoi to support such a conference, however, the other ruling parties—with the exception of the Albanians—might well have attended, greatly embarrassing Peking.

One clear purpose of Shelepin's visit—perhaps the major one—was to line Hanoi up on Moscow's side against Peking in exchange for Soviet military and economic aid. To this end, it was a limited success. Hanoi, while not agreeing to support a summit conference, did agree to send representatives to the Moscow Congress, which the Chinese were to denounce as a "conspiracy" that had "nothing in common with a congress of the party of Lenin." North Vietnam sent to the Congress a top-level delegation headed by Le Duan, who praised the Soviet Union as "my second fatherland,"[50] profusely thanked the Russians for their aid, and—in contrast to China's accusal that Moscow was restoring capitalism—praised Russia's progress toward communism.

Because Shelepin was so anxious to gain Hanoi's support against China, it is unlikely that he made any major moves toward negotiations. In fact, in some of his speeches, he hurled some of the harshest epithets ever used by the Russians against Washington.[51] Moreover, he stated unequivocally that the United States must understand that a settlement in Vietnam is "inconceivable" without NLF participation. And he cast doubt on Washington's peaceful intentions (there had been a bombing pause for thirty-seven days) by contrasting these "so-called peace initiatives" with the simultaneous increase in American troop commitments. Pham Van Dong later publicly thanked Shelepin for supporting Hanoi's rejection of U.S. peace offers.[52]

At the same time, there is some evidence to suggest that Shelepin continued to urge Hanoi to hold the door open to negotiations. He failed to echo predictions made by Hanoi leaders that they would ultimately triumph and to endorse their resolve to fight for "five, ten, twenty years or longer."[53] And Party Secretary D. F. Ustinov, who accompanied Shelepin, told an audience at Hanoi's polytechnic college that North Vietnam's impressive achievements in the building of socialism would be still greater were it not for American destructive acts.[54] He thus implied that North Vietnam had more to gain by peace than by a continuation of the war. Moreover, captured North Vietnamese documents dating from this period and reported by Joseph Alsop in April, 1967, indicated that Shelepin had made some moves to bring Hanoi to negotiations but had been turned down. "A number of socialist countries," said the Hanoi documents, held that "conditions favorable to negotiations" prevailed. Presumably this advice was given to Hanoi by the Russians during the bombing pause which accompanied Shelepin's visit.

Further evidence of Moscow's continued interest in a negotiated settlement of the war came from the Soviet delegate to the 18-Nation Disarmament Committee at Geneva who declared soon after the Tashkent meeting convened by Kosygin on January 4, 1966, to bring India and Pakistan together to work out a cease-fire agreement that:

> Recent developments furnish fresh evidence that, in this day and age, *no problem* can be solved by armed force . . . no matter how powerful. The key to settlement of pressing . . . issues can be found *only* at the conference table. Vietnam and Tashkent symbolize two diametrically opposed concepts in world affairs. And everyone can see which of these concepts benefits mankind.[55] (Emphasis added.)

Soviet newspapers agreed with this assessment. *Red Star*, the military paper, wrote after Tashkent: "The fruitful results of the Tashkent meeting convincingly show that even complex international issues can and should be solved by means of talks."[56]

Although Moscow was apparently trying to convince Hanoi that favorable conditions for negotiations existed, there is no indication that the Russians were urging Hanoi to make substantial concessions to the United States, or that they threatened sanctions if Hanoi did not negotiate. On the contrary, the captured documents cited above indicate that Hanoi was convinced that "the Soviet Union supports us under all conditions: whether we fight or negotiate or whether we fight and negotiate." One of the reasons for Hanoi's confidence was the existence of the Sino-Soviet split. Hanoi was well aware that Moscow valued good relations with the smaller Communist state in order to check Chinese influence in the international Communist movement. In order to maintain such good relations, Moscow could not afford to press Hanoi into negotiations against its own will. Thus, the Sino-Soviet split had certain advantages for Hanoi.

As the Vietnam war went on, the split between Russia and China intensified. For instance, when Marshal Rodion Malinovsky charged Peking with hampering Soviet weapons shipments, the Chinese Foreign Ministry called him a "liar" and claimed that China transported Russian materiel "with priority, at high speed and free of charge."[57] The Chinese then launched into one of the most lengthy and vicious assaults to that time on Moscow's Vietnam policy:

> Both in quantity and quality, the aid the Soviet Union gives to Vietnam is far from commensurate with its strength. It should have been easy for a big power like the Soviet Union to provide Vietnam with several hundred thousand tons of military supplies. But it has only given a few tens of thousands of tons, a deplorably meager amount. [Moreover] most of the Soviet supplies consisted of old weapons . . . and . . . even included some that were worn out and of no use at all. True, the Soviet Union has also given Vietnam some weapons of comparatively new types, but even these are already outmoded. As for those of truly good quality, the Soviet Union either does not supply them or is unwilling to supply them in large quantities. . . . The heart of the matter is that the Soviet revisionist leading group has already degenerated into an accomplice of U.S. imperialism. Its so-called aid to Vietnam is a sham. . . .[58]

Significantly, the Chinese statement added:

> . . . Malinovsky ought to know that besides ground and air communications, there are sea routes to link various countries. . . . The Soviet Union has no common boundary with Cuba . . . yet it could ship rocket-nuclear weapons [there]. . . . It is not even that far from Vietnam; why can't it ship even conventional weapons there?[59]

Peking was trying to goad Moscow into supplying North Vietnam by sea and thus to risk a confrontation with the United States. The Russians clearly understood this.

Official Soviet reaction to American bombing of oil depots around Hanoi and Haiphong in late June was mild, and no attempt was made to stress American raids on North Vietnamese population centers. Furthermore, both the June 30th official Soviet government statement on this issue and Brezhnev's July 1st speech to military academy graduates blamed American military leaders rather than the United States government for the bombing[60]—a device the Russians commonly employ to leave room for maneuver. Brezhnev said Soviet aid to Hanoi would increase, but he made no definite commitment. He emphasized only that the United States should give serious thought to the possible outcome of its policy.[61] Moreover, Moscow took pains to deny that the Soviet Union regarded withdrawal of United States troops from Vietnam as a condition for a nuclear nonproliferation treaty.

Although *Pravda* on July 8th published a rather harsh indictment of U.S. policy in Vietnam, the very next day it featured a more lengthy article on the overwhelming need to strengthen peace and security in Europe. In addition, a note from the Soviet Foreign Ministry to the U.S. Embassy complaining that air strikes near Haiphong had endangered Russian merchant vessels and sailors was decidedly weak.[62]

This Soviet attitude did not go unnoticed by Peking. The same day the Soviet note was delivered, Chou En-lai accused Moscow of committing a "most open, barefaced betrayal of the Vietnamese people" by allegedly stating that U.S. bombing of Hanoi and Haiphong would not affect Soviet-American cooperation and achievement of a disarmament accord.[63] China's strongest anti-Soviet propaganda at this time, however, was aimed against Moscow's interest in Vietnam peace talks even in the face of American escalation. The Prime Ministers of both Britain and India visited the Soviet Union in July to discuss the Vietnam war. Publicly, Moscow declared that if Wilson truly desired a peaceful settlement, he

> would have to demand from the United States the immediate and unconditional withdrawal of American troops, . . . the cessation of intervention in the internal affairs of the Vietnamese people, and the liquidation of foreign military bases in South Vietnam. A political solution of the Vietnamese problem can be found [only] on that basis.[64]

Mrs. Gandhi meanwhile told reporters: "The stand of the USSR is that any proposal should first have the approval of North Vietnam."[65] Privately, the Russians apparently told Wilson and Mrs. Gandhi—as well as U Thant, who visited Moscow shortly afterward—that

Soviet good offices would be available if and when Hanoi showed signs of wanting negotiations.[66]

A statement on Vietnam adopted by the Supreme Soviet on August 3rd offered the standard Soviet fare—including a pledge to send volunteers if North Vietnam requested them, reaffirmation of the four- and five-point programs of Hanoi and the NLF, and the demand that

> . . . the U.S. government . . . take the road of strict fulfillment of the Geneva Agreements . . . immediately, decisively and unconditionally stop bombing the . . . DRV, end the armed intervention in South Vietnam, withdraw American troops and the troops of its satellites from South Vietnam, remove all American military bases from that country, recognize the NLF as the only genuine representative of . . . South Vietnam, and recognize the right of the people of Vietnam to determine their own destiny without outside interference. . . .[67]

Kosygin, in his speech to the Supreme Soviet, sounded a hopeful note when he pointedly referred to the existence in the United States of "sound tendencies":

> . . . today the aggressive military forces increasingly set the tone in American policy. . . . Aggressive moods obviously predominate in Washington at the present stage. But we know that there are other, sounder tendencies there too. The strengthening of these tendencies will be received with due understanding on our part.[68]

And, emphasizing that Soviet policy remained based on peaceful coexistence, Kosygin observed that, although the Vietnam war poisons the atmosphere for the adoption of fundamental disarmament measures,

> . . . nevertheless, even now a number of important partial measures can be taken. . . . One such measure could be . . . a treaty for nonproliferation of nuclear weapons. . . . Another . . . could be the banning of all nuclear tests.[69]

A few days after the Premier's speech, the Soviet Foreign Ministry issued another mild protest to the U.S. Embassy about new "provocations" against Soviet merchant ships in Haiphong harbor. The Kremlin, in fact, seemed relieved that Washington had not yet instituted anything in Vietnam comparable to its blockade of Cuba during the missile crisis.

SOVIET REASSESSMENT

In the last four months of 1966, Moscow gave signs of undertaking a major reassessment of its foreign policy, and particularly its relations with China and the United States. This was doubtless brought about by three developments: the pursuit of the "cultural revolution" in China, which saw pro-Soviet factions led by Marshal Lo Jui-ching and Party leaders Teng Hsiao-ping and Liu Shao-chi routed by Mao and Marshal Lin Piao; increasing calls in the United States for greater flexibility in American policy toward China; and several speeches by President Johnson offering to radically improve Soviet-American relations and to lift export restrictions on a large number of nonstrategic items.

These developments compelled the new Soviet leaders to begin making long-avoided choices—particularly the one between Peking and Washington. Caught in the middle of the triangular relationship, for years Moscow had hesitated to move too close to Washington for fear of a break with Peking. At the same time, it had been reluctant to write off China as long as there was evidence—as there was—of the existence of a powerful pro-Soviet lobby within the Chinese party that wished a reconciliation with Moscow. From August, 1966, however, it was clear that Mao had defeated this pro-Soviet faction and, in an effort to discredit it at home, had deliberately sought to provoke the Russians into a diplomatic break. The reasons for Mao's policy will be discussed in a later chapter. It is sufficient to indicate here that Mao was genuinely concerned at the possibility of a "revisionist" capture of the Chinese revolution and that he was determined to prevent it. Mao came increasingly to look upon Moscow, the capital of "revisionism," as his main enemy.

Moscow had good cause for concern. It had to fear further tensions with China, and the fact that the United States might seek to exploit the opportunity by opening up its own relations with China. Soon after August, 1966, therefore, the Russians began a concerted effort to sound out American views on China and to make clear to the United States that Moscow would interpret any improvement of Sino-American relations as an anti-Soviet act.

As the Sino-Soviet split deepened, Moscow feared that while China and the United States had reached a tacit agreement not to become embroiled over Vietnam, China would cut off Moscow's overland supply route to Vietnam, forcing Russia to supply North

Vietnam by sea—thus setting the stage for a Soviet-American confrontation a la Cuba. Such a possibility had been long hinted at by Peking.

Such fears may have encouraged the Kremlin to press more strongly for a negotiated settlement of the Vietnamese war. Furthermore, because Peking had persistently refused to join in united action on Vietnam, the Kremlin may have seen a chance of pressing Hanoi toward talks and blaming Peking for the failure to achieve Communist goals.

Moscow began to do several things: first, for the first time since Khrushchev's ouster, it engaged in a violent propaganda campaign against China. Internally, such a campaign was designed to prepare the Russian party and people for a final break with China; externally, it was designed to censure Chinese policy through new and stronger efforts to arrange an international meeting of Communist parties. Second, Soviet diplomats in several countries began actively to explore the American position on how the war might be ended. Soviet envoys discussed privately with their American counterparts what could be done to induce U Thant to remain at his U.N. post. In private talks with the Secretary-General, the Russians assured him they would support his efforts to bring about a settlement of the war if he would stay on for another term.

The first sign of the new Soviet tactic came in mid-October with a sudden and unannounced conference in Moscow of Soviet, East European, Mongolian, and Cuban Communist leaders. The Russians said that a major purpose of the conclave was to coordinate the Warsaw Pact's Vietnam aid measures. "Coordinating aid to Vietnam" had by this time become a euphemism in Moscow for isolating Peking. China would not have attended under any circumstances, Hanoi—reluctant to join any anti-Peking conference despite its pretext—declined to attend, and North Korea refused to go without Hanoi. Hence, none of the ruling Asian parties turned up. Obviously, this conference of all ruling parties designed to coordinate aid to Vietnam was what Shelepin had in mind at his January visit to Hanoi.

Although the Communist representatives in Moscow promised to provide North Vietnam with financial and military aid totaling one billion dollars—800 million of it to come from Moscow—they also reportedly agreed "that it would be desirable for Hanoi to go to a peace conference and to make such a conference possible by helping to create the conditions that would lead to a halt in American bombing. . . ."[70]

There was additional evidence that the Soviet Union and its East European allies were now beginning to apply some pressure on Hanoi to negotiate. Shortly after the Moscow meeting had concluded, Ho Chi Minh told the editor of the French review *Événement* that

> . . . some people of good will, deceived by U.S. propaganda, have advised us to negotiate with the aggressors at all costs. They have forgotten that to end this war there needs only that the United States undertake to withdraw [from Vietnam]. . . .[71]

By late October, Russia's anti-China campaign was in full swing. Shelepin publicly blasted the Chinese for hindering Vietnam's war effort.[72] Brezhnev, speaking in Tbilisi on November 1, followed his lead. During a trip to Karachi, Soviet Academician Sverdlov revealed that Peking had refused permission to open camps in China for the training of Vietnamese to handle air defense weapons.[73] A Western correspondent in Moscow at this time summed up the Russian line: "The Soviets are discreetly spreading warnings that Peking is quite capable of doing something drastic in Vietnam . . . to make things awkward for the Kremlin and explosive for the U.S."[74]

Further indication of the new Soviet line—stepped-up aid to Vietnam with increased pressure for talks, all in the context of a violent anti-China campaign—came at the Bulgarian Party Congress that opened in Sofia in mid-November. At that time, Bulgarian Communist chief, Todor Zhivkov, made a call (approved and perhaps even inspired by Brezhnev, whose own congress speech echoed the proposal) for a world Communist conference, which, given the situation, clearly intended to rally the movement against China. Zhivkov's trial balloon fell flat.[75] The representatives from North Vietnam and the NLF, failing to join applause led by Brezhnev, were notably unenthusiastic.[76] Brezhnev had told the congress that Soviet aid to Vietnam was "concrete and effective" and that it would continue.[77]

Most significantly, however, a high Bulgarian official told Western correspondents covering the congress that the Soviet bloc's main objective was to bring about a peace conference on Vietnam; preconditions—such as a halt in bombing—were "of no great importance," he maintained.[78] This official also blasted Hanoi's "hawks" for their inflexible position on the war. At the same time, East German Premier Ulbrecht called for an early political settlement of the war.

It seems likely that the Russian and other East European delegations at the Bulgarian Congress used the meeting to discuss with the North Vietnamese and NLF representatives there the possibility of negotiations. The Poles evidently offered to act as intermediaries with Washington. Immediately after the Congress, in late November, according to a story by John Hightower published in May 1967, a Polish diplomat on the International Control Commission for Vietnam went to Hanoi for ten days of talks with North Vietnamese officials. The diplomat returned to Saigon in early December and told American Ambassador Henry Cabot Lodge that North Vietnam was now prepared to open secret talks with the United States. He did not make a bombing halt a condition of such talks. The stage was quickly set for secret exploratory talks between the United States and North Vietnam in Warsaw. At this point, American planes carried out the December 13th–14th raids on the outskirts of Hanoi. The North Vietnamese evidently regarded this as pre-talk pressure, for after this incident the Poles told the Americans that North Vietnam was no longer interested in talks because of the raids. The United States then ordered a halt in the bombing of Hanoi and its environs that lasted for four months, in an apparent effort to revive the Polish plan.

Evidently sensing that an opportunity for initiating talks had been badly bungled by the inopportune bombing of Hanoi, the United States, according to Hightower, made a major new effort to begin talks during the lunar New Year in February, 1967, reportedly after having sent a total of four messages to Hanoi containing peace proposals in January. In early February, President Johnson himself sent Ho Chi Minh a letter proposing secret talks. He offered to halt bombing of North Vietnam and to order a freeze in the build-up of United States forces in South Vietnam if North Vietnam stopped infiltration into South Vietnam.

Under obvious Soviet pressure to reconsider negotiations, North Vietnam announced publicly at the end of January that it would "consider" talks if the United States undertook a permanent and unconditional cessation of bombing of North Vietnam. This was the point of an important policy statement by Hanoi's Foreign Minister Nguyen Duy Trinh on January 28th [a statement which came right in the midst of the United States probes]. Ho Chi Minh's reply to President Johnson on February 15th dropped the demand that the bombing cessation be permanent, but insisted that it be "unconditional." By this Hanoi presumably meant to make clear that it was not prepared to enter discussions or to make any concessions in return for the bombing cessation.

The importance of these statements lay in the fact that they represented a departure from North Vietnam's previous public position, which had always been highly ambiguous about preconditions for negotiation. Previously, when asked whether they had any preconditions, Hanoi spokesmen would refer to the Four Points, leaving the impression that Hanoi wanted American recognition in principle of the Four Points before talks could begin. But Hanoi never flatly stated any preconditions for talks. Contrary to much opinion, careful study of Hanoi's public statements indicates that Hanoi never insisted on American withdrawal from Vietnam as a precondition for negotiations. Withdrawal is one of the Four Points but these, according to Hanoi, are to provide the basis for a "settlement" of the war and have never been called preconditions for negotiations.

Hanoi's adoption of a one-condition negotiating posture—an unconditional cessation of American bombing—seems to have been a gesture to the Russians who, unlike the Chinese, had long been suggesting privately and publicly that a halt in bombing was the only necessary precondition for talks. At any rate, Moscow clearly interpreted Trinh's January 28th statement as the "green light" from Hanoi it had been waiting for to reconvene the Geneva Conference. For, immediately after Trinh's statement, Soviet Premier Kosygin flew to London for talks with British Prime Minister Wilson.

In his statement in London, Kosygin for the first time in two years began to acknowledge Soviet responsibility for bringing peace to Vietnam. Previously Moscow's position had been that efforts to get negotiations going should be addressed to Hanoi. Now Moscow seemed confident that it had Hanoi's approval to reconvene the Geneva Conference. But Hanoi said it was willing to talk only if the United States stopped the bombing of North Vietnam. What is not clear, then, is whether Moscow expected the United States to stop bombing without a corresponding North Vietnamese concession, or whether Moscow sought and failed to get Hanoi to scale down its infiltration of South Vietnam, as Washington had demanded. What could no longer be doubted was that Russia was using its influence in Hanoi to bring about negotiations.

These efforts were, however, limited by suspicion in Hanoi of both American and Russian intentions and by continuation of the Sino-Soviet dispute, which made it possible for Hanoi to defy Soviet wishes by playing Peking off against Moscow. Indeed Sino-Soviet hostility may have made it possible for Hanoi to commit Moscow to a more dangerous course in Vietnam than Russia might otherwise have taken. For so long as Russia is concerned about its image as the leader of world Communism, and so long as Peking challenges its leading role, Moscow cannot afford to let Hanoi down.

As the war intensifies in mid-1967, it seems likely that Russia will step up its military aid to North Vietnam, while continuing to avoid a direct confrontation with the United States.[79] Moscow is anxiously seeking to estimate how far the United States might go in escalating the war and is beginning to appraise its own policy anew. It remains unclear to what extent the Soviet-American détente will be undermined by continuing escalation of the war.

CHAPTER THREE

Peking's Hawks, Doves, and Dawks*

THERE is, I believe, a consensus among those who specialize on Communist China that the crucial issues involved in the "Cultural Revolution" have to do with domestic rather than foreign policy issues. While domestic issues are central to the Chinese power struggle,[1] there are two fundamental reasons to consider foreign-policy questions. First, it is reasonably clear that American policies in Vietnam served as a catalyst to trigger long-standing political divergencies among the Chinese leadership, concerning especially China's relationship with the Soviet Union and the degree of risk it is prepared to meet in confronting the United States. Second, precisely because Mao regards his domestic opponents as "revisionists" who have come under Soviet ideological influence, and because he regards this influence as anathema to the future of the Chinese revolution, he has come to regard the Russians in some respects a greater enemy than the Americans.

Before pursuing the foreign-policy aspects of the Cultural Revolution, and their relationship to Vietnam, I want to make a few general remarks on the origins and the nature of the convulsion that has been shaking China since 1965 to establish the general framework in which Chinese foreign policy must be viewed.

---

* This chapter was originally prepared for a conference on Chinese foreign policy sponsored by the Center for Policy Study, University of Chicago.

The convulsion in China today is the result of three interacting processes: first, an attempted revolution from above that is surely unique in modern history—a pathetic effort by Mao and a few of his supporters against most of the party bureaucracy and vested interests in China to keep China in ferment and to prevent the kind of change (Mao would call it degeneration) that is the necessary fate of all revolutions; second, a premature power struggle to determine who and what will succeed Mao; and finally, a deep-seated and long-standing division of opinion among the Chinese leaders on basic questions of domestic and foreign policy.

Since the power struggle is both the most obvious and the most remarked-upon aspect of the crisis, I shall not dwell upon it except to say that Mao and his appointed heir, Marshal Lin Piao, are opposed by most of the central and provincial party leaders, by a substantial group of professionals within the army, by most of the cultural and educational leaders, and by most of the economic specialists and technocrats. Since the party and the army are the two major networks of power in Communist China, and since the intellectuals and specialists are crucial in any country—particularly an underdeveloped one—the opposition to Mao is clearly considerable. It is in fact so great that normal bureaucratic channels of power in the party and the government are no longer reliable instruments of power for Mao. He has therefore been forced to resort to such nonbureaucratic instruments as the Red Guards and specially created Cultural Revolution committees in the factories, farms, and schools in an effort to purge—or at least to "re-educate"—his opposition and to replace it with new leadership from younger and uncontaminated cadres.

In effect, Mao is attempting to push out—or at least to check— the present Chinese Communist political and economic elite and to bring in revolutionary elements drawn from the "purer" segments of society. These new Cultural Revolution committees are to become permanent organizations, periodically elected and replenished by the masses, modeled on the Paris Commune, and paralleling regular party and government bureaucracies throughout China. By creating these parallel organizations to challenge the regular bureaucracy, Mao is seeking to institutionalize a permanent revolution at home, to insure that after his death revolutionary ferment will continue, and to prevent the consolidation of a new class, a privileged stratum of Red bureaucrats.

In a real sense Mao is a tragic figure. Having been a revolutionary most of his life, and having overcome enormous obstacles on the road to power, Mao remains a revolutionary in power—an ideologue dedicated to remaking Chinese society and reshaping Chinese man, committed to the belief that the human will can overcome all obstacles no matter how insuperable they may seem.

In that he believes in the possibility of changing human nature, Mao's language is the language of unadulterated Marxism. The Cultural Revolution, said the Central Committee decision of August 8, 1966, is to "touch people to their very souls." Its aim is to revolutionize people's ideology. Mao, in other words, is convinced that to get on with the enormous task of industrializing China it is not only necessary to give material incentives in the form of higher wages or bonuses, but to transform man himself. It is this element in Maoism that has struck such responsive chords in many Western Marxists who have long since been disillusioned with Russia.

As I. F. Stone has pointed out, the Maoist Gospels read like early Christian homilies. "In Memory of Norman Bethune" urges Mao's followers to learn the "spirit of absolute selflessness" from the Canadian surgeon who served first the Loyalists in Spain and then the Communist guerrillas in China. In "The Foolish Old Man" Mao sets out to demonstrate in a parable that faith can move mountains. Mao's simple belief is that if he can mobilize China's gifted people to work together for more than self, under the impulse of revolutionary fervor, they can "leap forward" into the twenty-first century and eliminate backwardness.

To most of his exasperated followers—and to the second generation of bureaucrats who now replace those who made the revolution— Mao's call for 100 years of struggle and sacrifice, for creating a nation of supermen, for abolishing specialization, seems like the madness of a senile old man. They have seen the failure of the Great Leap Forward in 1959–1961; they are tired of ideological campaigns and mass mobilization; they want an end to the Permanent Revolution and the creation of bureaucratic normalcy.

What Mao did not understand—and what any Western political scientist might have told him—is that all revolutions in the modern era are made by the ideologues but devoured by the bureaucrats and the pragmatists. The men who make revolutions are guided by noble ideas and visions of a new society to replace the old order; the men who consolidate revolutions are guided by the exigencies of power, by the rising expectations of their own people, by the need to build rather than to destroy, and by the laws of economics rather than the rhetoric of ideology.

By waging war against the bureaucrats and technocrats, Mao is fighting a vain, rear-guard action against all Chinese society's natural tendencies to settle down and concentrate on rice rather than revolution—to move toward stability, order, and economic rationality.

(Thus, while Mao may win the battle, he will certainly lose the war. His revolutionary vision is doomed to eventual failure. Mao is dreaming impossible dreams, he lacks the necessary support within the bureaucracy to make them happen, and even the masses of Chinese peasants—whose substantial political and social grievances and deep nationalist fervor aroused by the Japanese invaders prompted them to follow Mao twenty years ago—are not likely to follow him now that he calls for a generation or more of struggle and sacrifice. Maoism is no longer relevant to the needs of Chinese society.)

It is in this context that the issues in debate between Mao and the opposition—one should say the oppositions—should be seen. These issues run the gamut of Chinese domestic and foreign policy. Should China adopt more pragmatic and more gradual economic policies at home—even if this means a slower rate of industrialization, and the creation of a new privileged stratum that could constitute the social basis for revisionism? Should China abandon its ultra-revolutionary foreign policy and turn inward—even if this means abandoning revolutionaries abroad until China grows stronger? Should China seek a reconciliation with Russia which would restore the Soviet nuclear umbrella and lay the groundwork for resumption of Soviet aid—even if this means accepting Soviet policies that have been anathema in the past? Or, should there be an attempt to normalize relations with the United States—even though this would mean a temporary acceptance of an American presence in Asia—particularly in Taiwan—that China has in the past found intolerable? Is Russia China's main enemy? Or is the United States still the main enemy?

These and related questions are at issue, and there is a wide range of views on them. Not since 1949—when the Chinese Communists took power—has there been such a far-reaching debate over basic policy alternatives.

THE DEBATE ON FOREIGN POLICY

In the analysis that follows, I shall explore the foreign policy views of three distinct factions within the Chinese elite: "hawks, doves, and dawks." In my view, the "dawks," "centrists," or more precisely, Maoists, have won. They have defeated both a hard-line group among the professional military that wanted a tougher line on Vietnam and a soft-line group within the party that wanted to turn inward and concentrate on building China's economy rather than expending China's energies to promote revolutions abroad and in confronting both superpowers at once. The latter group can be called the "rationalists" because they want to introduce economic policies more moderate and realistic than those favored by the Maoists.

Common to both groups of oppositionists—military hardliners and "rationalists"—was a desire for reconciliation with Moscow. The hardliners in the military (led by former Chief of Staff Marshal Lo Jui-ching wanted such a reconciliation because they felt "united action" with Russia was essential for deterring either American escalation of the war in Vietnam or an attack on China, or for fighting the United States if deterrence failed. The professional military has long been the principal interest group in China advocating a strong tie to the Russians, as the *Liberation Army Daily* has recently confirmed.[2] From 1953 to 1958, the military wanted to maintain the Russian tie in order to "regularize" and "modernize" the Chinese army, and particularly in order to obtain nuclear capability. In 1959, it was the Chinese Minister of Defense, Marshal Peng Te-huai, who sought to prevent the widening split with Moscow and was purged as a result.[3] In 1965, it was Marshal Lo Jui-ching, the Chief of Staff, who advocated a reconciliation with Moscow and was subsequently purged, a point I intend to develop here.

The army's persistent interest in maintaining close relations with Moscow is not difficult to understand. It has sought such ties for strategic reasons and because of its interest in obtaining modern weapons. Only the timing of its recent struggle with the party requires some brief explanation at this point. It was Khrushchev's ouster in October, 1964, and the American escalation of the war into North Vietnam in March, 1965, that together gave the army an opportunity to press its case for reestablishing the Russian connection. Its leaders argued that such rapprochement was both possible and necessary. It was possible because the new Soviet leaders were not revisionists like Khrushchev, had shown good will by not resuming open polemics against China, and had offered a program of united action to defend both China and North Vietnam from American attack—a program promising to bolster the defense of China and to prevent an American victory in Vietnam.[4]

The revisionists' interest in rapprochement with Moscow seems to have stemmed from different perspectives: primarily from their desire to concentrate on industrializing China. They probably calculated that a rapprochement with Moscow would facilitate the renewal of Soviet aid that was extremely important to China's rapid economic progress from 1952 to 1959. One of the soft-line slogans, said their accusers, was "construction before destruction."

The charges against this faction indicate that they mainly stressed domestic issues. They advocated a variety of revisionist measures to pump new life into the economy, including the expansion of private plots and free markets for the peasantry and using profitability as a criterion for small enterprises. They also opposed mass mobilization, a frenetic pace of economic development, and radical social and economic experiments—such as the ones adopted during the Great Leap in 1959—on the grounds that such frenzy could only impede China's industrialization. Their watchword was economic rationality, a policy that could best be promoted by a moderate foreign policy. Some of them were accused of advocating compromises with both Russia and the United States as well as a reduction of assistance to the national liberation movement.

This group, in short, represented a "Bukharinite" faction in China, evidently prepared to make considerable concessions to both foreign and domestic class enemies for the sake of industrialization. While the professional military saw reconciliation with Moscow as a necessary prelude to tougher measures against the Americans, this Bukharinite group probably saw it as a means to normalization of relations with both super powers and more leisurely industrialization.

In both cases, evidently, the oppositionists were prepared to make substantial concessions to Moscow. They were prepared, among other things, to give up the challenge to Soviet hegemony in the international Communist movement, to stop open polemics against Moscow, and to refrain from undermining Soviet authority in the third world.

The victorious centrist faction, led by Mao, Lin Piao, and Chou En-lai, can best be viewed as anti-Soviet. It regards the Russians and Russian revisionism as—in some respects—an even greater enemy than the Americans. It rejected the army's demand for a hard-line policy on Vietnam because it would have both greatly increased risks of war with the United States and meant temporary reconciliation with Russia on Russia's terms. This Maoist, anti-Soviet faction believes that the struggle with revisionism at home and abroad should take priority over everything else, including the war in Vietnam and the struggle against the United States.

As far as Vietnam is concerned, this now dominant faction has rejected Moscow's persistent offers of "united action," including one proposal to station Soviet planes in southern Chinese airfields and Soviet troops in North Vietnam. It discredits any and all such offers of Soviet aid to North Vietnam as tricks designed to establish Soviet influence in Hanoi in order to pave the way for a sell-out to the Americans.

As far as the United States is concerned, this centrist faction continues to regard "American imperialism" as its main enemy, but it increasingly sees the Soviet Union as a cancerous growth within international Communist ranks that must be excised if U.S. imperialism is eventually to be defeated. Otherwise revisionism, which has already led to a "restoration of capitalism" in Russia and has seriously infected the Chinese party, will spread.

Unlike the military "hawks," this Maoist faction, as of mid-1967, rejected any actions in Vietnam that would increase the risks of war with the United States. It has advised North Vietnam and the Vietcong—since the massive American intervention began—to prepare for a long war of attrition in which substantial help from other Communist states, including China, should not be expected, and in which the Vietcong should assume the defensive until the balance of forces eventually changes. Unlike the moderates, this Maoist group rejects compromise in Vietnam. It warns North Vietnam against negotiations that would lead to a "sellout" peace.

That the victorious centrist faction in Peking is in some respects more anti-Soviet than anti-American has been the cause of considerable concern to the Russians. After a two-year hiatus in their polemics against Peking, the Russians began in October, 1966, to revive their attacks on China. This followed the August, 1966, Chinese party plenum when the pro-Soviet factions in China were routed. The Russians' recent actions indicated they are digging in and preparing for long struggle with China.

THE "HAWKS"—RAPPROCHEMENT WITH RUSSIA, HARD LINE ON VIETNAM

The struggle between the professional military "hawks" and the Maoists over Vietnam reached its peak at some point between February, 1965, when the Americans began bombing North Vietnam, and November, 1965, when former Chief of Staff Marshal Lo Jui-ching was last seen in public. The scope and intensity of this struggle was suggested by the army newspaper, *Liberation Army Daily*, when it observed in August, 1966, that there had been since 1949 "three big struggles against representatives of the bourgeois military line who wormed their way into the Party and the Army."[5] The third "big struggle," the editorial said, "took place not long ago." Exposed in this struggle were representatives of the bourgeoisie who had "usurped important posts in the army." Lo Jui-ching was not mentioned by name, but since he has been purged as Chief of Staff—along with other high-ranking army officers—he doubtless is one of the usurpers.

The best outline of Lo Jui-ching's views is provided in an article he wrote in May, 1965, soon after the American bombing of North Vietnam began and half a year before he disappeared from public notice. Lo's views were advanced in the esoteric form the Communists use to engage in polemical discussion with their comrades, but their meaning is clear enough.

Lo's article ostensibly concerned the lessons that might be drawn from World War II on the 20th anniversary of its conclusion. As is well known by students of current Communist politics, however, such articles are not written for the sake of history; they almost always have contemporary relevance. The political relevance of Lo's article on this occasion is brought out by another written for the same occasion by the editorial staff of the party paper, *People's Daily*. The two articles appeared side by side in *Peking Review*. The differences between them are all the more striking.[6]

In a variety of ways, Lo called for unity with Russia and a hard line on Vietnam. He used the Munich analogy to inveigh against appeasement. *People's Daily*, on the other hand, rejected unity with the Soviet Union, took a softer line on Vietnam, and expressed less fear of the dangers of appeasement.

The approaches differ in a number of ways. First, it is apparent on a quantitative level. While *People's Daily* condemned the alleged perfidious role of both United States imperialism and Soviet revisionism, Lo placed much greater stress on the evils of the former. Approximately twenty-one paragraphs in Lo's article warned against the dangers of United States imperialism, while only about three denounced modern revisionism. In *People's Daily*, the ratio was about fourteen paragraphs to twelve. Again, in Lo's article, there were only four specific references to "Khrushchev revisionism" and forty-one to United States imperialism, while *People's Daily* referred specifically to "Khrushchev revisionism" (or "Khrushchev's successors") twenty-seven times as opposed to thirty-three references to United States imperialism.

Substantively, too, the entire thrust of Lo's article was a call for rapprochement with Russia aimed at deterring an American attack on China and U.S. escalation of the Vietnam war. *People's Daily*, however, argued that such a rapprochement was neither possible nor necessary. The differences in emphasis between the two articles are so great that it is inconceivable they could be accidental.

On the need for and possibility of rapprochement with Russia:

1. While Lo warned that the actions of the modern revisionists helped U.S. imperialism, and that China must relentlessly oppose such actions, he did not specifically condemn the principle of "united action." *People's Daily* labeled "united action" a "swindle" designed to realize Soviet-American world hegemony.

2. Lo specifically argued that a vitally important factor in the World War II victory was the rallying of a "united front with the Soviet Union and the world proletariat as its main force." The clear implication is that victory in the next world war—if it comes—will also require a united front. *People's Daily*, on the other hand, stressed the tremendous vitality of the Socialist system and Stalin's wise leadership as the main factors in Russia's ability to defeat Hitler. It implied that China's social system and Mao's leadership can do the same for China if a Sino-American war develops.

3. Lo consistently avoided use of the phrase "Khrushchev's successors" in his few attacks on Soviet policy. He criticized only "modern revisionists such as Khrushchev," thus leaving open the possibility that not all present Soviet leaders are revisionists. *People's Daily*, on the other hand, at several points lumped "Khrushchev's successors" with Khrushchev. While they are "more cunning," said the party paper, they cling to Khrushchev's revisionist line.

4. While both Lo and *People's Daily* referred favorably to Stalin, they utilized the Stalin symbol for quite different purposes. If one substitutes "Mao" for Stalin, the significance of these differences becomes apparent. Lo said that one of Stalin's major contributions was that he "correctly" analyzed the then current situation, identified the principal contradictions in the world arena, and was "therefore able to advance the correct slogan of an anti-fascist united front . . . with the Soviet Union and the world proletariat as its main force." In short, if Mao could only correctly analyze the present world situation, he too would recognize the need for a united front with Moscow. *People's Daily*, however, used Stalin to demonstrate that his infallible leadership before and after the outbreak of war made the Russian victory possible. Moreover, said *People's Daily*, it was only the revisionists who sought to besmirch Stalin's great deeds by arguing—as Khrushchev did—that Stalin "was not a great commander but an 'idiot.'" Only the revisionists tried to belittle or obliterate Stalin's role in the war. The implication seems clear that anyone in China today who doubts Mao's rejection of a united-front policy is a revisionist like Khrushchev.

5. Lo came close to saying that a U.S. attack on China could be deterred only by Chinese rapprochement with Moscow, while *People's Daily* pointed to a variety of other factors deterring the Americans. Thus, Lo said that U.S. plans for war and aggression could be frustrated, "provided that we are good at uniting the Socialist camp and the people's anti-imperialist forces in all countries as well as at making use of the contradictions within the imperialist camp." (Note the order.) *People's Daily*, on the other hand, concluded that the United States "is in a much worse strategic position than was Hitler in his day" and that "it is much more difficult for the United States to unleash a world war." It emphasized the struggle of the "revolutionary peoples and the peace-loving countries" as the main deterrent forces. Except to argue that such unity is impossible so long as the Soviet Union continues to align itself with U.S. imperialism, *People's Daily* said nothing about the need to unite the Socialist camp.

On the proper policy in Vietnam:

1. Both Lo and *People's Daily* warned against placing hopes for peace on negotiations and agreements, which the imperialists may

tear up at any time. But Lo gave much greater weight to this lesson than did *People's Daily*. He warned that firm opposition to any
"Munich policy" is one of the principal lessons (he lists seven) of
the Anti-Fascist War. He devoted five paragraphs to pinpointing
the dangers of appeasement, of cherishing illusions about pledges
or "fine words," of pinning hopes for preventing war on signing
treaties or other agreements. Moreover, his warning was not in
the context of an attack on revisionism, but in that of "our dealings with the imperialists and reactionaries." *People's Daily*, on the
other hand, did not consider the danger of appeasement one of the
four principal lessons it drew from reviewing the experience of
the Anti-Fascist War. In passing, it mentioned the danger of trying
to prevent war by relying excessively on negotiations; it quickly
pointed out, however, that only the Khrushchev revisionists might
be susceptible to this dangerous policy. Lo, in short, was evidently
warning that certain leaders in China and North Vietnam as well
as the revisionists were in danger of appeasing the imperialists. His
warning against appeasement was probably directed against those
Chinese, North Vietnamese, and Russian leaders who were then
thinking about the possibility of negotiating a Laos-type solution to
the Vietnam war at a new Geneva conference.

2. Lo was probably also cautioning against any Chinese steps
away from a confrontation with the United States over Vietnam.
It is interesting to note that Lo specifically promised that "we
will go on supporting and aiding the Vietnamese people, whether
or not U.S. imperialism bombs our country and whether or not it
enlarges the war." *People's Daily*, on the other hand, made only the
very general statement that "it is the bounden [sic] international
duty of all revolutionary forces . . . to support and aid the Vietnamese people in their struggle." Lo also promised to help the
Vietnamese people "materially to the limit of our capabilities" and
to "send our men to fight. . . ." *People's Daily* said relatively little
about what China was prepared to do to help the Vietnamese
people but spoke of what "all revolutionary forces" throughout the
world could do to help. This was later to be one of the principal
themes in Marshal Lin Piao's famous speech of September, 1965,
a speech that—as I shall try to show—was intended in part as the
response of the Mao–Lin Piao group to the "hawk" challenge posed
by Lo Jui-ching and his allies.

On preparations for a war with the United States:

Lo's image of a future war with the United States was quite different from that of *People's Daily.* Lo devoted one entire section to "active defense" as "the only correct strategy for Socialist countries in fighting against imperialist wars of aggression." This means "strategic pursuit to destroy the enemy," "energetically wiping out the enemy's effectives," "defending cities and other places," "actively supporting the anti-fascist armed uprisings of the peoples of other . . . countries," "close cooperation among the different armed services, of which the ground forces, and particularly the infantry, are primary." This, he said, was the historical lesson of World War II.

People's Daily, on the other hand, argued that World War II was won by means of a "people's war." "It was the people and not the fascists with their military superiority who proved really powerful." Elsewhere it wrote: "Given correct leadership in accordance with a correct line, the people will gradually grow stronger and become powerful in struggle, gradually change the balance of forces, and in the end they will defeat the fascist aggressors. The just people's war is bound to triumph." In short, while Lo was urging preparations for repelling an American attack by a variety of conventional means, *People's Daily* was stressing the efficacy of guerrilla warfare.

MAOIST RESPONSE TO THE HAWKS

A major broadside against revisionism released in midmonth—in which the Chinese leadership argued against any compromises with Moscow—indicates clearly that the question of a rapprochement with Moscow was still alive by June. That article was significantly entitled "Carry the Struggle Against Khrushchev Revisionism Through to the End." Lo Jui-ching's article in May had been subtitled "Carry the Struggle Against U.S. Imperialism Through to the End." There could be no better symbol of the difference in the two viewpoints. The army leaders saw the United States as the main enemy, against whom it was necessary to unite with Russia, while the Maoists rejected compromise with Russia.

That Lo Jui-ching's views were still very much alive in June was reflected in the party's warning against being "taken in" by Russia's "honeyed words." "The question confronting the Chinese Communists today," it said, "is whether to carry the struggle against Khrushchev revisionism through to the end or whether to stop halfway." The article went on to say how "of late, the new leaders of the CPSU have been loud in chanting honeyed words such as 'unity.' " Marxist-Leninists, however, must not be taken in by such words. "In our struggle against the revisionists, we must be able to deal with their tough and with their soft tactics; we must dare to resist all their pressure and must refuse to be *misled by any of their fine words.*" (Emphasis added.) Continuing in this defensive tone, the article asserted that flexibility was important; but "it would be wrong to exercise unprincipled flexibility, to create ambiguity and confusion on questions of principle on the pretext of flexibility." To "abandon our principled stand and accommodate ourselves or yield to the Khrushchev revisionists" would be a "grave historical mistake."

Clearly, some Chinese leaders were urging greater "flexibility" in dealing with the Russians, and calling for efforts to contain the Sino-Soviet dispute at some halfway point.

Further evidence to support this interpretation can be found in an article by the combined editorial departments of *People's Daily* and *Red Flag* which appeared in mid-November 1965, or about the time when Marshal Lo was last seen in public.[7] The entire article was devoted to defense of an uncompromising stand against Moscow. First, the article argued that there could be no "solid unity" without struggle against revisionism. It denied that China, by struggling against revisionism, was destroying unity—as some had apparently charged. Mao was merely seeking unity on a higher plane—without the Russians. Second, the article sought to demolish the idea—apparently held by some—that the Russians were in fact sincere in their offers of united action on Vietnam. It went into considerable detail to argue that the Russians were merely using "united action" slogans to increase their influence in Hanoi and thus to help the United States find a way out of Vietnam and to regain their influence in the international Communist movement. Third, the article explained why it was impossible to stop open polemics. It was necessary to carry the debate "to the finish," first because "the more the polemics, the higher the level of revolutionary consciousness." But the most important reason was that if China stopped open polemics—or equivocated in the struggle with Moscow—it would be tantamount to giving up long efforts to establish a new coalition of anti-Soviet but "pure"—i.e., pro-Chinese—

Communist parties throughout the world. As the article put it, adoption of a middle course would mean that the Chinese party would no longer be free to support or rebuild genuine revolutionary forces throughout the world, in effect, to challenge Soviet hegemony in the revolutionary world. The article went on to ask rhetorically why limited forms of united action with Russia could not be taken against the imperialists in Vietnam and elsewhere. After all, the Chinese party often cooperated for limited purposes with bourgeois nationalists and even with anti-American imperialists whose ideological perspectives it does not share. Why then could it not cooperate for limited purposes with Moscow?

"Some people ask, why is it that the Marxist-Leninists and the revolutionary people cannot take united action with the new leaders of the CPSU, yet can unite with personages from the upper strata in the nationalist countries, and strive for united action with them in the anti-imperialist struggle, and can even exploit the contradictions among the imperialist countries in the struggle against the United States?"[8] The Maoists answered that opposition to United States imperialism was the main criterion for deciding whether it was possible to engage in united action with others. Russia flunked the test.

Russia, said the party paper, continued to make "deals" with the United States on nuclear proliferation, to aid the Indian reactionaries, and to use the United Nations as a "stock exchange" to dominate the world with the United States. In short, it was possible from time to time and "in varying degrees" to unite with Morocco, the UAR, or France, in order to weaken the United States, but it was never possible to unite with the Russians. Doubtless, many of the oppositionists found this argument wanting. For, while it is true that Moscow and Washington share some overlapping interests, it is also true that Mao has consistently overstated the degree and purposes of cooperation between Russia and the United States for his own polemical purposes.

As the danger of a Sino-American confrontation over Vietnam grew daily in the summer and fall of 1965, it became increasingly clear that powerful groups within the professional military were calling not only for a rapprochement with the Soviet Union but also for reducing party control within the army to facilitate preparations for war. The extent of party control in the Chinese army had been a chronic problem since the Communists came to power.

Mounting danger of war and differences of view over how best to meet the American threat made the problem more acute than ever.

On August 1st, the 38th anniversary of the founding of the People's Liberation Army (PLA), Marshal Ho Lung took as his theme the "democratic tradition of the Chinese People's Liberation Army." What Ho Lung meant by "democracy" was the subordination of military professionalism to party leadership. He suggested this when he said:

> . . . The army's history over the decades proves that whenever any unit undermined or weakened the Party committee system, it inevitably developed a trend of warlordism characterized by individual arbitrariness and undermined . . . the Party's leadership over the army. . . .[9]

Ho pointedly warned against the danger of "left opportunism"—the call for abolition of the party-committee system in the army. Moreover, he insisted, "democracy" was "entirely feasible under conditions of modern equipment and modern war." It was not true—as those with "bourgeois views on military affairs" insisted—that in conditions of modern warfare "only those commanders and technical experts who had undergone strict professional training were to be depended on."

Throughout late summer and early fall in 1965, Washington and Peking exchanged ominous threats. Washington was intent on warning Peking that if the war in Vietnam turned into another Korean-type situation, China would be attacked and there would be no sanctuary. Peking tried to convince Washington that it would not be intimidated by such threats. Thus, on August 7, 1965, a Chinese government statement:

> We, the 650 million Chinese people, have repeatedly pledged to the Vietnamese people our all-out support and assistance, up to and including the sending, according to their need, of our men to fight shoulder to shoulder with them to drive out the U.S. aggressors. We warn the U.S. aggressors once more: We Chinese people mean what we say![10]

A week earlier, Marshal Lo Jui-ching specifically referred to U.S. warnings that it would permit no sanctuary this time—as it had in Korea—and said the United States was mistaken if it misjudged the strength and determination of the Chinese. Lo, in the next to last public appearance he made before he was purged, warned that if the United States imposed a war on China, the PLA "would not only take them on till the very end but would invite them to come in large numbers. And the more the better. . . ."[11] Lo also threateningly warned that "in the past year, too, we have successfully mastered the material [as opposed to the spiritual] atom bomb which we did not possess in the past."

It was in this context—a debate among the top Chinese leaders on how best to meet an American attack on China if it came, and how hard a line to pursue on Vietnam—that the famous article by Lin Piao appeared on September 3, 1965. There are two popular interpretations of this article. The first is that the article was mere 4th of July rhetoric, a profession of faith rather than a blueprint.[12] The second is that the article was intended to serve notice on the West of China's expansionist ambitions and can therefore be reasonably compared with Hitler's *Mein Kampf*.[13]

Let us briefly examine the first explanation. It has long been apparent to students of contemporary Communist affairs that major pronouncements by Communist leaders provide important clues to the outlook and assumptions of those leaders as well as to political differences within the leadership. Evidence to support this belief comes from numerous ex-Communists and from many scholars of Communist politics who, by using the speeches and documents of Communist leaders, have been able to suggest interpretations that were later validated. To regard Lin Piao's article—and articles by other Chinese leaders of his stature—as rhetorical professions of faith is to ignore why the "rhetoric" changes over a period of time, why it often is a matter of dispute between top leaders, and why Communist leaders are often accused of having violated the current "rhetorical" line.

Statements such as Lin Piao's, in fact, provide the very stuff of politics in any Communist state. To dismiss such statements is to deprive oneself of one of the few weapons available to us for studying contemporary politics in Communist China and to reduce all explanations of political phenomena to "deep" historical and cultural factors. While such historical and cultural factors are unquestionably necessary to a full understanding of politics in contemporary China, they are by themselves inadequate to explain specific political developments, as Benjamin Schwartz has so well brought out.[14]

The explanation equating Lin Piao's statement with *Mein Kampf* is equally misleading. First, Lin Piao's article was in many respects a rehash of what Chinese Communist leaders have been saying sporadically since 1949. The *Mein Kampf* analogy, to say the least, comes a little late. Also, such an analogy is misleading because the equation of Maoist and Nazi ideology evokes the specter of overt Chinese Communist military and territorial expansion in Asia. While few students of contemporary China would deny that Communist China is a dissatisfied power, equally few would assert that China regards direct military expansion as a major instrumentality of its foreign policy. Neither in the Lin Piao statement nor in the multitude of similar statements made in the past is there any suggestion of Chinese Communist intentions to engage in direct military expansion.

Nor—with the possible exception of its invasion of Tibet—has China been guilty of military expansion in the past fifteen years. The attack on India in 1962 was made for limited political objectives in disputed territory. China never intended to move into India itself. Moreover, the Indians had—by their "forward policy"—done much to provoke the Chinese action. Shelling of the offshore islands has been aimed at forcing Nationalist withdrawal from them. The Chinese have never made any serious attempt to invade the islands— much less to move against Taiwan, mindful that such action would lead to confrontation with the United States. Their intervention in Korea was defensive. China intervened only after General Mac-Arthur crossed the 38th parallel and moved toward her Manchurian border. Any careful study of Chinese foreign policy during the past fifteen years would have to conclude that although China is a revolutionary power opposing the present status quo, it does not aim to bring about change by its own military force.[15]

Third, the equation with *Mein Kampf* ignores one of the key messages in Lin Piao's article and one of the basic principles of "liberation wars"—that Communist revolutionaries throughout the world must make their revolutions on their own. Far from giving notice of any intention to intervene aggressively in Vietnam or in other "people's wars," Lin Piao was rationalizing Peking's unwillingness to intervene directly and massively in such wars. He was reiterating what is essentially a "do-it-yourself" model of revolution for foreign Communists. Lin Piao's article was—far from a sign of Chinese belligerence—a "dove" answer to the military "hawks" like Lo Jui-ching, who were clamoring for a tough line on Vietnam.

There are two plausible and not incompatible interpretations of Lin Piao's article. The first, initially suggested by D. Mozingo and T. Robinson,[16] argues that Lin Piao was addressing Hanoi and the Vietcong. According to this interpretation, he was urging on them a strategic retreat in the face of the massive introduction of American troops and firepower in mid-1965, which completely changed the military and political situation in Vietnam. This American intervention may well have given rise to two extreme points of view in North Vietnam, defeatism on the one hand, and pressures for a quick victory on the other. In response to such pressures, the Chinese were arguing that the Vietcong should prepare for a protracted struggle and for shifting to the defensive. This would mean avoiding regular warfare with the American units, consolidating the Communists' political grip on the base areas in the countryside, and seeking to build a broad anti-American united front to include the Buddhists, the various sects, and such other groups and strata as could be won over. Such a strategy of temporary retreat and digging in for protracted war, the Chinese argued, was the only alternative to costly Vietcong military setbacks at the hands of the larger and better-equipped American forces.

A number of points in the article substantiate such an interpretation.[17] First, there is the obvious parallel between the situation then confronting the Vietcong and the situation which Lin Piao was discussing—the dilemma of the Chinese Communists (in 1937) in the face of the Japanese invasion of a China rent by civil war. Much of Lin's article is an effort to show—by using the war against Japan as an example—"how it was possible for a weak country finally to defeat a strong country" and how it was possible "for a seemingly weak army to become the main force of the war." Second, Lin Piao expends much effort to explain how the Chinese Communist party "made a series of adjustments in its policies" to unite all anti-Japanese parties and groups, including the Kuomintang, after the Japanese invasion. Many of these "adjustments" are relevant to the Vietcong: for example, conciliating the rural rich and making political concessions to non-Communists in Communist-held base areas.

Third, Lin Piao's article clearly warns that "people's wars" should be carried out primarily by the efforts of the indigenous guerrillas without reliance on foreign assistance—even from countries such as China which "persist in revolution."

Fourth, Lin Piao emphasizes heavily the virtues of guerrilla—as opposed to conventional or mobile—warfare in a situation where the enemy is still stronger than the insurgents. Thus he says that Mao

> raised guerrilla warfare to the level of strategy because, if they are to defeat a formidable enemy, revolutionary armed forces should not fight with reckless disregard for the consequences when there is a great disparity between their own strength and the enemy's. If they do, they will suffer serious losses and bring heavy setbacks to the revolution. Guerrilla warfare is the *only way* to mobilize and apply the whole strength of the people against the enemy, the only way to expand our forces in the course of the war, deplete and weaken the enemy, gradually change the balance of forces between the enemy and ourselves, switch from guerrilla to mobile warfare, and finally defeat the enemy. (Emphasis added.) [18]

It is true that Lin Piao by no means ruled out mobile, or conventional, warfare. "Guerrilla warfare is basic, but lose no chance for mobile warfare under favorable conditions." Lin's major stress, however, was on guerrilla warfare as the main tactic during the initial stages of the war. Mobile warfare should be relied upon only at a later stage of the war, *after* the balance of forces has changed in favor of the insurgents and the cities are ripe for storming.

> In the later period of the war of resistance against Japan and during the third revolutionary civil war (i.e., 1945–49), we switched our strategy from that of guerrilla warfare as the primary form of fighting to that of mobilized warfare in the light of the changes in the balance of forces between the enemy and ourselves. By the middle, and especially the later period of the third revolutionary civil war, our operations had developed into large-scale mobilized warfare, including the storming of cities. [19]

Lin thus seemed to remind the Vietcong of the Chinese Communists' experience in their victory over Chiang Kai-shek between 1945 and 1949. In 1948, at a time when the Chinese Communists had forced the Kuomintang forces to retreat into the cities from the countryside, and when large-scale unit defections from the Kuomintang army had begun, the Chinese Communists began to launch frontal, conventional attacks on the cities. Only at that time did they consider the balance of forces to have changed sufficiently in their favor to risk such attacks. The implication for the Vietnamese seems clear: at a time when American ground troops were arriving in South Vietnam in large numbers to help defend the cities and to attack Vietcong base areas, the balance of forces was hardly propitious for conventional warfare.

Moreover, argued Lin Piao, whether fighting guerrilla or mobile warfare, whatever is best suited to waging "battles of annihilation" should be the guiding principle:

> A battle in which the enemy is routed is not basically decisive in a contest with a foe of great strength. A battle of annihilation, on the other hand, produces a great and immediate impact on any enemy. Injuring all of a man's ten fingers is not as effective as chopping off one, and routing ten enemy divisions is not as effective as annihilating one of them.[20]

In order to annihilate the enemy, it is necessary "in every battle" to concentrate an absolutely superior force (two, three, four, and sometimes even five or six times the enemy's strength); to avoid battles of attrition; to concentrate first on dispersed or isolated enemy forces and only later on strong enemy troops; to fight no battle "we are not sure of winning." Moreover, it is advisable to give up certain indefensible positions: "We are firmly against dividing up our forces to defend all positions and putting up resistance at every place for fear that our territory might be lost. . . ." This suggests that the Vietcong should not try to defend the heavily populated Delta but should instead retreat to the more difficult terrain of the Central Highlands.

Fifth, and perhaps most important, Lin said that successful revolutionaries have to be adept at assessing the balance of forces properly and careful not to yield either to defeatism or blind optimism. Pursuing the example of the Chinese war against Japan, Lin Piao said:

> The defeatists came forward with the assertion that China was no match for Japan and that the nation was bound to be subjugated. The blind optimists came forward with the assertion that China could win very quickly, without much effort.[21]

While advising against negotiations—presumably favored by the Hanoi defeatists—Lin was also advising against continuing on the offensive in light of the massive American intervention. His advice to Hanoi evidently was to retreat to the strategic defensive, concentrate on guerrilla warfare and united-front tactics, and avoid any premature actions that could spell disaster. Thus he repeatedly attacked "left-wing opportunist" views during China's own civil war. These leftists thought they could win the war quickly by attacking the cities; they moved too quickly to mobile warfare; they neglected painstaking work among the peasants; they failed to build rural revolutionary base areas; they neglected united-front tactics—and thus courted disaster.

Obviously, then, there were a number of points in Lin Piao's article pertinent to the situation facing the North Vietnamese and Vietcong forces in late 1965—particularly the crucial question of what to do in the face of a vastly superior enemy: negotiate, continue to take the military offensive, or dig in for a long, hard war by concentrating on guerrilla warfare. Lin seemed to advocate the last course of action.

It was a course of action that—if adopted—would serve two important Chinese strategic goals: first, it would reduce the dangers of escalation that might eventually result in an American attack on China; second, it would tie down U.S. forces in Vietnam to a long war of attrition with minimum Chinese involvement and risk.

LIN'S AUDIENCE IN HANOI

Perhaps the best indication that Hanoi and the Vietcong were among Lin's audiences is the fact that Hanoi first ignored him and then offered indirect but unmistakable criticism. There is no indication that Hanoi's newspapers or journals ever republished the text or even portions of Lin Piao's programmatic analysis, or that North Vietnamese leaders ever even referred to it in passing. By contrast, there has been persistent reference to General Giap's writings on guerrilla warfare and to North Vietnam's own rich revolutionary experience against the Japanese and French. For a document so broadly disseminated by the Chinese themselves, this slight on the part of the North Vietnamese was remarkable and was *prima facie* evidence of their disapproval of its contents.

Hanoi went on to reject Lin Piao's advice in several speeches delivered by top North Vietnamese leaders at an army conference in May, 1966—speeches which were not released until July. Other replies to Lin Piao appeared in the July issue of *Hoc Tap*, North Vietnam's party journal. The essence of these speeches was that Hanoi and the Vietcong could defeat the Americans by taking the offensive, and that no foreign revolutionary experience was valid for conditions that the Hanoi leaders knew best.[22]

Le Duan, Secretary-General of the Lao Dong party, pointedly remarked at the conference—as it was later broadcast by Radio Hanoi on July 26, 1966—that "we cannot automatically apply the revolutionary experiences of other countries in our country." Since only China was offering to apply its own experience, the implication of that remark was clear. Duan stressed the need for "creativity," for keeping the realities of the Vietnamese situation in mind when planning revolutionary strategy, and for not "mechanically" following "the experiences of the fraternal parties."

> Creativity is a very important problem. Without a spirit of creativity, we cannot successfully carry out the revolution. We cannot automatically apply the revolutionary experiences of other countries in our country. Our party line is correct, because it was conceived in a creative manner. It has cleverly associated Marxism-Leninism with the revolutionary realities in Vietnam. Our party has paid special attention to studying the experiences of the fraternal parties, but it has not studied them mechanically. We must have the requirements of the Vietnamese revolution in mind while studying these experiences. We must also know how to apply these experiences to the concrete conditions of Vietnam. Creativity is a manifestation of the spirit of independence and autonomy, patriotism, and a high revolutionary spirit. If we are obsessed with an inferiority complex and with a desire to rely on others, we cannot have a spirit of creativity. We are not genuine revolutionaries. We do not understand Marxism-Leninism.

Then Le Duan replied to Lin Piao's argument for a strategic retreat:

> It is not fortuitous that in the history of our country, each time we rose up to oppose foreign aggression, we took the offensive and not the defensive. . . . Taking the offensive is a strategy, while taking the defensive is only a stratagem. Since the day the South Vietnamese people rose up, they have continually taken the offensive.

Even during the recent dry season, he continued, when the U.S. imperialists introduced 200,000 troops into South Vietnam, the southern troops "unhesitantly and resolutely took the offensive," they repeatedly attacked the enemy and achieved great victories. Pointedly he noted that "without understanding the Vietnamese people and Vietnamese history, one cannot understand the strategy and tactics of the Vietnamese revolution, nor can one lead the Vietnamese people in fighting the enemy."

Evidently countering Lin Piao's argument that a basic principle of Maoist strategy was to make sure that the enemy was always outnumbered, Le Duan stated that

. . . our troops and people have invented unique tactical methods which enable a lesser force to attack a larger force. . . . In combat, there are times when we concentrate quite a strong force and firepower to outnumber the enemy by two or three to one, but there are also times when our ratios are one to one, one to ten, or even more, and we still win. Thus, our army and people have the methods, tactics and techniques which are suitable to the Vietnamese battlefields and to the Vietnamese themselves.

China, Le Duan hinted, had better limit itself to supplying weapons and leave the strategy to Hanoi:

We do not disregard foreign countries' weaponry and technology, but we have to know how to apply the . . . techniques which are suitable to *our* country's situation and characteristics and to *our* combat methods. (Emphasis added.)

At about the same time that Le Duan's speech was broadcast, another strong—if still indirect—attack on Peking came from Nguyen Chi Thanh, a powerful Politburo member, a member of the National Defense Council, and widely rumored to be Hanoi's man in charge of the war in the south. Writing in the July issue of *Hoc Tap*, Thanh warned against the man who "would cite profuse experiences from here and there to demonstrate vaguely that 'we can be successful,' but would accompany all this with a lot of 'buts'—thus making it impossible to understand what he meant and what his purpose was in speaking this way." With Lin Piao clearly in mind, he cautioned that some people pointed to enemy strength not to cope with it "but to threaten others, thus intentionally or unintentionally spreading pessimism. . . ." Of course, he went on, the Americans were stronger in certain respects, "but they absolutely do not have any peerless strength. . . ."

Thanh then turned to assess the balance of forces on the ground in South Vietnam and rejected the conclusion that the balance favored the enemy since the introduction of U.S. ground troops. Such a conclusion was "formalistic" and not dialectical, he declared. Although the enemy had increased its forces, "our strategic position has been much better than before. . . ."

If we only looked at the quantity of the enemy's strength . . . indeed the comparative balance of forces has clearly changed in favor of the enemy. Yet that was an evaluation made according to formalistic logic. . . . It is a fact that the enemy has considerably increased his troop

strength, but our strategic position has been [is] much better than before . . . the initiative on the battlefield is already ours. . . .[23]

Thanh branded as adventurists those who repeat obsolete experiences
from textbooks and invoke magic formulae instead of examining the
realities. Criticizing those who copied the "experiences of foreign
countries," he said that people who spoke of the necessary superiority of at least seven to one or nine to one, and so forth, were
"diviners" and not scientists. And those who "repeat exactly in a
new reality what belongs to history" are committing "adventurous"
acts.

Thanh also said one could not settle "in an old-fashioned manner
the question of relations between the delta and the mountainous
region and between the rural areas and the cities in the southern
revolutionary war." In this particular context, this reference would
seem to suggest—as indicated earlier—that the Chinese not only
advised the Vietcong to postpone attacks on the cities and to concentrate on rural areas, but also that they suggested less attention
to fighting in the heavily populated delta and more to battle in the
inaccessible mountainous regions.

Other attacks on Lin Piao's theses were launched by the Vietnamese. Writing in the June issue of the military journal *Quan Doi
Nhan Dan*, Truong Sen (a pseudonym) asserted that the Vietcong
attacked strong as well as weak enemy positions. Moreover, he
argued that during the past dry season, "had we retreated to the
strategic defensive position," serious consequences would have followed. With apparent reference to Lin Piao's thesis that in order
to maximize the united-front appeal, the main blows should be
directed against the Americans—not the Saigon military—Truong
Sen said, "We aimed our blows at both the Americans and [their]
puppets." His conclusion, like that of the other North Vietnamese
leaders, was that the Communist troops maintained the initiative
despite the American intervention.

Such Vietnamese arguments support the idea that one of Lin
Piao's target audiences was Hanoi. Further, they support the asser-
tion that the Hanoi leaders did not take kindly to Peking's lecture
on how to fight revolutionary wars, particularly at a time when the
Chinese were sabotaging North Vietnam's war effort by refusing to
engage in united action with the Russians to deter American escalation.

LIN'S AUDIENCE IN PEKING

If Hanoi and the Vietcong constituted one audience for Lin Piao, his other audience was the Chinese military. As we have seen, one question of debate between the military and the Chinese Communist Party concerned the best way to meet an American attack—by launching guerrilla warfare, retreating to mountain and rural bases and sacrificing Chinese cities, or by fighting a conventional war. Sometimes, Lin's analysis seems directed to Chinese generals who wanted to fight the United States by conventional means. Thus, at one point, he says:

> In order to annihilate the enemy, we must adopt the policy of luring him in deep and abandoning some cities and districts of our own accord in a planned way, so as to let him in. It is only after letting the enemy in that the people can take part in the war in various ways and that the power of a people's war can be fully exerted. It is only after letting the enemy in that he can be compelled to divide up his forces, take on heavy burdens, and commit mistakes. In other words, we must let the enemy become elated, stretch out all his ten fingers and become hopelessly bogged down.[24]

Lin continues:

> We are firmly against dividing up our forces to defend all positions and putting up resistance at every place for fear that our territory might be lost and our pots and pans smashed, since this can neither wipe out the enemy forces nor hold cities or localities.[25]

Elsewhere, the Marshal says:

> The Chinese people definitely have ways of their own for coping with a U.S. imperialist war of aggression. Our methods are no secret. The most important one is still mobilization of the people, reliance on the people, making everyone a soldier and waging a people's war. We want to tell the U.S. imperialists once again that the vast ocean of several hundred million Chinese people in arms will be more than enough to submerge your few million aggressor troops.[26]

The strategy of "letting the enemy in" and drowning him in people's war clearly is different from that outlined by Lo Jui-ching, which advocated fighting the Americans with the Chinese infantry, Korean-war style. Lo called this "active defense," meaning, he said, "close cooperation among the different armed services, of which the ground forces, and particularly the infantry, are primary."

Lin Piao's article can be thus understood in part as a rejection of this hard line advanced by Lo Jui-ching and the military professionals—rapprochement with Russia, a get-tough policy in Vietnam, and preparation for conventional war with the United States. Lin was rejecting cooperation with Moscow, advising the Vietcong that they could win only by preparing for a protracted guerrilla war which they would wage themselves, and arguing that an American attack on China was unlikely.

Perhaps the most striking difference between Lin Piao's formulations and the much tougher ones of Lo in May was that Lin minimized the danger of Chinese-American confrontation in Vietnam and insisted that the United States would be defeated not by China but by a number of people's wars throughout the underdeveloped areas:

> The more successful the development of people's war in a given region, the larger the number of U.S. imperialist forces that can be pinned down and depleted there. When the U.S. aggressors are hard pressed in one place, they have no alternative but to loosen their grip on others. . . . Everything is divisible. And so is this colossus of U.S. imperialism. It can be split up and defeated. The peoples of Asia, Africa, and Latin America and other regions can destroy it piece by piece, some striking at its head and others at its feet. That is why the greatest fear of U.S. imperialism is that people's wars will be launched in different parts of the world. . . .[27]

Whereas Lo had suggested that the Chinese army would defeat the United States, Lin was saying that Vietnamese, Peruvian, and Angolan peasants would do the job.

Meanwhile Lo Jui-ching and his followers were continuing to take a harder line than Mao and Lin Piao on Vietnam. This is suggested in the last public statement made by Lo, on the very same occasion that Lin Piao spoke on "people's war."

Lo, although stepping up his attack on Soviet revisionism, stressed the threat of United States imperialism and the urgent need to take preparatory steps to meet a likely attack. The United States, he warned, "will not reconcile itself to defeat, still less give up altogether. It is bent on accelerating the war in Vietnam, recklessly shouting about spreading the war to China." He continued:

> It is possible that U.S. imperialism may go mad in trying to save itself from its doom; we must take this into full account and make prepara-

tions against its expansion of the war of aggression in Vietnam and against any war it may impose on us. A thousand and one things need to be done. . . .[28]

While Lin and other regime spokesmen were making it clear—as we shall see in a moment—that China would not intervene in the war unless the United States attacked the mainland, Lo was calling for unspecified preparations not only against an attack on China, but even against U.S. "expansion of the war of aggression in Vietnam." Apparently he was intent on lowering the threshold at which China should intervene. This interpretation is supported by his injunction—quite contrary to Lin Piao's "do-it-yourself" approach— that China must "give still more effective support to the Vietnamese . . . in their struggles against U.S. imperialism."

Lo dismissed Lin's article on people's war as a good textbook on which "there is . . . no need for me to dwell . . . ." He also paid the proper obeisance to Mao by arguing that the most important of the thousand and one things to be done was to hold high the great red banner of Mao's thought. It was undoubtedly such tactics that prompted the army paper a year later to observe that the military-firsters in the army "had waved 'red flags' to oppose the red flag" and had overtly agreed with Mao's thought while "covertly opposing" it and putting military affairs and techniques first.[29]

By the winter of 1965, however, there were several indications that the regime had decided against Lo and was intent on limiting support to the Vietnamese and reducing risks of war with the United States. First, China's warnings against U.S. military provocations—more than 400 of which have been issued since 1958—reached high points in October, 1964, after the Gulf of Tonkin incident, then again in April, 1965, after the American bombing of North Vietnam began, but dropped off sharply beginning in the summer of 1965.[30] While these warnings bear some relation to reality—inasmuch as U.S. ships and planes unquestionably violate Chinese boundaries as Peking conceives them—it is also clear that the Chinese manipulate such warnings for political purposes. Perhaps the best proof is, as Mr. Tretiak observes, that there is no necessary relationship between China's serious warnings and U.S. violations the Chinese list elsewhere. For example, from June 29, 1964, to April 5, 1966, according to a Chinese statement on the latter date, there were 241 intrusions of Chinese territory. Yet in this period Peking issued only 100 serious warnings. The fact that such warnings sharply declined during the summer of 1965 and remained low in 1966 seemed to reflect a desire on the part of Peking to reduce Sino-American tensions.

Further signs of such a desire can be found in Chinese statements since the winter of 1965 which implied that Peking will not intervene in the Vietnam war unless China itself is attacked. For example, in October, 1965, Foreign Minister Chen Yi declared: "Should the U.S. imperialists *invade* China's mainland, we will take all necessary measures to defeat them. By then, the war will have no boundaries."[31] Premier Chou En-lai, speaking at a reception for an NLF delegation on December 20th, listed a number of actions that the United States might take in Vietnam. The actions include: bombing Haiphong and Hanoi, blockading the Bac Bo [Tonkin] Gulf, bombing the central and southern parts of Laos held by the Pathet Lao, invading the southern portion of Laos bordering on Vietnam, and intensifying attacks against Cambodia in order to seal off the borders between Cambodia and South Vietnam. He said nothing about Chinese counteractions. He went on to say that if the United States failed to achieve its purposes by such means— and it certainly would fail—it might then "go a step further and extend its war of aggression to the whole of Indochina and to China. And indeed U.S. imperialism is now making preparations for this eventuality." Chou strongly implied that only at that point would China fight. Again, on New Year's Day, 1966, *People's Daily* editorially said that it was necessary to plan for a large-scale war that the United States might launch. It again implied that China would fight only if invaded: "If the U.S. aggressors should dare to invade our country, we shall wipe them out resolutely, thoroughly, wholly and completely."[32] An April, 1966, editorial in *People's Daily* amplified the threat somewhat by warning: "Should U.S. imperialism dare to attack China, either on a limited scale or in full strength, the only result will be the total annihilation of the U.S. invaders."[33] The threat of Chinese action was still conditional on U.S. invasion, however.

Finally, in May 1966, Chou explicitly said that "China will not take the initiative to provoke a war with the United States." However, if the Americans started such a war—"once in China"— the United States would not be able to pull out. Chou also warned that once the war breaks out, it will have no boundaries. "If you can come from the sky, why can't we fight back on the ground?"[34]

It may therefore be conjectured that by the winter of 1965 the Chinese "hawks" had been defeated and a policy of restraint in Vietnam decided upon. A decision not to intervene directly in the Vietnamese war unless the Americans actually attacked China had been made. The Chinese had probably also decided not to give the United States any pretext for attacking the mainland. That would explain why they have not used Chinese airplanes or bases in southern China to help North Vietnam shoot down American bombers. Such action, the United States has warned, will lead to retaliation against the bases themselves in line with the doctrine of "hot pursuit."

The point at which China would intervene in the Vietnamese war is, however, not certain. In late 1966 and early 1967, Peking was suggesting that it would intervene if the United States attacked North Vietnam or if there were a danger of a "sellout" peace. Because success in the war is so crucial to Maoist foreign policy, it would be unwise to write off threats of Chinese intervention. It is possible to conceive of a future situation in which one faction in Hanoi, unwilling to accept an American victory, calls on Chinese "volunteers" and gets them.

THE FOREIGN POLICY VIEWS OF THE PARTY OPPOSITION*

The foreign policy positions of party opposition leaders like Liu Shao-chi, Teng Hsiao-ping, and P'eng Chen—all of whom were demoted during the Cultural Revolution—remain to be discussed.

To begin with, it is apparent as Uri Ra'anan has brought out, that P'eng Chen and the Liu-Teng group had diametrically opposed views on the desirability of a reconciliation with Moscow. P'eng, like the Maoists, opposed such a reconciliation; the Liu-Teng group, like the military "hawks," favored it. It seems likely, therefore, that P'eng was purged more for his domestic views—or for power reasons—than for his views on foreign policy, which are almost indistinguishable from those of the Maoists.

The best indication of conflict in the views of P'eng Chen and Teng Hsiao-ping on the desirability of a reconciliation with Russia can be found by comparing speeches they made in the summer of 1965. By that time, as we have already seen, the issue of

---

* An article by Uri Ra'anan, soon to be published by the Center for Policy Study at the University of Chicago, modified my thinking on this subject after I had written the first version of this chapter.

united action had been raised by Lo Jui-ching. P'eng Chen, in a speech in Indonesia on May 25, 1965, made one of the most virulent attacks any Chinese leader has ever made on the Soviet "revisionists." Much of his argument foreshadowed the "third world strategy" that was later to be unfolded by Lin Piao.[35] Apart from railing against the "bourgeois privileged stratum" that had usurped power in Russia, and vigorously rejecting the idea that there had been any change in Soviet policies since the fall of Khrushchev, the most significant portion of P'eng's polemic was his reply to questions "some have asked": "Haven't you Marxist-Leninists established very good united-front relations with many non-Marxist–Leninists and non-Communists? Why can't you enter into united action with the modern revisionists?" While it is true that Asian Communists—including many in Hanoi—were undoubtedly asking these questions, the questions were also in the minds of the Chinese military and members of the Liu-Teng group.

P'eng's reply was that the Russians "really cannot be compared with the anti-imperialist and revolutionary representatives of the national bourgeoisie in Asia, Africa, and Latin America, nor even with the anti-imperialist and patriotic representatives of the royal families and the nobility." These were "objectively revolutionary" while the revisionists were "reactionary."

The best reflection of Teng Hsiao-ping's different ideas on this score is in his July 20, 1965, speech to the Ninth Congress of the Rumanian Communist Party.[36] In that speech, Teng concentrated his fire on U.S. imperialism rather than Soviet revisionism. He even went as far as saying, "we have constant international support and encouragement from Rumania and *other fraternal countries* . . . for which we express heartfelt gratitude." Moreover, Teng concluded his short speech with a forecast that the Chinese people will always march forward "hand in hand" with the "fraternal peoples of the Socialist camp." (For the Maoists and P'eng Chen, the term "Socialist camp" was already an anachronism.) Moreover, Teng implied that a united front with Moscow was still possible if only the Russians would adhere to the principles of the 1957 and 1960 Moscow Declarations guiding fraternal relations among parties. This was a far cry from the views of the Maoists and P'eng, who both insisted that revisionist degeneration in Russia had gone beyond talk of unity. Finally, and most important, Teng spelled out the reasons for his interest in a reconciliation with Moscow:

The Chinese people are determined to build their country into a power-ful socialist state with modern agriculture, modern industry, modern national defense and modern science and technology in not too long a historical period. We are by no means isolated in our struggle. We have constant international support from Rumania and other fraternal countries . . . for which we express heartfelt gratitude.[37]

With its obvious emphasis on China's backwardness this statement unquestionably represents the main reason that many of the opposi-tion leaders—particularly those whom we call "rationalists"—want a reconciliation with Russia: because they realize that such a recon-ciliation may be the only way to obtain the aid that is necessary for them to modernize China. Teng's deliberate and unusual repeti-tion of the adjective "modern" was undoubtedly designed to point up the backwardness of Chinese economy, defense, and technology and, in this context, to stress the need for an understanding with the Russians.

Many in the Chinese party evidently shared Teng's view that the main problem confronting China was that of modernization—and that this could be done best through reconciliation with Russia. This can be inferred from the kinds of attacks made against the opposition by the Maoists during the course of the Cultural Revo-lution. The opposition was accused of wanting: a reduction of the struggle with both Russia and the United States, a lessening of as-sistance to foreign revolutionaries, and a revisionist economic pro-gram that would afford greater scope to private plots and free mar-kets, use profitability as a criterion for small enterprises, and the like.

The Maoists, moreover, clearly intended to establish a link be-tween some of the party oppositionists and the pro-Soviet army group. Thus, in May, 1966, the following charges were leveled against Wu Han, former deputy mayor of Peking, and Teng To and Liao Mo'sha, two of P'eng's senior aides on the municipal commit-tee. Their writings, the article charged, had been directed "against the Lushan meeting" of 1959, at which Peng Te-huai had been purged. They sought to "reverse the decisions of that meeting." The message of Wu Han's drama, *Hai Jui Dismissed from Office*, published in 1961, was that the "Right opportunists" should come back to "administer 'court affairs.' " The attack also criticized one of Teng To's essays for advocating "learning from" and "uniting with" countries "stronger than our own," and for arguing that "we should be pleased if a friend is stronger than we are." In one essay the attack continued, Teng To had said, "If a man with a swelled head thinks he can learn a subject with ease and kicks his teacher out, he will never learn anything." This, said the article, was a "vicious attack on our struggle against modern revisionism and a demand that we ask the revisionists in and let the wolves into the house."[38]

The Chinese "rationalists" wanted a reconciliation with Moscow for reasons quite different from the army's. They seemed to desire a reconciliation with Moscow not to get tough on Vietnam—as the military faction did—but to reduce the danger to China from Russia and the United States. Such a policy would have enabled China to concentrate on its main task of internal economic development.

And, in fact, it is clear that the burden of their attack was on Mao's frenetic economic policies. As stated above, the revisionists were accused specifically of opposing the Great Leap Forward, wishing to extend private plots and free markets, and of wanting to use profitability as a criterion for small enterprises.[39] Their talismans included "construction before destruction." The charges against them suggest that some of them were even inclined to modify drastically the collective farm system.

SOME IMPLICATIONS

Having supported the contention that the Chinese power struggle has in part concerned vital foreign policy issues—particularly Vietnam—I would now like to raise some questions and offer some conjectures about recent events in China and their implications for international relations.

First, there seems little doubt that a major dispute developed in the past two years between army professionals and party leaders over *how* to fight a war with the United States if such a war occurred. As Morton Halperin and John Lewis have indicated, it seems likely that the party and the army agreed that the first stage of an American attack would involve the nuclear bombing of China's main centers.[40] Disagreement centered largely on how to meet the second stage, an American ground invasion. As the two analysts point out: "Basically, the Party proposes reliance on a strategy of people's war—the strategy which the Party pursued in the Japanese war—while the PLA proposes to rely on the modernized military forces to fight a positional war against the American ground forces."

While the army wanted to fight a more conventional, offensive, war, the party argued the need for a defensive war in which China would take whatever punishment the United States could mete out in air attacks, and then force American troops to fight against Chinese guerrillas on Chinese soil.

The reasons for army objections were many. First, such a strategy meant upgrading the role of the people's militia and downgrading that of the professional army;[41] the professional army leaders look with contempt on the "amateurs" of the militia.

It meant withstanding a U.S. invasion without support from the Soviet Union, which Mao continued to alienate for what many army professionals must have thought were foolish reasons.

Also, such a strategy meant reconciling the army to a passive rather than active role. Few armies appreciate this.

Finally, it meant being willing to sacrifice China's cities and urban population and retreating to rural bases.

Another point which merits further discussion is that it was both the "hawks" in the Chinese army and the revisionists in the party who called for a rapprochement with Moscow. What were the perspectives of each group? More particularly, why did the "hawks" believe they could persuade Moscow to support them in a tougher policy on Vietnam, and what price were they willing to pay for such support?

There are several possible explanations of the military perspective. First, as we have seen, sometime in mid-1965 Moscow did in fact propose sending Soviet airplanes to southern China and troops to North Vietnam as part of its offer of "united action" with China to defend Vietnam. Mao and the party leaders rejected this proposal on the grounds that Moscow was only interested in laying the groundwork for a Cuban-type deal with the Americans that would sell out Hanoi and the NLF. The military, on the other hand, may well have argued—like the Japanese, North Korean, and North Vietnamese Communists—that this was an unjust interpretation of Soviet purposes, or that even if it was a correct interpretation, the Soviets could not back out of a commitment. Furthermore, in military eyes, such a deployment of Soviet forces in China and North Vietnam—regardless of Soviet motives—would give the Americans pause about further escalation of the war. The military may also have believed that not all the Soviet leaders were "revisionists" and that some might be willing—given the proper inducements from China—to stand up to the United States in Vietnam. They may have argued that the Chinese party should make concessions to the Soviet Union within the international Communist movement in order to obtain Soviet support in Vietnam. Such concessions might have included an offer to tone down—if not eliminate—the Chinese challenge to Soviet authority in the Communist world and in the third world generally.

What, then, were the perspectives of the Chinese moderates who desired a normalization of relations with Moscow? Perhaps they believed that such normalization might eventually lead to a restoration of Soviet economic aid; or, that a reduction of tension with both Moscow and Washington would give Peking a much-needed breathing spell to concentrate on economic development and to reduce defense spending.

Clearly, it is this particular school of thought in China that the Johnson Administration has hoped to encourage. The vigor with which this faction challenged Mao is ample testimony to its strength. It will undoubtedly be heard from again, particularly once Mao dies or the present transient coalition dissolves.

Particularly interesting about this faction is that it may want to opt out of the international chess game temporarily while it concentrates on modernization at home. This should give hope both to Washington, which fears a Sino-Soviet reconciliation at its expense, and to Moscow, which dreads a Sino-American rapprochement.

The future relationship among the three great powers, however, could evolve in a variety of ways. Much depends on both Soviet and American policies and how these policies are perceived in Peking. Much depends on when and how the Vietnam war will end. Clearly the possibility that most concerns Moscow is a Peking–Washington understanding, however unlikely this now seems. Such an understanding would expose the Russians to powerful adversaries on two fronts. At present the Soviets can take some comfort from the fact that its two potential foes are at one another's throats. Any Sino-American understanding, no matter how slight, could alter that situation to enable either—or both—to exert greater leverage on Russia.

There are some indications that such thoughts have occurred to certain leaders in Peking. Thus, a recent French emissary to the Chinese capital was told that the Americans, although enemies, were to be respected, while the Russians were "traitors" who could never be forgiven. A delegation of Japanese parliamentarians who talked with Chen Yi on September 6, 1966, were told by the Chinese Foreign Minister:

> We shall not attack the United States. As a matter of fact, China is not strong enough to attack America. To tell the truth, America is afraid of China and China is somewhat afraid of America. I do not believe that the United States would invade present-day China. . . . I do not take a particularly pessimistic view of relations between the United States and China.[42]

Commenting on these remarks, the Polish party newspaper, *Trybuna Ludu,* pointed out that

> The calm, businesslike tone of this statement would arouse no objections were the PRC to pursue a policy of unity and cooperation with the Soviet Union and the entire socialist camp. However, in the light of the disruptive policy of the CPC, this statement acquires a somewhat different complexion.
>
> Commenting on Chen Yi's statement, *France-Presse* observed that it undoubtedly confirms the opinion held by many observers that China is sharpening its conflict with the Soviet Union in order to prepare the ground for direct negotiations with the U.S. government.[43]

Obviously the Russians and some of their East European allies are interested in portraying the Chinese as anxious to make a deal with the American "imperialists" in order to discredit Peking. The Chinese have, of course, used the same argument to try to discredit Moscow. But there is sufficient evidence to suggest that this is not mere polemics, that Moscow is frankly alarmed at the possibility of improved Sino-American relations in the context of deteriorating Sino-Soviet relations. The Russians have not been slow to observe that recent Chinese statements have tended to concentrate their attack on the dangers of revisionism, while mentioning imperialism "only in passing."[44] Nor are the Russians unaware of a strong school of thought in Europe—particularly in West Germany—that the United States should ease relations with China in order to compel concessions from Russia.

For Peking to ease tensions with the United States at this time, however, it would be necessary for it to make a major and far-reaching change in the strategy it has been pursuing without let-up since 1958. This strategy has identified U.S. imperialism as the main enemy of all peace-loving peoples, and has involved Peking's active encouragement of all anti-American groups and countries through-out the world. Any substantial adjustments in Peking's relations with the United States would alienate it from the most extreme anti-American forces in the third world, which it has most assiduously cultivated in recent years. Moreover, since it is unlikely that the United States would make any major concessions to Peking—and perhaps not even any minor ones, given the present policy of the American Administration—any such adjustment would have to be made on the basis of the present status quo in the Far East, which Peking finds intolerable.

Finally, it is apparent that Washington is at the moment—and for the foreseeable future—more interested in reaching an accom-modation with the Soviet Union than in reaching one with Peking. Indeed, Washington recently suggested that one of its major reasons for continuing to oppose Chinese admission to the United Nations was its fear of disturbing its relationship with the Soviet Union.[45] Under these circumstances, Peking's room for maneuver is limited.

Nevertheless, the future shape of relations among the three powers is fluid. The present realities of the international situation are more conducive to a Soviet-American understanding than to either a Sino-Soviet or Sino-American accommodation. This situation could easily change under circumstances that are not yet foreseeable.

CHAPTER FOUR

Hanoi Between Moscow and Peking

THERE are four questions that seem central to any discussion of North Vietnam's role in the war: What is the relationship between Hanoi and Moscow and Peking? What is the relationship between Hanoi and the National Liberation Front in South Vietnam? What is Hanoi's strategic outlook on the war in Vietnam? What is its attitude toward negotiations?

Ideologically, of course, the roots of Vietnamese communism, like those of all other Communist parties in the world, go back to Moscow. Ho Chi Minh started, after all, as a Comintern agent in South China, subsequently in Southeast Asia. From 1930 to 1945 the Indochinese Communist Party (ICP), as it was known at the time, loyally followed the twists and turns of the Comintern line. The ICP opposed French colonial rule prior to 1935—when the Comintern adopted the Popular Front line—but refused to oppose the French between 1935 and the Nazi-Soviet Pact in 1939. As a result, it lost much ground in Cochin China—the only part of Vietnam in which it was legal during the 1930's—to the Trotskyites and other southern parties which persistently opposed French colonial rule.

{Throughout the 30's and 40's, the Vietminh's relations with Moscow were channeled through the French Communists—an indication both of Moscow's distant paternalism and its Europe-centric attitude.} After Ho Chi Minh proclaimed the Democratic Republic of Vietnam (DRV) in 1945, it took Moscow a full five years to recognize the

DRV, and by 1950, Ho had already been dispossessed of his capital, Hanoi, and was fighting a war against the French from the bush— with Chinese Communist help.

As suggested earlier, there was not much evidence of serious Soviet interest in Vietnam until after the beginning of the Korean War in 1950. Even then, Soviet military aid to the Vietminh did not arrive until the very last stages of the first Indochina war.

For the first four years of its existence, the DRV fought as an isolated and besieged extension of what was a developing Communist bloc centered in Europe. When the war against the French began in December, 1946, potentially sympathetic Communist parties in Europe were in no position to render effective aid. This was especially true of the French Communists who, at the time, participated in a coalition government in Paris, and had reason to believe that they could eventually exercise the leading role in a revitalized French Union. To this belief, French Communists subordinated everything else. They were particularly anxious to prevent Communist-led rebellions in the French colonies from interfering with their political prospects at home. Moscow did not want to see a Communist-led movement in distant Asia obstruct the increasingly promising outlook for a successful Communist political maneuver in France.

HANOI-PEKING, 1949–1957

The situation changed drastically for the Vietminh when Mao's armies reached the borders of Vietnam in 1949. Almost immediately, the Chinese Communists provided substantial economic and military assistance to the struggling forces of Ho Chi Minh—assistance which proved decisive in the DRV's six-year struggle with France. To the eve of the Sino-Soviet split, it seems plausible that Soviet leaders were satisfied with having the Vietnamese Communists rely mainly on China, leaving the impression that Vietnam was regarded as properly within a Chinese sphere of influence. This, in effect, was an extension of the agreement reached between the Allied Powers (including Russia) prior to the Communist take-over in China, when the Chinese nationalists were assigned the task of occupying Vietnam to the 16th parallel and accepting the Japanese surrender in that area.

Whatever doubts and suspicions Vietminh leaders may have had regarding China's interest in Vietnam, they gratefully accepted

Chinese Communist aid and support. China sent munitions and artillery, DRV troops were trained on Chinese soil, Vietnamese cadres went to China for political training and Chinese cadres, in turn, were infiltrated into the areas controlled by the resistance fighters to give advice and direction. Certainly, in this period a very close working relationship developed between the struggling Vietnamese Communists and their Chinese comrades.

Chinese political influence in the DRV remained paramount for the first few years that followed the signing of the Geneva Accords. Contrary to what might logically have been expected of a native leadership fully aware of a complex social and economic situation far different from that of China, Chinese prestige and influence were so high that the Hanoi regime (in 1953) instituted a slavish imitation of the Chinese land-reform campaign.[1] Chinese advisers were brought in to assist Vietnamese Communist cadres in classifying land ownership in the villages, and so-called landlords and rich peasants were executed by the thousands.

The disastrous results of this poorly-thought-out land reform, in the end acknowledged by the Hanoi leadership with the demotion of its leading advocate, Party Secretary-General Truong Chinh, led to the first serious reassessment of the validity of the Chinese model. In the very first effort to remodel the social order, the example provided by China proved inapplicable to an area fundamental to the structuring of a Socialist society.

This failure of the Chinese land-reform program in North Vietnam coincided with a growing realization in Hanoi that the reunification of the whole of Vietnam held out by the Geneva Accords was not to be brought about. By 1957, the deadline set by the Geneva Conference for elections to reunify Vietnam had passed, and there was no chance that they would be held. The United States had committed itself to the support of the anti-Communist government of Ngo Dinh Diem, and had made it clear that it regarded the partition of Vietnam as an indefinite Cold War truce line in Asia, pending an overall Asian settlement. Moreover, the Russians gave every indication that they too regarded the 1954 partition as a Cold War truce line. When the July 1956 deadline for elections arrived, the Russians, who were cochairmen with the British of the International Control Commission, agreed to extend *sine die* the functions of the commission beyond the term initially fixed but, much to the annoyance of the Hanoi government, did not press for elections.[2] Moreover, at the beginning of 1957, the USSR proposed the simultaneous admission of the two Vietnams to the United Nations.[3]

As prospects of early reunification faded, Hanoi had to come to grips with its acute economic problems. No longer able to count on incorporating the rice-rich South into its economy, it began to look for alternative sources of foodstuffs for the North and to lay the groundwork for a self-sustaining economy. It now came to believe that its best hope for eventual reunification lay in building up its own strength. Official recognition of this was reflected in January 1957, when the Hanoi government announced that the "struggle for unity would be long and difficult" and that an essential prerequisite for unity was the consolidation of the North.[4]

In this situation, it was both necessary and logical for the DRV to turn to the Soviet Union. DRV requests were met with surprising alacrity by Moscow, despite the fact that the Soviet Union was already cutting down on its aid to China. Thus, then Soviet chief of state Klement Voroshilov went to Hanoi in May, 1957, and generously proffered offers of Soviet assistance to the Northern economy. His visit was described by the Hanoi press as a "most important historical event." A month later Ho Chi Minh toured Eastern Europe for the purpose of soliciting aid. Within a year the Soviet Union and Eastern Europe had replaced China as the principal source of economic aid to the DRV.[5] Not unnaturally, Hanoi media began to give increasing play to Soviet points of view on relations within the Communist bloc and international affairs in general. These media also adopted the Soviet view that reunification of Vietnam could only come about peacefully and gradually as a result of the eventual merger of the two Vietnams.

SHIFT TO MOSCOW (1957–1960)

The apparent shifting of loyalties did not come about without serious conflict within the Hanoi leadership. It is largely taken for granted by analysts of the Hanoi political scene that at least two and probably three tendencies are reflected in the group immediately around Ho. These tendencies may very broadly be described as looking for guidance to Peking; depending on Moscow for economic— and right now for military—aid; and exploiting Sino-Soviet divergencies for Hanoi's own purposes.

It is important to be clear on what it means for a group in Hanoi —or, for that matter, in any small Communist party—to be "pro-Moscow" or "pro-Chinese" under present conditions of growing pluralism in the international Communist movement. It means, primarily, that there is a common outlook between the local group and the larger party on crucial local issues. In the case of most non-ruling parties, for example, factional tendencies generally develop around the question of the proper strategy for gaining power. One group tends to emphasize the need for violence while another stresses political struggle. In most Communist parties, the first group often—but not always in recent years—tends to look toward China for ideological guidance and legitimacy, while the second group looks toward Moscow. The two big powers have, in turn, tended to favor the representatives of one or the other local group. In the case of ruling parties, local issues have centered on the methods and pace of economic development, military security, and foreign policy.

What distinguishes the divided Communist states—East Germany, North Korea, and North Vietnam—is that the crucial local questions have to do with both sets of issues. That is, each Communist state must concern itself not only with economic development and military security, but with the question of reunification: how to take power in the other half of the state.

At the risk of some oversimplification, it can be stated that since 1957—when it became clear to North Vietnam that reunification was going to be neither quick nor easy—the crucial local issue has revolved around the relative priority to be assigned to economic development of the North and struggle in the South. Between 1957 and 1960, Northern leaders agreed on the need to concentrate on economic development. But between 1960 and 1963 a continuing debate seems to have gone on between an "economist" faction and a "southern-oriented" faction, the first placing primary emphasis on building up the North, the second on giving support to the burgeoning anti-Diem struggle in the South. Because the Russians—between 1960 and 1963—gave their support to the first group and the Chinese gave theirs to the second, we can refer to the first group as "pro-Soviet" and to the second as "pro-Chinese," with the understanding that the orientation pertained for a given time and issue. Under different circumstances a few years later, some of the individuals who were in the "pro-Chinese" group would be found on the "pro-Russian" side of the argument.

In other words, factional tendencies in North Vietnam—as in any small country attempting to maintain viability in a big-power world—have to be seen in terms of local issues. The postures and alignments assumed from time to time and event to event by Communist leaders in Hanoi are largely a reflection of their views on these local issues. There is, in short, no "China lobby" in Hanoi in the sense that any group wishes to promote Chinese interests when those interests conflict with Hanoi's. Indeed, the DRV leaders most often cited as members of the "China lobby" and who have sometimes identified with Chinese positions have also been those who have most openly rejected Chinese military advice.[6] They have expressed the most unquestionably prevalent sentiment in the Vietnamese Communist elite—which, after all, can look back upon a unique national revolutionary experience, and was the first Communist group to take over state power outside the Soviet Union—that the Vietnamese revolution need not copy any foreign models, and that attempts to imitate the experiences of Communist movements abroad are foolish.

In this context, it is not surprising that the North Vietnamese leaders as a whole have attempted to steer a middle course between Russia and China, sidestepping issues not immediately germane to their own problems and being careful to maintain communication with both protagonists. Such divergencies of view as there have been—and continue to be—in Hanoi have revolved about the problems of immediate concern: reunification, economic development of the North, and the war in the South. Hanoi's policy on these issues has shifted over the years, in accordance with what the prevailing group within the DRV elite deemed best to promote North Vietnamese interests in the given situation.

THE NORTHERN VERSUS THE SOUTHERN OPTION (1960–1963)

Since the late 1950's, by which time the Southern anti-Diemist movement had acquired considerable momentum, the Hanoi leaders have been faced with a dilemma. Should they give all-out support to the Southerners even if this would mean a war with the United States that would devastate their country? The idea that Hanoi set out, in the late 1950's or early 1960's, with a plan for the conquest of South Vietnam which they have been following ever since is a myth. Indeed, there is good evidence to suggest that Hanoi initially strove to restrain the Southern resistance fighters. The truth of the matter seems rather that as the anti-Diemist struggle in the South gained intensity, and as the North came to believe that the risks of outright American intervention were minimal, it increasingly dropped its restraint. But throughout the period from 1959 to 1965, there were a number of signs of debate within the Hanoi leadership and between Hanoi and the NLF over the proper course of action to pursue in the South.

One sign was given in a speech delivered by Le Duan in April, 1960, shortly before the formation of the NLF. Duan stressed the problems of industrializing the North and building up its agriculture and then went on to make a frank plea for "restricting" the Southern resistance movement so that it would not interfere with world peace—a clear warning of the danger of a larger war with the Americans if the Southerners pushed too hard.

> The Northern people will never neglect their task with regard to one half of their country which is not yet liberated. But in the present conjuncture, when the possibility exists to maintain a lasting peace in the world and create favorable conditions for the world movement of socialist revolution and national independence to go forward, we can and must guide and restrict within the South the solving of the contradiction between imperialism and the colonies of our country.[7]

Elsewhere in the same speech, Duan frankly conceded that putting priority on Northern development over Southern revolution created "complications" for the Southerners, but he insisted that there would be advantages in such a gradualist strategy for the Southerners as well. His idea seemed to be that once the North had consolidated itself, it could then lend greater assistance to the Southern resistance.

> In the world, the socialist forces are becoming stronger than the imperialist forces. In our country, the socialist forces in the North are also being developed strongly. Though this situation has created a number of complications for the revolution in the South, the advantages are fundamental. We must know how to make use of this supremacy of the socialist forces adequately and in good time to help the revolution in the South develop favorably.

Duan even seemed to be advising against a Southern strategy based on violence and for a strategy based on political maneuver. He argued that the Diem regime would fall apart under conditions of peace and reached new dialectical heights in claiming that preservation of peace was revolutionary.

If peace can be maintained, the aggressive schemes of the United States–Diem clique will rapidly fail, and their totalitarian fascist regime will rapidly decay. If peace is maintained, the revolutionary forces will enjoy necessary conditions to develop strongly. Hence to maintain peace is a revolutionary slogan.

Thus, as of mid-1960, on the very eve of the formation of the NLF, Hanoi was doing its best to contain the Southern resistance movement and was warning it against adventurism. Hanoi was clearly more intent on developing its own economy with an ambitious new Five Year Plan to be announced later in the year than on giving support to the Southerners.

It was against this background that the Third Congress of the Lao Dong Party met in September, 1960. Doubtless one of the key questions before it was whether to continue to give priority to economic development of the North, or to increase support to the Southern guerrillas with all the attendant risks. The Russians supported the first alternative and the Chinese the second. The Soviet delegate to the Congress emphasized the importance of peaceful coexistence, while the Chinese delegate denounced revisionism and stressed the comradeship in arms between the Chinese and Vietnamese people, as if to express complete Chinese support in the event of a showdown with the United States.

North Vietnamese leaders, although divided in their emphasis, came down on the side of simultaneously developing the North and increasing support to the South. The new line was apparent in Le Duan's report to the Congress on behalf of the Central Committee.[8] Whereas a few months earlier he had advised caution for the Southerners, and had given priority to building up the North, he now spoke of the close connection of Northern development and Southern revolution and the need to make "simultaneous progress." He contended that "so long as South Vietnam is not yet liberated . . . there can be no peace in the minds of our people." Abandoning the previous emphasis on developing the North first, he now said that the South "must play a direct role" in bringing about its own liberation. The immediate task of the revolution in the South, he argued, was to overthrow the Diem government and to form a "national democratic coalition government in South Vietnam. . . ." Toward this end he urged "our people there" to organize a "broad National Front." A few months later the NLF came into existence.

Although the Third Congress marked a new departure in Hanoi's attitude toward the Southern struggle, there were apparent differences among the leaders both as to the wisdom of the new line and its possible effects. Premier Pham Van Dong, a consistent moderate, continued to adhere to the old formulation that strengthening the North was the best way to help the Southern revolution.[9] Dong also placed great emphasis on the Soviet Union as the leader of the socialist camp and on the importance of maintaining peace. General Vo Nguyen Giap, on the other hand, in what seemed a clear rebuff to Dong, who had stressed the importance of "peaceful" reunification, said:

> . . . while speaking about our Party's policy of peaceful reunification, a number of our comrades are not fully aware of the plots of the United States imperialists and their lackeys; they do not understand that while our policy is to preserve peace and to achieve peaceful reunification, we should always be prepared to cope with any maneuver of the enemy. That is due to the fact that a number of our comrades have no all-sided understanding of the present world situation; they see only the possibility of winning a lasting peace and not the danger of war which still exists . . . they are not fully aware of the plots of imperialism. . . .[10]

The main thrust of Giap's argument was that developments in the South could eventually lead to an American attack on the North, and the North had to be prepared.

> They are openly sabotaging the Geneva Agreements, ceaselessly introducing reinforcements in military personnel and war materials into South Vietnam, building up strategic roads and military bases, and actively preparing for an aggressive war. . . . If some day the United States imperialists . . . dared to launch an aggressive war against the North, all our compatriots in the South would certainly rise up as a single man to stop them. . . . However, this is no reason why we should underestimate the enemy and disregard his plots.[11]

While the argument between Giap and Dong may have concerned differing views of American intentions, it seems likely that it also concerned differing views about the proper amount of risk to run in the South.

In any event, by the time the Congress ended, the North had made several substantial concessions to the advocates of greater militancy. Le Duan, a former Southern resistance leader, was named the new Secretary General of the Lao Dong party in an obvious effort to assure the Southern guerrillas that the North would not forsake them. And the new party line called for pushing the revolution in the North and South "simultaneously."

Throughout 1961 and the early part of 1962, Hanoi's attention was concentrated on Laos and the civil war that followed the Kong Le coup in late 1960. The civil war ended with the neutralization of Laos at Geneva in July 1962, after it had threatened to erupt into a confrontation between Russia and the United States. The Laotian settlement had certain obvious advantages for the Communists. It left the Laotian Communists or Pathet Lao—who were trained, organized and guided by Hanoi—as members of a coalition government; it called for the withdrawal of United States military personnel, robbed SEATO of all pretexts for interfering in future Laotian developments, and left the Pathet Lao in control of the strategically important eastern portion of Laos through which the Ho Chi Minh trail from North to South Vietnam ran.

United States willingness to agree to a "neutralized" Laos greatly strengthened the belief in Hanoi that it would also agree to a "neutralized" South Vietnam on the Laotian model.[12] For this reason, from July 1962, when the Laos agreement was signed, until about mid-1963, Hanoi held up the Laotian settlement as a model for South Vietnam and scaled down military operations in an effort to reach a settlement. Only after it had become clear that the Americans had no intention of using the Laotian model in South Vietnam did Hanoi and the NLF increase military pressure on the South. At the same time, there was a decided turn toward China and away from the Soviet Union, presumably because the Hanoi leaders were increasingly frustrated with Soviet counsels of restraint in the South.

TURN BACK TO CHINA

The switch back toward China was signaled in April 1963, when Party General Secretary Le Duan made the case for a violent versus a peaceful path to power. His speech was reprinted in full by the Chinese party newspaper, *People's Daily*, and was subsequently disseminated by Peking's Foreign Languages Publishing House.[13]

Although Hanoi moved closer to China in the spring of 1963, its shift was not as unequivocal as China would have liked. This was made clear at the time during a state visit to North Vietnam by Liu Shao-chi, then Mao's heir apparent. Speaking to the Hanoi Party School on May 15th, Liu pointedly warned against following a "middle course" in the Sino-Soviet dispute:

> The international communist movement is now in a crucially important period. There is an acute worldwide struggle between Marxist-Leninists and modern revisionists over a series of important questions of principle. . . . We cannot look on with folded arms or *follow a middle course* [Italics added] with regard to this important question of the struggle between conflicting principles.[14]

It seems quite likely that the North Vietnamese leaders were still divided both on the extent to which Hanoi should associate itself with Peking's position and on the extent to which it should encourage and support armed struggle in the South that could lead to a larger war with the United States. But the more militant line was obviously gaining.

It was probably in this context that in July, 1963, *Hoc Tap* published an article by Nguyen Chi Thanh, "Who Will Win in South Vietnam?" With Moscow clearly in mind, Thanh said:

> We do not have any illusions about the United States. We do not underestimate our opponent—the strong and cunning U.S. imperialism. But we are not afraid of the United States. . . . If, on the contrary, one is afraid of the United States and thinks that to offend it would court failure, and that firm opposition to United States imperialism would touch off a nuclear war, then the only course left would be to compromise with and surrender to United States imperialism.[15]

Thanh went on to call for increased aid to the Vietcong from Hanoi, arguing against the position—apparently taken by some of his comrades and the Russians—that the best aid to the insurgents would be to consolidate the North.

> A powerful North Vietnam will be a decisive factor in the social development of our entire country. But this does not mean that simply because the North is strong, the revolutionary movement in the South will automatically succeed. The powerful North Vietnam and the revolutionary movement of the South Vietnamese people are mutually complementary and must be closely coordinated; the building of the North itself cannot replace the resolution of the inherent social contradictions of South Vietnam.[16]

Not surprisingly, the Chinese promptly republished Thanh's article. In August, Hanoi came out vigorously against the test-ban agreement Moscow had signed with the United States. By September, *Hoc Tap* was making violent attacks on revisionism and stressing the superiority of armed struggle over peaceful revolution.[17] These and other things indicated that Hanoi was moving farther from Moscow toward Peking as it became increasingly committed to support of the Southern guerrillas seeking to overthrow the Diem government.

Le Duan's speech at the Ninth Plenum of the Central Committee in December, 1963, reflected the reasons for Hanoi's growing disgruntlement with Moscow.[18] Duan sharply criticized those who did not have the proper fighting will and revolutionary spirit and could not "see clearly the boundless prospects of revolution held out before the world. . . ." The "revisionists" had "mistaken" views on international questions, continued Duan, because they had not fully understood the development of Marxist-Leninist theory in recent decades, the major contribution to which had been by Mao in answering a whole series of questions about "uprisings in the rural areas, the relying on the rural areas, the establishment of rural bases, the encirclement of cities by villages, and questions concerning the mobilization of peasants, the protracted armed struggle . . . and so on." In other words, Russia had little to offer—either in experience or, presumably, advice—on the war in the South.

Duan then proceeded to attack the line—evidently taken by Moscow—that the Communists should follow a more long-range strategy in South Vietnam:

> If we Communists follow a strategic line with nuclear weapons as its mainstay, the logical result can only be a defensive strategy . . . to adopt such a defensive strategy is the same as to repudiate revolution both objectively and subjectively.

He went on to slap at "some people" who argued that the economic progress of the Socialist camp would be decisive in Vietnam:

> But the point is this. Is it necessary to wait until the socialist camp has surpassed the capitalist camp in industrial and agricultural output before carrying the revolution forward to eradicate imperialism?

"Some people" placed the desire to reach a détente with imperialism above everything else and, "whether you like it or not, the outcome will only be to hamper the development of revolution."

"The strategy of revolution," warned Duan, "should not be a defensive one." It should be an "offensive strategy" which, while it rejects world war, nevertheless promotes "revolutionary struggles in order to repulse imperialism step by step and overthrow it bit by bit." To "remain on the defensive" would only encourage imperialism. To pursue a policy of peaceful coexistence "can only lead to a stalemate . . ."

In short, the main objection of the Hanoi militants to Soviet strategy was its refusal on various pretexts to give sufficient support to an offensive strategy in South Vietnam. From Duan's final remarks, it is clear that a more cautious line was also favored by a group in the DRV itself.

> Some comrades in our Party have come under the influence of modern revisionism. Although their number is small, it is not a good thing and we must pay attention to it.

Otherwise, revisionism would "corrode our Party"—particularly when the revolution meets with difficulties.

By July, 1964, Hanoi had so irritated Khrushchev by its developing ties with Peking that he was preparing to disengage from Indochina by resigning Soviet cochairmanship of the International Control Commission. Between late 1964 and early 1965, however, Hanoi shifted back to a more neutral position, due mainly to the increasing threat of American attack highlighted by the Tonkin Gulf incident in August, 1964. To meet the American threat Hanoi obviously required Soviet assistance. When Khrushchev was ousted in October, 1964, and the new Soviet leadership made a special effort to restore ties with the Asian sector of the Communist movement, the North Vietnamese were responsive. It was under these circumstances that Soviet Premier Kosygin made his trip to Hanoi in February, 1965. Since that time, Hanoi's relations with Moscow have been growing closer while relations with Peking have cooled.

One of the best indications of the change in Hanoi's attitude toward Moscow in early 1965, was the sudden drop in the number of denunciations of modern revisionism which had been standard fare in the previous year and a half. These references became very rare after Kosygin's visit.

An even better indication of the shift was the invitation given by Hanoi in early April to the Italian Communist Party to send a delegation to North Vietnam. The Italian party is the most "revisionist" of all the European Communist parties and has been vigorously attacked by the Chinese.

By April 1966, Hanoi was, in stark contrast to Peking, waxing enthusiastic in its comments on the Twenty-Third Congress of the CPSU. At the same time Hanoi, clearly unwilling to go too far in antagonizing Peking, made a special point of refuting Soviet charges that the Chinese were hindering Soviet arms deliveries to Vietnam. Premier Pham Van Dong, addressing the North Vietnamese National Assembly, went out of his way to "thank China . . . for her devoted help in the transit of the aid from the Soviet Union and other fraternal East European countries according to schedule."[19] It was by sticking to such tactics that Hanoi finally was able to get Moscow and Peking to agree, in early 1967, on an arrangement for transporting Soviet weapons and supplies through China to Vietnam. The agreement provided for the North Vietnamese to pick up the shipments at the Soviet-Chinese border and to escort them through Chinese territory. This agreement would reduce chances of Sino-Soviet friction over weapons shipments and was obviously intended by both powers as a gesture of aid to Hanoi's war effort rather than as a prelude to a Sino-Soviet reconciliation. It thus provided still another example of Hanoi's leverage on its Communist allies arising from their conflict.

HANOI AND THE NLF

The relationship of the Hanoi government to the National Liberation Front in South Vietnam is extremely complex. This relationship is often oversimplified in one of two directions. Some claim that the NLF is a mere puppet of the North, while others insist that it is completely autonomous. The truth, it seems to me, lies somewhere in between.

On the one hand, the evidence is overwhelming that the People's Revolutionary Party (PRP), which was set up in 1962, and has the decisive voice in the NLF, is, in fact, the Southern branch of the Lao Dong Party which rules Hanoi.[20] Prior to the Geneva settlement of 1954, the Vietminh operated as one movement in North and South Vietnam. The present Secretary General of the Lao Dong Party in the North, Le Duan, is a Southerner who was one of the principal leaders of the resistance fighters in the South during the first Indochina war. Moreover, although there are non-Communist, Southern political forces represented in the NLF, there is little evidence of their organizational independence. The so-called Democratic and Radical Socialist parties included in the Front do not

have newspapers and give no other signs of political life. The Democratic Party has been controlled by the Southern Communists since
1946.

On the other hand, there are non-Communist individuals and
forces in the Front, some of whom unquestionably believe that
they can push the NLF toward democracy, and many of whom do
not want to subordinate themselves to the North. The Southern
resistance movement was begun by a variety of anti-Diemist forces
including the Communists. This movement, for a long time fighting
on its own, with only minimal Northern assistance and with considerable indigenous support, developed a strong sense of dis-
tinctiveness and will not easily be turned into a mere tool of the
North. On several key issues, at any rate, there have been persistent
signs of disagreement between the North and the NLF. On the question of negotiations, for example, the NLF has consistently displayed
an independent attitude. Thus, while Hanoi has recently indicated
that a halt in the bombing of the North would open the way to
talks, the NLF has insisted that its acceptance as the interlocutor
is central. Moreover, the NLF has seemed consistently less interested than Hanoi in reunification.

The relationship between Hanoi and the NLF is further com-
plicated by the fact that there are significant historical differences
in the development of the Communist movements in North and
South Vietnam. In part, these differences stem from the governmental and administrative environments in which Communism had
to operate. With its nerve center in Saigon, South Vietnam was a
full-fledged French colony tied directly to France, while the Northern
protectorate of Tonkin remained much further removed from Paris.[21]
In a certain respect there was a hothouse atmosphere surrounding
the Communist plant in the South nurtured by periodic infusions
from the French Communist Party, many of whose internal disputes were mirrored by the budding comrades in the Saigon cafés.
Essentially, Communism in Saigon and its hinterland was an in-
tellectualized movement that attracted adherents from a prema-
turely displaced bourgeois stratum, heavily tinged with an early
and violent anti-French nationalism. It revealed many traces
of an undisciplined leftism, which gave rise to factionalism on
a wide scale which weakened the Communist movement in the
South.

Communism in North Vietnam was initially built up on a far less

popular basis but during World War II, when it led a national resistance movement, it acquired an indigenous character devoid of
the pseudo-Europeanism of Southern Communism and of its predilec-
tion for ideological hair-splitting. Consequently, while the Communist movement in the South lost its vitality soon after the French
return in 1945, the movement in North Vietnam—small but tightly
knit and monolithically directed by native Northern Vietnamese—
was able to flourish, profiting from the antiforeign grass-roots sentiment aroused by the Japanese occupation. The Communist party in
the North emerged as the foremost and most effective champion of
native rule, and it was to uphold this image to the point of victory
over the French.

At the same time, as Douglas Pike says in his excellent discussion
of North-South divergencies within the Vietminh, Vietminh fortunes
in the South can best be described as a "successful failure."

"The Cochin-Chinese," says Pike, "regarded the resistance as
Northern-oriented: the center of the fighting was in the North, the
Vietminh was strongest in the North, most of its leaders were Northerners, and the French were most vulnerable in the Red River
delta. . . . The communication channel between Hanoi and Saigon
was undependable, and liaison within the South was difficult. The
Northern leadership exhibited little knowledge about Southerners
and even less patience with Southern lethargy. Finally, the international situation was such as to favor more active pursuit of the
resistance above the 16th parallel." [22]

The Southern Communists had been carrying on a far less effective struggle against the French, not only because the French political
and military administration in Saigon was stronger, but also because
the Northern sense of unity and purpose was lacking. The French
had succeeded in fractionalizing Southern regionalist groups and
encouraging the particularism already indigenous to the area. This
played a major role in the failure of the Vietminh's Southern branch
to either rally around it or unify the anti-French militant resistance
groups who insisted on carving out for themselves their individual
resistance enclaves. [23]

Moreover, as already pointed out, the Southern Communists,
instead of having created a unified and purposeful movement, were
themselves rent by factionalism and disputes, and could not take
advantage of the weakness of the other parties to achieve unchal-
lenged supremacy in the fight against the French. They must have

had reason to hope that the victory of their comrades in the North would give to them the chance they themselves had failed to earn; great was their disappointment, therefore, when Ho Chi Minh accepted the Geneva Accords and the partition which threw them back on their own resources.

The biographical accounts of NLF leaders (as published by DRV media)[24] and other evidence leave little doubt that, within six months after the 1954 Geneva Conference, and even before the Hanoi leadership had reached a valid assessment of the situation in South Vietnam, the Lao Dong party undertook the difficult and delicate task of reorganizing the Communist movement in South Vietnam. Because the movement had to organize support among the peasantry in the Delta, and because many of its leaders had either defected or gone underground the task was difficult. The problem of securing adherence of the non-Communist regionalist-particularist groups consistently apprehensive of Northern domination and for that reason among others, refusing to lend their support to the local Communists, made the task a delicate one.

Hanoi had to carefully choose men to whom leadership in the South could be entrusted. Accordingly, it selected men, who on their own could generate a following, but who would be responsive to direction and whose past performance gave promise that they would become neither factionalists nor traitors. In most instances Hanoi gave preference to men who had held second-level, third-level, and even lower leadership positions in the pre-1954 years, and who were not tarred with the factionalist brush. Such men might be expected to welcome an opportunity to gain prominence within the movement. Moreover, because they lacked a personal following in the local party apparatus, they would be more amenable to control and would not give competition to party hierarchs in Hanoi. For example, one of the top leaders of the PRP today is an individual with a relatively obscure past. Tran Nam Trung, the present secretary-general of the PRP and possibly the single most important figure in the Southern Communist organization, has a history of only middle-level leadership posts in the anti-French struggle during the 1930's and 1940's. He left South Vietnam shortly after June, 1954, and is said to have stayed in North Vietnam until 1963 as an officer in the Vietnamese People's Army.[25]

The population exchange that took place shortly after the Geneva Accords were signed undoubtedly provided the Hanoi regime with the opportunity to infiltrate cadres into South Vietnam very quickly. At the same time, many Southern Vietnamese went north to be "re-educated" and trained for party tasks in the South.

An intensification of clandestine political work was undertaken shortly after Diem's repudiation of the village elections scheduled for 1956, and the movement—carefully nurtured, financed, and publicized by Hanoi—continued to gain ground. Diem's grievous political errors, and above all his intransigent persecution of any and all political opposition, certainly gained for the insurgency many of those adherents among the sects—and populace as a whole—previously denied pre-Geneva resistance.

The structural framework of the present relationship between the Hanoi leadership and the NLF can best be understood in the context of this history and development. In its internal structure, the NLF is a "broad-based pyramid with the villages at the bottom and the central committee at the top. . . ."[26] The PRP—the Southern branch of the Lao Dong party proper—is a "thinner and harder-core pyramid within the NLF."[27] Moreover, the main task of the PRP within the NLF is that of control. The political officers in all NLF military units are—with rare exceptions—PRP cadres. Overt or secret PRP members serve as liaison personnel in the non-Communist groups within the NLF. In sum, the main function of the PRP is to insure political control of the military arm of the NLF and to guide the movement's political struggle. According to captured NLF documents, PRP secretary-general, Tram Nam Trung, has overall responsibility for the NLF armed forces. PRP chairman Vo Chi Cong supervises agitprop and indoctrination, recruitment, and organization building.[28]

The PRP Central Committee is frequently referred to as "COSVN," which stands for "Central Office, South Vietnam." COSVN, however, whose offices were thought to be in Tay Ninh province, is essentially the general staff of the entire NLF military organization in the South, and may well be the site of the physical location of the PRP Central Committee as well.[29] It has, in any case, direct communication with the reunification department of the Lao Dong party in Hanoi under General Nguyen Van Vinh. During the past two years, DRV media have given ample publicity to General Nguyen Van Vinh's public views on the reunification struggle in South Vietnam.[30]

Notwithstanding this elaborate control machinery, whose threads all lead back to Hanoi, the NLF has emerged as a viable movement in its own right. It has acquired momentum growing out of nearly a decade of struggle on the firing line. Certainly the NLF includes very significant political forces that are not Communist and still harbor long-held apprehensions about both Communist domination and domination by Northerners. Additionally, the NLF has managed to attract very substantial support among the Southern peasantry. Indicative of the genuinely indigenous Southern wellsprings that the NLF had succeeded in generating was Hanoi's formal constitution of the PRP as late as January, 1962. The long delay in announcing this party was implicit recognition by Hanoi that many forces so far outside DRV political control were advancing DRV aims in the South. The PRP had to be set up formally at this stage in order to reinforce and, indeed, insure control by Hanoi.[31]

The problem of control—and it is worthwhile emphasizing this point—is probably one of the most sensitive areas in Hanoi's relationship with the NLF and with the PRP leadership of the NLF. Hanoi fears the growth of independent attitudes among the Southern resistance fighters and their leaders. On the other hand, the DRV must publicly foster recognition of the NLF as an independent force, and must enhance its claims to legitimacy. In this sense, Hanoi's dilemma is strikingly parallel to that of both Moscow and Peking.

To a certain extent, Hanoi has not had to face up to its dilemma because of the unquestioned charismatic role played by Ho Chi Minh for all of Vietnam, and because of the great authority exercised by Ho in Hanoi. Nevertheless, Hanoi has—with increasing frequency—given public endorsement to announced goals and aims of the NLF, and on several occasions has obviously had to bargain with the NLF when the latter's position was not in line with Hanoi's programs.[32] At the same time, Hanoi has deliberately sought to underplay the role of NLF leaders, and has not been willing to permit the emergence of a Southern resistance personality around whom an independent leadership could coalesce. I have been informed on good authority that a recent documentary film, made by the NLF in South Vietnam, was sent to Hanoi for clearance and subsequently edited to tone down the activities of Nguyen Huu Tho, chairman of the NLF Central Committee. Moreover, it seems significant that at no time in recent years have DRV media given meaningful publicity to the speeches or activities of any Southern Communist (PRP) leader.

Nevertheless, DRV leaders must now—with whatever qualms—live and deal with the NLF leadership on terms that will assure an effective and viable, mutually advantageous relationship over the next decade or more. It must by this time be very clear to Hanoi that reunification of Vietnam by military means is virtually impossible because of U.S. opposition, and that reunification by political means—even after a possible settlement of the fighting in the South—is a long way off. This has, in effect, now been conceded by both the NLF and the DRV. The DRV is consequently obliged to accept the lesser goal of a recognized status for its Southern creation.

Moreover, there is and has consistently been a limit to the extent to which the DRV can assume the major share of military and political management of the struggle in South Vietnam without running certain definite risks: (1) alienation of the local support which has been so laboriously built up around Southern particularism; (2) damage to the image of the genuinely popular nature of the liberation movement in South Vietnam; (3) exacerbation of the already existing frictions between DRV army units (PAVN) in South Vietnam and NLF guerrilla units; and (4) increasing the apprehensions of the Laotian and Cambodian governments with respect to the well-known pan-Indochina aims of the Vietnamese Communists.

These considerations, needless to say, will not deter the DRV's giving all possible help to the NLF—from logistic aid to heavy military infiltration of PAVN units—in order to counter the U.S. military build-up in the South and to attempt to achieve a position of strength for bargaining purposes. However, it is clear that this type of escalation, on both sides, cannot continue indefinitely without turning the entire struggle in South Vietnam into a kind of war locally and internationally different from what it has been up to now.

Logically, therefore, the DRV has a stake in reciprocal de-escalation, and so does the NLF. In other words, a lessening of the military confrontation is a major point on which DRV and NLF interests coincide, albeit for different reasons. Certainly the NLF is loath to be taken over lock, stock, and barrel by the DRV. However, even in the face of this desire for de-escalation, neither the DRV nor the NLF would accept a one-sided de-escalation, or a settlement which would leave the NLF without legitimized political status. By the same token, Hanoi cannot agree to Washington's demand for reducing the DRV commitment to the NLF in exchange for a cessation of the bombing of North Vietnam. Hanoi cannot afford even to hint that it would be prepared to abandon the NLF. The NLF has displayed a strong sensitivity to any such possibility, as is strikingly illustrated by the January 20, 1967, public statement of NLF Secretary-General Huynh Tam Phat. In that statement he pointedly omitted mention of DRV Foreign Minister Nguyen Duy Trinh's January 18th tie-in of a cessation of bombing to negotiations. Phat went so far as to leave the impression that, in fact, Trinh had placed a major emphasis on the indivisible unity between Hanoi and NLF. This element had, in fact, been conspicuously underplayed in the Trinh statement.[33]

This episode points up the question of the diverse elements which are dynamically at play in the DRV–NLF relationship. These elements involve alternatives and prospects about which agreement between the two parties has probably not been conclusively worked out. As a first consideration, there is the outlook for the immediate future of South Vietnam. The NLF has reason to fear that Hanoi may be forced to look at South Vietnam in terms of certain minimal goals only, without necessarily abandoning the long-range goals of unification. To the NLF leaders, such a prospect poses two equally distasteful alternatives: (1) a settlement in South Vietnam in which the PRP leadership of the NLF would be subordinated to a non-Communist South Vietnamese government in which the NLF—as a whole—would be allowed to participate on the most tenuous terms, or in which the emerging "unity" government of Saigon would attempt to come to terms primarily with the non-Communist elements of the NLF; (2) at the worst, a repeat of 1954, which would oblige the PRP to operate strictly underground in South Vietnam and would force many of its leaders to flee to the North.

On the other hand, neither of these alternatives is likely to be imposed by Hanoi simply because the DRV can neither afford to accept the political emasculation of the NLF, nor repeat 1954. Hanoi is in the position of having an irrevocable commitment to the NLF. Just as Moscow cannot afford to write off the DRV—even for the sake of a meaningful détente with the United States because the power and prestige of the Soviet Union in the international Communist movement is at stake—Hanoi cannot afford to write off the Communist-led NLF in South Vietnam. Such abandonment, it must fear, could set the stage for a relatively stable, viable South Vietnamese regime based on the broad support of the non-Communist sectors of South Vietnamese society. This regime could—not least because of the important U.S. economic support it could mobilize—eventually emerge as a strong contender for the support and loyalties of Vietnamese both North and South.

Contrary to the pessimistic estimates which American governmental circles entertain about the prospects of a non-Communist regime in South Vietnam, there is reason to believe that such a regime could emerge on a viable basis in the absence of Communist-inspired terror and guerrilla war. To this extent, those American advocates of a policy giving priority to pacification are probably quite correct. Key indicators of this potential are the facts that only a few, if any, of the political oppositionists originally jailed by Diem and released after his fall have gone over to the NLF, and that some of the participating groups of the NLF under the Diem regime subsequently abandoned the NLF. Very much aware of this Achilles heel, the NLF has recently gone out of its way to woo anti-Ky elements in South Vietnam in a broad united-front appeal.

In the context of these alternatives and prospects, both Hanoi and the NLF, nevertheless, operate in the framework of maximal and minimal goals, by no means identical, the priorities of which change according to external and internal pressures. Hanoi's maximal goals—the very best that Hanoi could hope to achieve—are: (1) the reunification of Vietnam under the aegis of the DRV; (2) international guarantees and recognition of this unification, and eventual entry into the United Nations; (3) assumption of a significant role in Southeast Asian affairs, and especially general acceptance of a Vietnamese sphere of influence in Cambodia and Laos; and (4) the ability to stand up to Chinese pressures by using the enhanced DRV status within the Communist camp and by manipulating big-power support for its own ends.

The maximal goals of the NLF are far more circumscribed: (1) inclusion of the NLF in a Saigon coalition regime which it could hope to influence substantially from the very outset, and to dominate in a relatively short period of time; (2) international recognition of such a coalition regime, including recognition by the major powers with specific political guarantees and pledges of economic aid for reconstruction; and (3) eventual reunification of Vietnam on terms that would insure the significant participation of South Vietnamese Communist leaders in an all-Vietnam government.

Hanoi's minimal goals, in essence announced in the Four Points and later elaborated, are: (1) unconditional cessation of U.S. bombing of North Vietnam, and an end to further U.S. military buildup in South Vietnam; (2) an international conference on Vietnam for working out an arrangement which would insure NLF political status in South Vietnam and possibly participation in a coalition government; (3) major power guarantees for the neutralization of South Vietnam, Laos, and Cambodia, including removal of the major U.S. military force from South Vietnam (Hanoi would probably not insist on a total withdrawal of all U.S. forces, and might even accept the maintenance of certain Guantanamo-type U.S. bases); and (4) the establishment of a skeletal machinery, with international supervision, to program the eventual reunification of Vietnam; Hanoi is likely to accept broad, general terms toward this end, with indefinite or at least not rigidly fixed deadlines.

The NLF's minimal goal is replacement of the present Saigon regime by a broad coalition in which it would be allowed to achieve status and play a role. It is open to question whether, under minimal conditions, the NLF would insist on holding one or two ministries in a coalition cabinet. It is interesting that quite recently, in a conversation with a French journalist, NLF spokesmen not only failed to mention cabinet representation but, quite defensively, asked what guarantees they could expect so as to be spared the fate suffered by the Communist Party in Indonesia.

There is some evidence to suggest that both Hanoi and the NLF are considering a settlement on the basis of minimal rather than maximal goals. The January 28, 1967, statement of DRV Foreign Minister Trinh represented, in effect, a major shift from Hanoi's previous position. Whereas up to that time Hanoi had repeatedly implied that the United States would have to accept the Four Points in principle, Trinh took pains to state only one condition for negotiations—a cessation of American bombing. This shift was probably due, in part, to Soviet pressure, and it will be recalled that the implications of Trinh's statement reflected what had been the Soviet position for some time. Hanoi's new accommodation to the Soviet line does not, however, mean a reduced commitment to the NLF, nor should it be interpreted as an indication of weakness. Indeed, this accommodation to Moscow was most probably made as a quid pro quo for greatly increased Soviet military aid—which, in fact, has been given in recent months.

The recent emphasis by Hanoi on a cessation of U.S. bombing also should not be interpreted as a sign of weakness or flagging morale with regard to pursuit of the war. It is quite clear that the North Vietnamese are preparing for the worst—including the bombing of the dikes—and are relocating their people and resources in difficult mountainous terrain.

HANOI'S ATTITUDE TOWARD NEGOTIATIONS

(Since the American bombing of North Vietnam began, and the North Vietnamese set down their four-point proposal for a settlement of the Vietnamese conflict, there has been widespread misunderstanding in the United States of Communist preconditions for negotiations. Much of this confusion was due to the calculated ambiguity on the part of the DRV and NLF leaders. Much was also the result of sloppy American reporting. Never had the Hanoi leaders said flatly that acceptance of the Four Points—or any one of them, e.g., American withdrawal—was a precondition for talks. Since the Four Points were first released in April, 1965, they have been saying these points were a "basis for a settlement."/

In a report to the National Assembly in Hanoi on April 12, 1965, Premier Pham Van Dong set out the Four Points and went on to say the following:

> The government of the DRV is of the view that the stand expounded above is the basis for the soundest political settlement of the Vietnam problem. If this basis is recognized, favorable conditions will be created for the peaceful settlement of the Vietnam problem and it will be possible to consider the reconvening of an international conference along the pattern of the 1954 Geneva conference on Vietnam.[34]

In the following months, |Hanoi leaders adhered closely to Pham Van Dong's formulation that the Four Points provided a "basis for settlement." Sometimes they said that the Four Points were "the most correct solution,"[35] or the "most correct way to a peaceful settlement of the Vietnam problem,"[36] but they never said that recognition of the Four Points was a precondition for negotiations| On several occasions, perceptive French reporters phrased questions to the DRV leaders in such a way as to elicit from them a response as to whether acceptance of any of the Four Points was a precondition for negotiations, but the usual response was to reaffirm the Four Points themselves.[37]

What Hanoi did seem to be insisting on was an American acceptance *in principle* of the Four Points prior to negotiations. Thus a North Vietnamese statement of September 23, 1965, asserted that

> The United States Government must solemnly declare its acceptance of this four point stand before a political settlement of the Vietnam problem can be considered.[38]

And on September 27, 1965, a leading North Vietnamese spokesman said:

> If the United States accepts the above four-point stand . . . we shall be ready to come to the conference table and talk with them at any time and in any place.[39]

As I have already indicated, the statements by Hanoi's foreign minister and Ho Chi Minh in January and February 1967, constituted a revision of this position. What Hanoi is now insisting upon as a precondition for negotiations is an unconditional cessation of American bombing of North Vietnam.

Another ambiguity in Hanoi's statements concerned whether the Four Points were open by discussion once talks began. On September 23, 1965, *Nhan Dan*, in an article titled "What 'Signs' Is Johnson Waiting For?" seemed to indicate they were not:

> Our government's four points are a basis for settling the Vietnamese problem and are no longer problems subject to discussion. In proposing only to 'discuss Hanoi's conditions' . . . Johnson insolently put the question whether or not to allow the Vietnamese people to enjoy independence.

However, in Pham Van Dong's interview with a *New York Times* correspondent in January, 1967, the North Vietnamese Premier said the Four Points were to be considered as "valid conclusions" for discussion."[40]

Several other points can be made about Hanoi's attitude toward negotiations on the basis of a close study of its public statements.

First, Hanoi has never insisted on American troop withdrawal as a precondition for negotiations. Indeed, one spokesman said pointedly on this matter:

> Concerning the way of conducting this withdrawal [of American troops] the imperialist side has many experiences: The French have withdrawn from Indochina and Algeria, and the Americans have withdrawn from Laos and other areas in the world.[41]

In all three cases cited, negotiations took place while French or American troops remained in the country.

Second, Hanoi has persistently rejected the idea that the NLF should be included in the North Vietnamese peace delegation to any peace talks—a possibility left open on various occasions by the Administration—and insisted that the United States must recognize the NLF as an "independent party" in any negotiations.[42]

Third, Hanoi seems to rule out the possibility of a cease-fire followed by protracted negotiations because it contends that a prolonged cease-fire would benefit the United States.[43] It seems to fear that the United States would deliberately drag out the negotiations in order to consolidate its position and that of the Saigon government. This is the exact opposite of the American fear: that negotiations without a cease-fire would benefit the Communists and would degenerate into a bitter repetition of the Panmunjom talks in Korea which dragged on while fighting continued.

Finally, Hanoi rejects the idea that American troops might be withdrawn from South Vietnam in exchange for a withdrawal of its own troops to North Vietnam. This, it said, would be tantamount to acceptance of a United States victory.[44]

Perhaps the most important point to make about Hanoi's attitude toward negotiations is that at the moment it sees little to negotiate about so long as the United States is unwilling to make any major concessions on future political arrangements in South Vietnam. Hanoi and the NLF seem confident that they can frustrate American efforts at pacification, that there will be increasing political instability in Saigon, that the NLF forces can deliver crushing blows to the Saigon and American armies, and that there will be increasing domestic pressures in the United States for a negotiated settlement. For all these reasons, Hanoi and the NLF probably calculate that they have more staying power than the Americans and the Saigon army. This was presumably what Pham Van Dong had in mind when he told Harrison Salisbury in January 1967:

> It's no use to make haste [to reach a settlement]. If we show haste, the question will be put wrongly and we will have to wait again. So let the situation ripen.

CHAPTER FIVE

Conclusions

THE main purpose of this book has been to clarify the positions of each of the Communist protagonists involved in the Vietnam war—Moscow, Peking, Hanoi, and the Communist-dominated NLF—and to show the special interests and outlook of each on the war. In this concluding chapter I want to highlight the main factors that help determine the position of each, to indicate the significance of the differences among them for United States policy, and to assess the impact of the war on the relations among the three great powers—Russia, China, and the United States.

The Communist protagonists in Moscow and Peking view the war as major powers who have global interests. The war is therefore assessed in terms of whether it serves or hinders their numerous foreign policy priorities. The other two, Hanoi and the PRP which leads the Front, view the war more simply—as a small state and party respectively, each more directly involved than either Peking or Moscow and each having a greater stake in the outcome.

Because the global interests and priorities of Moscow and Peking differ, and even conflict, they have sharply different attitudes toward the war. Although both of them support Hanoi, they refuse to cooperate in rendering such support. Soviet-Chinese differences in approach to the Vietnam war result from conflicting interests and priorities in the larger international arena and, above all, in their differing relationships with the United States.

The Soviet Union and the United States, because of their mutual interest in avoiding a nuclear holocaust, have become adversaries rather than enemies. This adversary relationship is one in which elements of cooperation and conflict coexist. Typical of this mixed relationship is that Russia and the United States are on the same side in some areas of the world and on opposite sides in others. In India and Indonesia, for example, Russia and the United States are basically on the same side against China. But they are on opposing sides in Vietnam and Germany. Also characteristic of this relationship is that neither necessarily considers a gain for one a loss for the other. For example, Soviet efforts to mediate the Indo-Pakistan conflict at Tashkent—although they improved Soviet prestige on the Asian subcontinent—were regarded with approval by Washington.

The adversary relationship between Russia and the United States imposes certain inhibitions and restraints on each of them. For example, neither has yet been willing to let the Vietnam war block cooperation in other areas or on issues of important national interest such as halting nuclear proliferation, limiting the arms race, and the like. Neither wants to humiliate the other in Vietnam because this would endanger cooperation elsewhere and might even endanger the adversary relationship itself. Finally, because of a strong mutual desire to contain China, neither Russia nor the United States wants to see the war end in a way that would enhance Chinese power and prestige.

China and the United States, on the other hand, have an entirely different relationship—one that is characterized by almost total conflict and one in which there are virtually no overlapping interests. In every area and on every global or local issue, Peking and Washington act as if a gain for one is a loss to the other. The conflict relationship between Peking and Washington is best illustrated in Vietnam. Even though their forces are not directly opposed, and both want to avoid a direct military confrontation, China and the United States are in effect fighting each other. Both are seeking in Vietnam to undermine the other because the realization of larger, global interests depends on one's blocking the other.

For China, the war in Vietnam represents *the* test case for its liberation-war strategy—the avowed purpose of which is to foment a series of guerrilla conflicts. This liberation-war strategy would diffuse American power throughout the underdeveloped areas and facilitate China's primary goal of driving the United States out of Asia—a goal which the Chinese are too weak to accomplish themselves by direct means. Although well aware that China did not start the war in Vietnam, American leaders fear that a Communist victory would greatly enhance Chinese power and prestige in Asia and vindicate the Chinese revolutionary strategy. Their confidence in the United States undermined, the smaller Asian states would then be forced to accommodate in one way or another to China.

Thus, two of the three big powers involved in the war—China and the United States—see a successful outcome of the war as crucial to their wider interests. The optimal outcome for China is a protracted war that bleeds the United States and encourages guerrilla armies in other underdeveloped areas to open second fronts: For the United States, the optimal outcome is a negotiated settlement that leaves the 17th parallel intact as the dividing line between North and South Vietnam, preserves a non-Communist government in South Vietnam, and serves as a negative object lesson to other Communist parties throughout the underdeveloped areas.

The third big power—the Soviet Union—views the war not as an Armageddon but rather as a potentially dangerous, nuisance-like intrusion that only complicates its foreign policy and adds to its dilemmas. Russia has little to gain in Vietnam and much to lose. Its goal there is shaped not by its own ambitions, but by the goals of its two adversaries—China and the United States. Russia wants neither an American nor a Chinese victory, either of which would undermine Soviet prestige. The best outcome for Russia is a draw. It is for this reason that Russia has been working hard to promote a compromise settlement that falls short of both Chinese and American optimal goals, but which is acceptable to Hanoi. By the same token, both China and the United States are likely to continue to urge more rigorous peace terms on their respective Vietnamese allies. China has already warned North Vietnam that a cessation of American bombing of the North is not a sufficient concession for talks. The United States has tightened its own terms for negotiations, insisting now on a reciprocal military concession from Hanoi in exchange for a cessation of bombing.

Before turning to Hanoi and the NLF—which hold the key to negotiations—it is appropriate to say a few words about the probable impact of the war on each of the three major powers. So far as Russia is concerned, I have already suggested that the war is not likely to lead to any permanent or fundamental shift in Soviet foreign policy. The Russians have eagerly seized upon and exploited opportunities open to them as a result of the war. In Europe, they have benefited from fears that the United States is neglecting its European commitments and alliances and from increased pro-Communist and anti-American feeling caused by the war. In the international Communist movement, Russia has benefited from China's doctrinaire refusal to form a united front against the United States. It is doubtful, however, that either of these temporary gains can be converted into more lasting ones. The future of Soviet diplomacy in Europe hinges on factors other than Vietnam and the degree of Soviet influence in the international Communist movement is likely to change in accordance with changing circumstances.

For China, the war in Vietnam is likely to represent an important turning point. It may well be the crucial setback in a series of foreign-policy catastrophes that have befallen Peking in the past two years. In several respects Peking has already suffered severe set-backs in Vietnam—particularly when the war is viewed against a background of Chinese objectives. Chinese liberation-war strategy was originally intended to disperse American power away from China, and to eventually compel American withdrawal from Asia. Instead, more American troops are in Southeast Asia than ever before. Moreover, the original strategic conception was to foment several guerrilla wars or local military conflicts simultaneously in order to stretch the United States beyond its capacities. To this end, China unsuccessfully sought to initiate similar actions outside Vietnam. It failed to get North Korea to open the South Korean front. It was also unable to persuade the Japanese Communists to open an anti-American terror campaign in Japan and it was unable to get the Russians to put pressure on Berlin.

A further testimony of Chinese failure is that Vietnam has in-creased Soviet rather than Chinese influence in the international Communist movement. Also, China had hoped to use the war to break up the Soviet-American détente. Although the war has put some strain on Soviet-American relations, it has not hampered agreement—or at least continued discussion—on a large number of issues. Finally, if a settlement of the war is negotiated in the near future, China's most important objective in Vietnam—to humble the United States—will collapse.

Together with the whole series of foreign-policy setbacks suffered since late 1965, a setback in Vietnam could force a long-overdue reassessment of Chinese foreign policy. Indeed, as I have suggested earlier, there is evidence to suggest that the opposition to Mao has already made such a reassessment. If the opposition wins, this could lead to a turning inward, to a rapprochement with the Soviet Union, or to a normalization of relations with the United States—perhaps to all or some combination of them.

The war in Vietnam is likely to have a far greater effect on the United States than on either Russia or China. It has already provoked a far-reaching debate over: American goals in Asia, the limits of American power, the criteria for intervention in civil wars, and the future relationship between the United States and the underdeveloped countries. If—as Arthur Schlesinger contends—Vietnam is a triumph of the politics of inadvertence, it is almost certain that future American commitments in underdeveloped areas will be made with due and deliberate consideration of their ultimate consequences.

On balance, the war in Vietnam has not altered the international climate as much as might have been expected. The Soviet-American détente goes on; some would contend it has been accelerated by the war. The Soviet-Chinese relationship has deteriorated more rapidly as a result of the war, but it seems unlikely that it would have improved in any case. The Chinese-American relationship remains in the same impasse it has been in during most of the decade. Thus, while the war may have speeded certain trends in international relations and arrested others, it has not had a decisive impact on them.

What are the prospects for the United States' having to cope with future Communist-led "wars of liberation" on the model of Vietnam? Let me begin by noting that few if any Communist parties in Asia today—or anywhere else in the underdeveloped areas—have the kind of rural revolutionary base from which to launch a guerrilla war. It is not generally understood why the Communists in Vietnam have such a base while few others do. Principally, it is because the Vietnamese Communists were able to mobilize the peasants under the banner of nationalism in a struggle first against Japanese invaders, then against French colonialists during and after World War II. In the course of that long and popular struggle, the Communists gained control over and began to administer large sections of the Vietnamese countryside where Japanese—and later French—authority was weak. In order to secure the loyalty of the peasants, they redistributed the land. In many areas of Vietnam, consequently, the Communists appeared both as leaders of a popular national cause and as social reformers redressing longstanding grievances over inequitable distribution of the land. In the absence of a strong non-Communist nationalist movement, they gained the loyalty of a substantial section of the peasantry.

It is important to note that this recipe for Communist success was followed also in both China and Yugoslavia, where local Communists captured a nationalist movement in the course of a struggle against a foreign invader during and after World War II. Moreover, if one carefully examines Communist strength in those underdeveloped countries where they are still struggling for power, it becomes evident that Communism is successful only when it can exploit powerful national or regional—as well as social—grievances. In India, for example, Communism is strong only in the three states in which it has successfully harnessed regional or sub-national sentiment.

In other words the record suggests that Communism in underdeveloped areas is not—in Walt Rostow's phrase—the scavenger of the modernization process so much as it is related to the nation-building process. Where Communism is unable for one reason or another to relate itself to national or regional feeling, it is weak. It is strong where it is able to do so.

It would take us too far afield from our present purposes to analyze the reasons why some Communist parties are unable to exploit nationalist feeling. Suffice it to say that the task is not easy, and that World War II and the decolonization process immediately thereafter provided a massive opportunity to the Communists in the former colonial areas which most of them failed to exploit. Where that opportunity was lost, where the non-Communist nationalists outmaneuvered the Communists in the post-colonial struggle for power, the Communists must hope that a fortunate and unusual combination of circumstances will provide another such opportunity. The Indonesian Communists, for example, got a second chance in the mid-1960's, but were unable to convert it into lasting gain.

It is possible that if the process of modernization fails and social tensions mount, Communism in the underdeveloped areas will find another opportunity comparable to the one it had during the decolonization period. At this historical moment, however, it seems unlikely. Communist success in Vietnam will not be easily duplicated.

Having briefly summarized the positions of the major powers involved in Vietnam, it now remains to consider the two smaller Communist protagonists who hold the key to negotiations: Hanoi and the Communist-dominated NLF. Perhaps the first and most important question concerning Hanoi is why it refuses to negotiate with the United States. Even if one assumes that the United States is not interested in serious negotiations—as some Administration critics do—it is a fact that Hanoi has not seemed anxious for talks at any time since 1965. One explanation for this is Hanoi's apparent confidence that it has greater staying power than the United States. North Vietnam recalls that it won the first Indochina war in Paris rather than in Indochina and signs of discord in the United States encourage it to believe that the longer it waits, the better the settlement it will get.

A compatible explanation is that North Vietnam has a sanguine outlook on the situation in South Vietnam based on the following calculations spelled out by Hanoi itself in its own strategic writing:

1. An alien army is incapable of pacifying South Vietnam.

2. The NLF armed forces can bring about the disintegration of the Saigon army and thus leave military action wholly in the hands of the United States forces, exposing once and for all the foreign "imperialist" nature of the war and strengthening the NLF appeal for a popularly-backed united front.

3. The widespread United States bombing of North Vietnam is ineffectual against a war effort based on a primarily agricultural economy.

4. The NLF can inflict an increasingly heavy toll of casualties on the American forces, thereby strengthening American domestic pressure for a settlement.

5. The number of American troops actively fighting in South Vietnam will never be sufficiently large to reach the ten-to-one (or greater) ratio required to defeat a guerrilla force.[1]

Still another explanation is that Hanoi may simply doubt Washington's desire to negotiate anything other than its unconditional surrender. It seems unlikely, for example, that Washington is prepared to accept either a partition of South Vietnam or a coalition government including Communists. More likely, Washington envisages a Korean-type settlement in which a non-Communist government in South Vietnam would be protected by some continuing American military presence. If Hanoi reads Washington's intentions in this way, it may simply feel that the time is not yet ripe for negotiations—precisely the phrase used by North Vietnamese Premier Pham Van Dong in a recent conversation with *New York Times* correspondent Harrison Salisbury.

Also, Hanoi probably has the same fear as Washington—that a compromise of its own tenuous position in South Vietnam now could lead to disaster in a year or two. Washington fears that the non-Communist parties in South Vietnam, not yet strong enough to compete with the NLF, will inevitably be devoured by it. Hanoi, on the other hand, fears that a resurgence of non-Communist political life in South Vietnam could submerge the NLF and eventually challenge Hanoi itself.

Then, too, Hanoi may believe that it will get better terms for negotiations in 1968 prior to the American elections. Or, it may feel that any reciprocal concessions to the United States in exchange for a cessation of American bombing would appear as a sign of weakness and would only encourage the American hawks—or possibly, that such a concession would legitimize the American interpretation of the war as an aggression from the North.

Last, Hanoi may be unwilling to make any military concessions regarding infiltration into South Vietnam that might be interpreted by the NLF as a Northern sellout.

Meanwhile, in the background of Hanoi's intransigence is the memory of the 1954 Geneva Conference at which it got much less than it thought it was entitled to. This earlier experience with a negotiated settlement whose provisions were never met has undoubtedly produced a kind of Communist "Yalta complex"—a feeling that the "imperialists" never live up to their agreements and have to be defeated on the battlefield. Moreover, this experience has left an attitude of distrust toward the Russians who played a key role in arranging the Geneva Conference and who once again seek to bring pressure on Hanoi to negotiate.

Concerning the NLF, I have already presented evidence to indicate that while the Front is Hanoi's creature, it has developed a personality and vitality of its own and cannot now be dismissed as a mere Northern puppet. Although both Hanoi and the NLF share the objective of removing the United States from South Vietnam, their interests regarding the future of South Vietnam are not identical. Hanoi wants a government that will eventually lend itself to reunification on Northern terms and will not develop a personality of its own in the interim. It fears any political arrangements in South Vietnam that could lay the groundwork for a popular government to ultimately threaten North Vietnam itself. Some of the Communists and most of the non-Communists in the NLF, on the other hand, want a government free of Northern control—a government in which they can exercise maximum influence. They have much less interest in reunification than the North.

Both Hanoi and the NLF are suspicious of each other's intentions. Hanoi fears that an NLF compromise with non-Communist political groups in South Vietnam could lead to a popular and independent South Vietnamese government. The NLF fears that Hanoi will make concessions to the United States in order to get the bombing stopped and might—under Russian pressure—repeat the 1954 settlement in which the Southerners were left to the tender mercies of the anti-Communist government.

IS A BARGAIN FEASIBLE?

In a recent issue of the *New York Times Magazine*,[2] Max Frankel, in an extremely perceptive analysis of the prospects for peace in Vietnam, wrote the following:

> Deep down, they believe—and also hope—in Washington that when North Vietnam comes to terms with its own predicament it will choose to quit the battlefield as quietly as it arrived rather than sign an agreement that would define the proportions of its failure.

At another point he wrote that

> . . . by yielding South Vietnam to the A.R.V.N. forces, the Communists could probably buy an amnesty for their own fighters in the South . . .

If Frankel's analysis is correct, the current assumption in Washington is that Hanoi can be militarily coerced into capitulation in South Vietnam.

Such an assumption seems to me profoundly in error. It grossly minimizes the skill, determination and both the military and political assets of Hanoi and the NLF. It bears no relation to the sense of confidence they display. It ignores the considerable leverage that Hanoi has on both Moscow and Peking. It fails to take account of the strong commitment that Hanoi has made to the NLF. And it fails to take account of China, which is unlikely to stand by while North Vietnam capitulates, particularly if a faction in either Hanoi or the NLF calls for Chinese intervention to avoid such a capitulation. There are many signs of a growing Chinese belief that the Americans will use the Vietnamese war as a pretext for attacking

China. Such a belief could prompt the Chinese leadership to take risks in Vietnam in support of Hanoi.

If the surrender of North Vietnam and the NLF is not a feasible goal for the United States to pursue in South Vietnam, what is? Frankel—reflecting current Washington views—contends that "each side still expects its own victory or the enemy's exhaustion and these are not attitudes that can be translated or bargained into a settlement." While this may be an accurate assessment of our own government's attitudes, I am not at all certain it represents an accurate assessment of the position on the Communist side.

Peking has already made known its opposition to what it calls a "sellout peace" and has disassociated itself from Hanoi's offer to talk if the United States stops the bombing of North Vietnam. This suggests that Peking is fearful that Hanoi, under considerable Soviet pressure, is willing to bargain. I have already provided evidence to suggest that the NLF itself has similar concerns about Hanoi's position. It can be assumed that both Peking and the NLF have at least as good an insight into the current thinking of the Hanoi leadership as Washington has.

Moreover, as I have indicated, there has been a loosening of Hanoi's terms for negotiations. Whereas Hanoi earlier insisted on American recognition in principle of the Four Points, it has now indicated a willingness to talk if the United States stops the bombing of North Vietnam.

There is also considerable evidence to suggest that there has long existed in the Hanoi leadership a moderate group inclined to strike a bargain with the United States if the bargain were a genuine one and not a concealed demand for capitulation. According to no less an authority than Politburo member Le Duc Tho, there are some comrades in Hanoi who have displayed "pessimism, perplexity, and a reluctance to carry on protracted resistance" and who "fail to realize clearly the deceptive peace negotiation plot of the enemy."[3] This warning came shortly after the thirty-seven-day bombing pause in 1965–1966. Pike, in his exhaustive study of the Vietcong, indicates the existence of a minority group that has long favored a political settlement of the war.

Finally, the events of December 1966, to February 1967, which came very close to producing negotiations, clearly indicated some willingness on the Communist side to bargain.

If a bargain is possible, on what terms could it be made? It is not possible to foresee the details of such a bargain, but it is obvious that both sides would have to be prepared to make major concessions concerning future political arrangements in South Vietnam. The eventual outcome of such an arrangement would be a coalition government. There are several reasons why such a coalition government could prove to be viable in the short run at least. First, it is very likely that the Communists would act with circumspection to avoid uniting non-Communist forces in South Vietnam against them. Admitting them to a coalition government might well encourage them to concentrate on political maneuver rather than military action. There would be an added inducement to such restraint on their part if the United States maintained token forces in the South for a year or two which would act as a tripwire in the event of an attempted Communist coup. Second, there are a variety of non-Communist forces in South Vietnam, including the army, which would unquestionably make every effort to resist a Communist coup. In my view, we have consistently underestimated the capacity of non-governmental political forces to withstand Communist pressure. By so doing, we have defeated our own purpose of stimulating non-Communist political life. This is but another example of our failure to put "politics in command," as the Chinese Communists say.

Obviously any real compromise solution in South Vietnam means that there will be attendant risks. But such risks need to be measured against the costs of escalation or a protracted war of attrition. My own judgment is that the risks of such a compromise would be much smaller. The first step toward compromise on our part must be the cessation of American bombing of North Vietnam and the indication of our willingness to recognize the NLF.

Pondering our intervention in Vietnam some years ago, Theodore H. White wondered whether "we have the proper personnel, the proper instruments, the proper clarity of objectives to intervene successfully." As of mid-1967, the answer to that question seemed, to this writer, to be in the negative. We have been unable to subordinate our military power to feasible and well-conceived political objectives. Our action has resembled that of a bull in a china shop more than that of a surgeon performing a delicate operation on the body politic of a distant and strange nation. One can only hope that the lesson of this tragic experience is being learned. But the signs are not hopeful. We continue with what must be a vain effort to rescue political failure by crude military pressure.

At the time of this writing, the war in Vietnam is approaching the point where a compromise settlement of any kind seems increasingly difficult to attain because of an apparently mindless American escalation. This escalation was based on a series of highly questionable assumptions. While the nation's leadership is evidently willing to take enormous military risks, it seems unwilling to take any political risks. It is increasingly losing the support of those who share the views of neither the "hawks" nor the "doves." If "victory" in Vietnam is to be our goal, we should ponder the experience of a Greek king of Epirus called Pyrrhus with the Romans at Asculum.

APPENDICES

Sino–Soviet Relations Since the Fall of Khrushchev

1964

Oct. 16 Khrushchev's ouster officially announced.

Nov. 1 Zëri i Popullit article entitled "Khrushchev's Fall Hasn't Brought About a Disappearance of Khrushchev Revisionism."

Nov. 7 Chou En-lai leads delegation to Moscow to celebrate anniversary of Bolshevik Revolution; uses occasion to explore attitudes of new Soviet leaders. Russians refuse to disavow major policies and doctrines but offer to resume aid to China and to stop public ideological polemics.

Subsequently, 26-party preparatory conference that Khrushchev had called for mid-December is postponed until March; Russians also assure Chinese that no "excommunication" of China from world Communist movement is intended during meeting.

Nov. 21 Hung Ch'i editorial on "Why Khrushchev Fell": "Although Khrushchev has fallen, his supporters—the U.S. imperialists, the reactionaries, and the modern revisionists—will not resign themselves to this failure. These hobgoblins are continuing to pray for Khrushchev . . . so that 'Khrushchevism without Khrushchev' may prevail. . . .''

1965

Feb. 14 15th anniversary of Sino–Soviet Treaty of Friendship, Alliance, and Mutual Assistance. Chinese Ambassador to Soviet

Union, Pan Tzu-li, says in Moscow: ". . . if the imperialists dare to attack the Soviet Union, the Chinese people without the least hesitation will fulfill their treaty obligations and together with the great Soviet people . . . will fight shoulder to shoulder until the final victory. . . ."

Jen-min Jih Pao editorial of Feb. 14: "It is our firm belief that, whatever storm may arise in the international arena, the two countries and two peoples of China and the Soviet Union will inevitably fight shoulder to shoulder and wipe out . . . all aggressors who venture to invade the Socialist camp."

Just before March interparty meeting begins in Moscow, China resumes—after lull in immediate post-Khrushchev period—public polemics on almost all issues at stake in Sino–Soviet dispute. Attacks extend to Soviet foreign policy; thus, not limited to ideological differences between the two parties, but include state-level relations too.

Mar. 1 18-party consultative meeting opens in Moscow (several parties of the original 26 invited back out at last minute).

Mar. 4 Chinese students in Moscow demonstrate at U.S. Embassy to protest American bombing of North Vietnam but clash with Soviet police. Soviet press emphasizes that "foreigners" rather than Russians were involved.

Mar. 5 Several Chinese students leave Moscow for home after clash with police; some wear bandages, others are carried on stretchers. Receive heroes' welcome on arrival in Peking.

Mar. 10 Communiqué of 18-party meeting advocates preparations for new international Communist conference "at a suitable time" to promote unity.

Official Chinese comment on Moscow meeting: *Jen-min Jih Pao* and *Hung Ch'i* editorials claim that ". . . in essence, the new leaders of the CPSU have taken over Khrushchev's revisionism and splittism lock, stock, and barrel, and they carried out his behest for a divisive meeting very faithfully. . . . It is now possible for people to see . . . that these new leaders . . . had to oust Khrushchev, not because they had any difference of principle with him, but because Khrushchev had become too . . . stupid in . . . his practices and because

Khrushchev himself had become a serious obstacle to the carrying out of Khrushchev revisionism. In replacing Khrushchev . . . the new leaders of the CPSU are continuing to practice Khrushchev revisionism. . . ."

"Since there are differences of principle between Marxism–Leninism and modern revisionism, and since the modern revisionists have maligned us so much . . . we have the right to refute them publicly. . . . It will not do to call for an end to the public polemics . . . for a single day, for a month, a year, 100 years, 1,000 years, or 10,000 years. If 9,000 years are not enough to complete the refutation, then we shall take 10,000. . . . It is imperative to isolate to the maximum the modern revisionists and to carry the struggle against Khrushchev revisionism through to the very end."

Mar. 26 Peking Review publishes Chinese reaction to Chou En-lai's meeting with Kremlin leaders in November; claims that Brezhnev and Kosygin "explicitly stated that there was not a shade of difference between themselves and Khrushchev on . . . questions of the international Communist movement and in their attitude toward China. . . ."

Mar. 26 Resolution of plenary session of CPSU Central Committee says it would be desirable to strengthen Communist solidarity by holding in the near future a preliminary consultative meeting of representatives of the 81 Communist parties present at the 1960 Moscow meeting; adds that preparations should be made for new international Communist conference "at a suitable time."

Apr. 3 Moscow proposes summit meeting between Soviet Union, China, and North Vietnam; also suggests sending via China 4,000 Soviet troops to Vietnam. Peking refuses.

Time of serious deterioration in Sino–Soviet economic relations; China refuses cooperation with Russia in carrying out several industrial projects provided for in 1961 Sino–Soviet trade agreement.

June 18 Peking Review reprints *Jen-min Jih Pao* and *Hung Ch'i* editorial entitled "Carry the Struggle Against Khrushchev Revisionism Through to the End": "Revisionism has always been . . . a force serving imperialism. To combat imperialism, and above all U.S. imperialism, it is imperative to carry the struggle against Khrushchev revisionism through to the end. . . ."

July Last Chinese scientists leave Joint Atomic Institute at Dubna in Soviet Union.

Sept. 29 Brezhnev speech regrets that China had not supported "major moves" by CPSU to improve relations but says that "despite this, we must consistently continue to search for ways of settling the disagreements."

Nov. 6 Polyansky speech says CPSU had done "everything that is possible" to improve relations with China; rest is up to the Chinese. Speech made to international Communist rally in Kremlin Hall of Congresses on 48th anniversary of Russian Revolution.

Nov. 7 Chinese greetings to Soviet Union on anniversary of Revolution: Message addressed to Brezhnev, Kosygin, and Mikoyan (then President of Soviet Union) and signed by Mao, Liu Shao-chi, and Chou En-lai. Message extends "warm greetings" to Soviet leaders and praises Soviet people; no tribute to CPSU or Soviet Government.

Jen-min Jih Pao says "difficulties in Soviet–Chinese relations" only an episode on the scale of history.

Nov. 10 *Jen-min Jih Pao* and *Hung Ch'i* publish 30,000-word polemic detailing Chinese charges against Soviet Union on Vietnam and other questions. Chinese also demand "a clear line of demarcation, both politically and organizationally, between the Marxist–Leninist parties and the revisionists."

Nov. 11 TASS says Chinese attack of the previous day was "crude and slanderous." This is first official revelation to Soviet people of great sharpening of China's anti-Soviet campaign; earlier Chinese attacks not reported in Soviet press.

Nov. 28 *Pravda* editorial contains most sweeping denunciations of Chinese policy since Khrushchev's fall; editorial covers two-thirds of *Pravda's* first page.

Dec. 21 *Jen-min Jih Pao* reprints *Pravda* editorial and publishes Chinese reply: ". . . you are carrying out Khrushchevism without Khrushchev. . . ." Also accuses Russians of "plotting new deals with the United States on the 'prevention of nuclear proliferation,' 'disarmament,' and the question of Germany. Why are you afraid to answer any of these charges?"

1966

Jan. 18 Chinese charges that Russians are further aggravating Sino–Soviet relations by signing defense treaty with Mongolia, holding Tashkent mediation meeting with India and Pakistan, and concluding new aid agreement with North Vietnam.

Feb. 2 Jen-min Jih Pao "Observer" article suggests that Sino–Soviet dispute has shifted main emphasis from ideological issues to national differences affecting security; article adds that Soviet policy toward India, Pakistan, and Japan aims at encirclement of China.

Mar. 21 Die Welt publishes excerpts from alleged CPSU Central Committee secret letter to ruling Communist parties in East Europe and to lower party bodies in Soviet Union; letter contains detailed review of current state of Sino–Soviet relations as viewed from Moscow. Letter is indictment of Chinese leaders, particularly on questions concerning Vietnam. Also claims that China hopes for Soviet–American war so it can be "sitting on a hillside and watching the battle of the tigers." Letter adds that China refuses to resume talks regarding delineation of Sino–Soviet border which broke off in May, 1964, and that Peking threatens to solve border problems "with other means" and is preparing the Chinese people for possible military clash with Russia.

Mar. 26 P'eng Chen accuses Soviet leaders of "criminal activities," and *Hung Ch'i* calls them "renegades and informers," "freaks and monsters."

In general, Chinese criticism of Soviet Union mounts in period immediately preceding 23rd CPSU Congress.

Mar. 29 Opening of 23rd CPSU Congress in Moscow; Chinese boycott it, along with Albanian, Japanese, and some minor Asian Communist parties. Brezhnev speaks more in sorrow than anger about Chinese boycott and repeats offer to meet to "reexamine existing difficulties."

May 28 Chen Yi says Soviet Union and United States might "jointly want to start a war against us."

June 8 In speech during Supreme Soviet election campaign, Kosygin advocates Communist unity and says differences between Chinese and other parties are "not insurmountable." Also says ". . . we are convinced that . . . the Communists of China will close ranks with the Communists . . . of the world. . . ."

June 16 Chou En-lai arrives in Rumania, where spurns pleas for easing of Sino–Soviet tension and for expediting Soviet and Eastern European aid to North Vietnam.

July 9 Chou En-lai speaks at closing session of two-week Afro–Asian writers' conference; accuses Soviet Union of betraying Vietnam by allegedly claiming that bombing around Hanoi and Haiphong would not affect Soviet–American collaboration or achievement of disarmament accord.

July 10 At Peking mass rally to condemn U.S. bombing of Hanoi–Haiphong oil depots, Chen Yi accuses Soviet Union of "making military deployments along the Chinese border in coordination with U.S. imperialist encirclement of China." Also says Russians are seeking a relaxation of tension and reduction of forces in Europe so United States can "draw away forces to cope with the Vietnamese people."

Aug. 1–12 Plenary session of Central Committee of CCP; first session in four years and 11th plenum of 8th Central Committee. Followed by series of demonstrations at Soviet Embassy in Peking. Plenum resolution says China must struggle against three enemies: "imperialism, world reaction, and modern revisionism."

CPSU Central Committee statement says "the documents of the [Chinese] plenary meeting show that the CCP's leadership has given its anti-Soviet line the form of official policy. . . ." Adds that Peking—not Moscow—"renders a big service to imperialism and reaction."

In late August, Russians begin propaganda campaign against China, after having refrained from public polemics since Khrushchev's ouster.

September Brezhnev tours Eastern Europe to test rulers' opinion on anti-Chinese offensive.

China expels foreign students, claiming that professors are preoccupied with "cultural revolution." Russia reacts by expelling 65 Chinese students. These actions mark virtual end of Sino–Soviet cultural relations.

Oct. 1 Soviet and East European diplomats walk out of Chinese National Day festivities when Chinese leaders attack Soviet policies in Vietnam and elsewhere.

Oct. 3 Chou En-lai says both United States and Soviet Union consider China the "main enemy."

Oct. 10 Rusk–Gromyko talks open in Washington; Gromyko allegedly tells Rusk that Sino–Soviet break is "quite fundamental."

Mid-October Conference of Soviet, Eastern European, Mongolian, and Cuban Communist leaders is held in Moscow; major objective is to unify world Communist movement against China.

Nov. 2 Opening of 5th Congress of Albanian Communist Party in Tirana; Chinese use it as platform from which to attack Soviet policies.

Nov. 6 Several thousand youths demonstrate at Soviet Embassy in Peking.

Nov. 7 CCP Central Committee, Parliament, and Government send telegram on occasion of Bolshevik Revolution anniversary; message addressed only to Soviet people (not to CPSU, Supreme Soviet, or Government), and not signed by any Chinese leader personally.

For first time in history of Sino–Soviet relations, no toasts proposed at reception given by Soviet Embassy in Peking in honor of Revolution. (By this time, Soviet Ambassador, P. Lapin, back in Moscow, and only Chargé d'Affaires, Y. N. Razdukhov, remains in Peking.)

Nov. 12 Chou En-lai, in speech commemorating anniversary of Sun Yat-sen's birth, calls Soviet leaders "a clique which has betrayed Lenin, which is collaborating with the Americans against China, and which is working for the restoration of capitalism in the Socialist world." Soviet diplomats walk out in protest.

Nov. 15 Brezhnev at Bulgarian party Congress supports Todor Zhivkov's call for world Communist conference on China. Soviet Union probably sponsored Zhivkov's call as trial balloon, but finds lack of support among many Communist parties.

Nov. 18 Soviet friendship delegation breaks off visit to China when Chinese officials and Red Guards harass them, blocking their path and shouting anti-Soviet slogans. Chinese official at Friendship Society meeting also claims Soviet policies are as villainous as Nazi Germany's.

Nov. 22 The New York Times reports that Soviet Union has recently transferred special intelligence equipment—formerly used to follow U.S. military activities—to Sino–Soviet border to monitor Chinese nuclear tests.

Nov. 27 4,500-word *Pravda* editorial summarizes Soviet charges against Chinese leaders: Abandonment of world Communist line adopted at 1957 and 1960 Moscow Conferences; jeopardizing of CCP by purging Mao's opponents; damaging of North Vietnamese war effort by refusing joint Communist aid program; brainwashing of Chinese people to instill anti-Soviet attitudes; discrediting of communism around the world through excesses and violence of "cultural revolution"; harming national liberation movements.

Editorial continues by claiming that "the interests of unity of all revolutionary forces in the struggle against imperialism demand that the nationalist, anti-Soviet policy and the attempts to distort Marxism–Leninism and replace it by the ideology and practice of Mao Tsetungism should be overcome." Says China had proclaimed Soviet Union as "Enemy No. 1," against which it planned "to struggle to the end." But insists that "Marxist–Leninists cannot be interested in the isolation of any Socialist country. . . ."

Editorial also talks of "growing dissatisfaction" with Mao's policies among Chinese party, army, and intellectuals and accuses China of trying to involve Communist bloc in war with United States.

Editorial represents first Soviet attack on Mao.

Editorial distributed to U.N. delegates just before vote on whether to seat China.

Nov. 28 Jen-min Jih Pao calls Soviet leaders a "group of renegades" and predicts their overthrow. Says "the days of imperialism, modern revisionism, and reaction . . . are numbered. They will all be overthrown, defeated, and eliminated by the revolutionary people."

Nov. 28 Janos Kadar, Hungarian Communist chief, tells opening session of 9th Hungarian party Congress that pro-Soviet parties have given up idea of demanding that virtually every Communist party in the world participate in anti-Chinese conference.

Nov. 29 Brezhnev speech at Hungarian party Congress: ". . . the capitalist press has lately been trumpeting . . . that the aim was a meeting of Marxist–Leninist parties to 'excommunicate' somebody from our movement. Surely this is complete nonsense circulated by the imperialists as provocation." Says interparty meeting would be a "comradely discussion" to "elaborate a common line for the future."

Dec. 2 *Jen-min Jih Pao* editorial accuses Soviet Union of working behind the scenes to keep China out of U.N.

Dec. 10 Danillo J. G. dos Santos, Brazilian lawyer just back from China, reports on interview with Chen Yi, who told him that China expects Soviet–American attack. Chen also reportedly said that "today's Soviet Union is still run by Khrushchev's gang. Nothing changed with the fall of the former Premier, and the oligarchy that runs the country lives in luxury, forgetting the people. . . ."

Dec. 13 CPSU Central Committee ends two-day meeting by endorsing Brezhnev's proposal for world Communist conference on China. Central Committee statement says the "anti-Soviet policy of Mao Tse-tung and his group has entered a new, dangerous stage" and that "favorable conditions are now being created for a new international conference." But adds that conference "should be well prepared in the course of mutual discussion among the parties."

Dec. 16 China orders three of the six Soviet correspondents stationed there to leave by Christmas; accuses them of anti-Chinese reporting and of spreading rumors about "cultural revolution."

Dec. 23 Moscow calls expulsion of correspondents an "unprecedented action" against a fellow Communist country. Soviet Foreign Ministry protest note warns that Moscow's three Chinese correspondents might be expelled in retaliation if they keep writing "slanderous concoctions" about Soviet policies.

1967

Jan. 25 Melee in Red Square between visiting Chinese students en route home from Western European schools and Soviet policemen and citizens in line at Lenin's mausoleum. Soviet Foreign Ministry protest note says Chinese, in laying wreaths at mausoleum and on Stalin's tomb, had interfered with other visitors to mausoleum, blocked their entry, and shouted anti-Soviet slogans.

Jan. 26 Chinese students, many wearing bandages for effect, leave Moscow by train for Peking, which claims that eight students so badly injured were unable to leave.

Jan. 27 Thousands of Red Guards and students demonstrate all day at Soviet Embassy in Peking; protest alleged Soviet repression of Chinese students in Moscow.

Jen-min Jih Pao editorial: "Listen, you handful of filthy Soviet revisionist swine! The Chinese people . . . are not to be bullied! The blood debt you owe must be paid!. . . . How closely your atrocious, bloody suppression of Chinese students resembles the atrocities committed by the Czar, by Hitler, and by the Ku Klux Klan! This clearly shows that what you are practicing in the Soviet Union is in fact a most reactionary and most savage fascist dictatorship."

Jan. 28 Chinese Army troops join demonstrations at Soviet Embassy in Peking. Posters on Embassy gates say "Shoot Brezhnev" and "Fry Kosygin."

Rival Chinese and Soviet news conferences in Moscow, each accusing the other side of responsibility for Red Square incident with Chinese students.

Jan. 29 Brezhnev and Kosygin burned in effigy in Peking and Shanghai.

Feb. 3 Chinese say Soviet police removed from sidewalk at Chinese Embassy some display cases containing pictures of Red Square clash; also say police beat up Embassy personnel trying to protect the display. Moscow denies beating.

On same day, Chinese harass Soviet advisers passing through China en route home from North Vietnam.

Feb. 4 First planeload of Soviet wives and children leaves Peking in emergency evacuation; harassed by Red Guards when try to board plane. Moscow says all Russian women and children in China will leave, and about 60 men will remain behind at besieged Peking Embassy.

Soviet Government note warns Chinese to halt campaign of violence against Russians in Peking or face retaliatory action. Note denounces "anti-Soviet hysteria" in China and says "the restraint and patience of the Soviet people are not boundless." Also calls demonstrations at Soviet Embassy in Peking "without precedent in the history of diplomatic relations."

Feb. 5 As demonstrations at Soviet Embassy enter 11th day, Chinese try to stop Russian women and children from leaving for airport.

Feb. 6 Jen-min Jih Pao editorial entitled "Outcome of a Savagery Seldom Seen in the History of World Diplomacy" protests Soviet removal of display cases at Chinese Embassy. Editorial also puts future of Sino–Soviet diplomatic relations in doubt: Says recent actions "prove that the Soviet revisionist authorities can no longer insure the legitimate functions and necessary safety of the diplomatic mission of a foreign country. Is your country still able to maintain normal diplomatic relations with other countries? Should your country still be considered a state or not?"

Chinese Government statement demands that Soviet Union "publicly admit mistakes" by apologizing to Chinese "victims" of Red Square melee, punishing Soviet personnel involved, restoring Chinese Embassy display, and guaranteeing against recurrence of such incidents.

Jen-min Jih Pao: "We want to warn the Soviet revisionist authorities that you must do as we say and completely fulfill all these demands. Failure to comply with even the smallest point is out of the question. You will be held responsible for all serious consequences arising from any such failure."

In Moscow, factory workers arrive at Chinese Embassy with resolutions protesting Chinese harassment of Russians in Soviet Embassy in Peking. First demonstration ever against a Communist Embassy in Soviet Union. When Chinese refuse admittance to Embassy, workers paste protests on Embassy gates.

Feb. 7 Russian students and workers enter Chinese Embassy in Moscow and exchange epithets with staff. Meanwhile, demonstrations at Soviet Embassy in Peking enter 13th day. Chinese warn that Russians cannot safely leave Embassy compound; thus, Russians become virtual prisoners.

Feb. 10 Suspension of Sino–Soviet consular agreement allowing travel without visas.

Feb. 13 Chinese lift siege of Soviet Embassy after 18 days; Soviet Chargé d'Affaires Razdukhov leaves Embassy for first time since start of demonstrations.

Proposals for Negotiations

1964

May 20 French call for international conference on Laos to be held in August; Soviet Union agrees but United States rejects proposal.

July 7 Pravda proposes conference on Laos; Soviet Union threatens to resign cochairmanship of permanent body of ICC if proposal is not accepted by other nations.

August Encouraged by Soviet Union, Hanoi relays message via U Thant to Washington; agrees to meet privately with U.S. representatives for talks on settlement. Thant arranges meeting in Burma, but Washington backs down.

October Cairo Conference of Nonaligned Nations advocates new international conference on Indochina.

1965

January Washington rebuffs second invitation to meet with Ho.

Chinese say Kosygin relayed to Hanoi an American message asking Moscow to try to persuade Hanoi to halt military aid to Vietcong and cease attacks on South Vietnamese cities as conditions for peace talks.

Feb. 6 Kosygin delegation arrives in Hanoi in hope of persuading North Vietnam to seek negotiated settlement of war.

Feb. 8 During Hanoi rally, Kosygin calls for international conference on Laos "without any preliminary conditions"; also expresses support for new international conference on Indochina as proposed by 1964 Cairo conference.

Feb. 11 Soviet–North Vietnamese Joint Statement issued on Kosygin's departure; advocates international conference on Laos "without delay and preconditions"; doesn't specifically mention reconvening Geneva conference, but endorses "struggle for . . . peaceful coexistence . . . and for the settlement of international disputes through negotiations." Statement also indicates Soviet willingness to resume duties of ICC cochairman in Vietnam.

Feb. 12 U Thant appeals for "shifting the quest for a solution away from the field of battle to the conference table."

Feb. 16 According to Chinese charges, Moscow officially proposed to Hanoi and Peking a conference on Indochina without prior conditions.

Feb. 20 Prime Minister Lal Bahadur Shastri of India presents proposal for neutrality and independence of both North and South Vietnam.

Pope Paul VI says he has tried to contact various countries to plead for peaceful end of war.

Feb. 22 Brezhnev and Gromyko reportedly tell visiting Indian Minister of Information that convening a conference would be "a step in the right direction" toward preventing escalation of war.

Deputy Soviet Foreign Minister Lapin tells British Ambassador in Moscow that Soviet Union will cooperate with Britain as cochairman of Geneva conference.

Feb. 23 Soviet Ambassador in Paris receives French agreement to press jointly for international conference on Vietnam.

Feb. 25 U Thant, during news conference, reveals that he has presented "concrete ideas and proposals" for peace to "some of the principal parties directly involved in the question of Vietnam."

Mar. 22 NLF issues five-point program as basis of settlement.

Apr. 1 Belgrade issues 17-nation appeal for talks "as soon as possible without posing any preconditions." Hanoi and Peking both ridicule this idea, and Peking attacks "Tito clique" for allegedly whitewashing U.S. aggression.

Apr. 7 Johnson makes speech at Johns Hopkins advocating "unconditional discussions"; also offers $1 billion for Mekong River development project and asks Soviet Union and others to join. Communist reaction notes that Johnson in fact imposes conditions for talks.

Apr. 8 Hanoi announces four-point program as basis of settlement.

May 12–18 U.S. bombing pause; no response from Communist side.

June 24 Soviet Union refuses to receive British Commonwealth peace mission seeking to promote Vietnam peace talks.

June 25 China and North Vietnam refuse to receive Commonwealth mission.

June 26 Johnson plea at 20th anniversary of U.N. being celebrated in San Francisco: "I call upon this gathering of the nations of the world to use their influence . . . to bring to the [conference] tables those who seem determined to make war. We will support their efforts, as we will support effective action by any agent or agency of these United Nations."

July 15 U.S. Ambassador-at-Large W. Averell Harriman arrives in Moscow for informal talks with Kosygin about Vietnam.

July 28 Johnson at news conference: "I have stated publicly . . . many times . . . American willingness to begin unconditional discussions. . . . But there has been no answer." Adds that he has told Goldberg to give U Thant "a letter from me requesting that all the resources and . . . immense prestige of the U.N. be employed to find ways to halt aggression and to bring peace in Vietnam."

Dec. 24 Beginning of 37-day bombing pause.

Dec. 27 Promulgation of Johnson's 14 points for peace.

Dec. 28 Moscow announces Shelepin mission to Hanoi.

Dec. 29 Harriman arrives in Warsaw to open U.S. "peace offensive."

1966

January "Peace offensive" continues: Harriman travels to Yugoslavia, Goldberg to Italy and meeting with Pope, and Humphrey to Far East and Southeast Asia.

Jan. 1 Pravda denounces U.S. "peace offensive" as "very much like a diversionary propaganda maneuver"; says military offensive parallels diplomatic one.

Jan. 7 Shelepin mission arrives in Hanoi.

Jan. 14 North Vietnam officially rejects U.S. "peace offensive." Ho calls it "a trick, merely the repetition of old themes."

Jan. 24 In midst of bombing pause, and after Shelepin's departure, Ho Chi Minh in letter to heads of state of many countries says, "If the United States Government really wants a peaceful settlement, it must accept the four-point stand of the government of the DRV and prove this by actual deeds: it must end unconditionally and for good all bombing raids and other war acts against the DRV. Only in this way can a political solution to the Vietnam problem be envisaged." Although call for acceptance of four-point stand as basis for settlement is standard Hanoi line, as is demand that United States must prove its acceptance of four points by "actual deeds," new element is implicit statement that cessation of bombing will be taken as proof of U.S. acceptance of four points. Thus for first time Hanoi hints at possibility of talks if U.S. bombing stops.

Jan. 31 U.S. resumes bombing of North Vietnam.

Feb. 2 U.N. Security Council meets in emergency session at Washington's request to seek end to Vietnam war. Moscow denounces the ". . . clumsy attempt to link the Geneva Agreements with the U.N., although . . . neither these agreements nor the Vietnam question as a whole are within the competence of the U.N. . . ."

Feb. British Prime Minister Harold Wilson arrives in Moscow; Chinese charge that he and Kosygin tried to initiate Vietnam peace talks.

Feb. 26 Pravda ridicules Humphrey's Far East and Southeast Asian tour: His " 'mission of peace' . . . was in fact a mission of war. . . ."

Mar. 6 U Thant proposes 3-point peace plan: Halt of bombing, reduction of military activity by both sides, and participation of NLF in peace talks.

July 13 Indian Prime Minister Indira Gandhi arrives in Moscow; suggests that Soviet Union and Britain reconvene Geneva conference. But adds before departing that "the stand of the USSR is that any proposal should first have the approval of North Vietnam."

July 16 Harold Wilson visits Moscow to discuss the war, but Russians again refuse to reconvene Geneva conference.

July 19 U Thant confers with Soviet leaders in Moscow; Russians tell him that their good offices will be available if and when Hanoi indicates it seeks negotiations.

August According to unconfirmed reports Pham Van Dong makes unpublicized trip to Soviet Union; tells Russian leaders that Hanoi will accept any "favorable possibility" of beginning talks.

August Thai Foreign Minister Thanat Khoman proposes all-Asian peace conference on Vietnam. *Pravda* reaction: ". . . The Vietnamese people themselves will decide their own fate, without any outside interference." Russians reiterate that only Hanoi's four points can bring a settlement.

Sept. 22 U.N. Ambassador Arthur Goldberg unveils 3-point peace proposal at General Assembly session: (1) United States will halt bombing of North Vietnam if Hanoi takes "corresponding and timely" steps to reduce its military activity; (2) United States willing to agree to scheduled withdrawal of troops if North Vietnam does the same; (3) Washington does not consider participation of NLF in peace talks "an insurmountable problem." *Pravda* and *Jen-min Jih Pao* both reject proposal, but Russians give some private signs that it offers some chance of bringing about eventual settlement.

October Reiteration of U Thant's 3-point peace plan. *Nhan Dan* rejects second and third points but says first point "conformed to the requirements for a settlement." *Jen-min Jih Pao* rejects all three points.

British Foreign Secretary George Brown presents 6-point peace plan: Conference of all parties (including NLF) involved in Vietnam, to be preceded by bombing pause and halt to both U.S. and North Vietnamese military buildups; cease-fire to be instituted during the conference, which should provide for free elections in both Vietnams, an amnesty, and eventual reunification of the country. Vietnam to be neutralized as aftermath of withdrawal of both American and North Vietnamese troops from South Vietnam. During talks in United States, Gromyko gives Brown the Soviet reaction: Moscow would take no initiatives toward peace talks without prior authorization from Hanoi. *Nhan Dan* rejects Brown plan as evidence of Anglo–American collusion on Vietnam question.

Soviet, East European, Mongolian, and Cuban Communist leaders meet in Moscow; take tough public stand toward United States but reportedly agree in private that Hanoi should attend a peace conference and help make it possible by taking some action that would lead to U.S. bombing pause.

United States, at Manila conference, pledges troop withdrawal within six months of a truce; but Russians insist that in fact there are reservations to this pledge.

Oct. 10 Paul Martin, Canadian Secretary of State for External Affairs, urges Soviet Union to authorize specific new functions to strengthen ICC as initial step toward peace in Vietnam. Gromyko replies that Moscow will not enter peace talks without prior mandate from Hanoi; that a bombing halt is "the essential precondition" to any diplomatic moves in Vietnam; that such a halt must be unilateral, with no reciprocal action by North Vietnam; and that bombing halt must be indicated to be only the first step toward U.S. withdrawal of troops.

Oct. 26 Communiqué of Tito–Nasser–Gandhi summit in Belgrade calls for "immediate" and "unconditional" bombing halt, fulfillment of Geneva accords, withdrawal of all foreign troops from Vietnam, and participation of NLF in peace talks. *Pravda* calls this "a realistic approach toward an understanding of the conditions prevailing in Southeast Asia." Peking denounces it.

November During Bulgarian party Congress, high official tells Western correspondents that Soviet bloc's main objective is to bring about Vietnam peace conference; adds that preconditions, such as halt in bombing, are "of no great importance."

November–December According to report by John Hightower of Associated Press, Hanoi and Washington arranged through Polish intermediary to meet for secret talks in Warsaw. Poles claim that American bombing of Hanoi in early December made Hanoi back out; Washington claims that Hanoi used the bombing as a pretext for not coming.

Dec. 19 Ambassador Goldberg gives U Thant letter from Johnson authorizing Thant to take any steps he considered necessary to bring about Vietnam cease-fire.

Dec. 30 British Foreign Secretary Brown calls for immediate cease-fire talks among representatives of United States, North Vietnam, and South Vietnam; Brown sends notes to this effect to Dean Rusk, North Vietnamese Foreign Minister Nguyen Duy Trinh, South Vietnamese Foreign Minister Tran Van Do, Gromyko, and U Thant. Russians call Brown proposal a political maneuver to quiet criticism of Harold Wilson's support of U.S. policy in Vietnam; *Izvestia* also says proposal is intended to help Washington, which "has come under fire from world opinion" because of alleged bombing of North Vietnamese population centers. Washington and Saigon accept Brown proposal, but Hanoi rejects it.

Dec. 31 Thant replies publicly to Goldberg letter of December 19 by asking United States to halt bombing of North Vietnam "even without preconditions"; also suggests extension of New Year cease-fire to allow time for "private contact and diplomatic explorations" that might lead to peace.

1967

Jan. 3 In an interview with Harrison E. Salisbury, Premier Pham Van Dong refers to four points as matters for "discussion." In past Hanoi had indicated that four points were not a matter for discussion.

January Secretary-General U Thant makes known his view, after two weeks of probing views of both sides, that the only thing which stood in the way of peace talks was the question of unconditional cessation of the United States bombing of North Vietnam.

Jan. 28 In an interview with Wilfred Burchett, North Vietnamese Foreign Minister Nguyen Duy Trinh says that if the United States "really wants talks, it must first halt unconditionally the bombing raids and all other acts of war against the DRV. It is only after the unconditional cessation of U.S. bombing and all other acts of war against the DRV that there could be talks between the DRV and the United States." This represents important departure from previous North Vietnamese statements which either related talks to recognition of four points or were deliberately vague in preconditions for talks.

Feb. 8 Soviet Premier Kosygin arrives in London for talks with Prime Minister Harold Wilson. Kosygin pointedly refers to Trinh's offer to negotiate in return for an unconditional cessation of bombing and approves the offer. There is reason to believe that the Russians, in this period, are transmitting American messages to Hanoi stating American terms for negotiations, a practice Moscow had not followed in the past.

Feb. 8 President Johnson's letter to Ho Chi Minh, dated February 2, is delivered to a North Vietnamese representative in Moscow. The letter was not made public until March 21. The President acknowledges that "in the past two weeks" he has noted public statements by representatives of the Hanoi Government indicating they would enter "into direct bilateral talks with representatives of the U.S. Government, provided that we ceased 'unconditionally' and permanently our bombing operations against your country and all military actions against it." He adds that "in the last day, serious and responsible parties have assured us indirectly that this is in fact your proposal." This apparently refers to the Russians. The President rejects this proposal. Offers to cease bombing only if "I am assured that infiltration into South Vietnam by land and by sea has stopped." If North Vietnam agrees to this, President offers not only to stop bombing but also to call halt in augmentation of American forces in South Vietnam.

February Harriman, in television program, replies to question whether United States would accept NLF as an equal in negotiations: ". . . we will not . . . accept them as a government," but "they could come with Hanoi" [to conference table]. Also says Saigon might seek peace talks by talking to "some of the groups . . . among the Vietcong or the Liberation Front." Feels this might be possible because there is "even some indication that among the Liberation Front there is a group that doesn't want to be dominated by Hanoi in the future," and these men might prefer mixed Socialist to Communist society.

Feb. 10 U Thant urges extension of four-day Tet truce which expires on this day. Premier Kosygin and Prime Minister Wilson also urge extension of truce for two days, indicating their continued hope for talks.

Feb. 12 New York Times notes "intense" diplomatic activity in White House and State Department.

Feb. 13 President Johnson announces resumption of "full-scale hostilities" including renewed bombing of North Vietnam.

APPENDIX THREE

North Vietnamese Government Organization

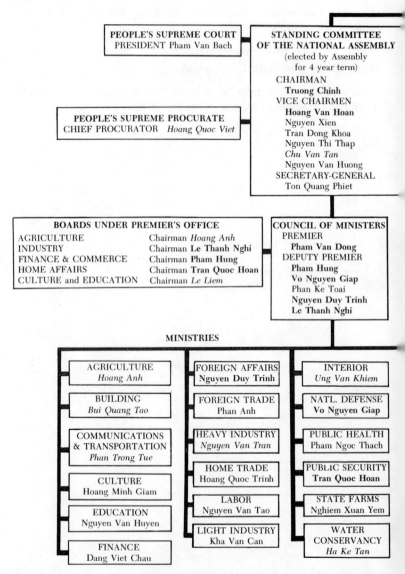

PEOPLE'S SUPREME COURT
PRESIDENT Pham Van Bach

STANDING COMMITTEE
OF THE NATIONAL ASSEMBLY
(elected by Assembly
for 4 year term)
CHAIRMAN
Truong Chinh
VICE CHAIRMEN
Hoang Van Hoan
Nguyen Xien
Tran Dong Khoa
Nguyen Thi Thap
Chu Van Tan
Nguyen Van Huong
SECRETARY-GENERAL
Ton Quang Phiet

PEOPLE'S SUPREME PROCURATE
CHIEF PROCURATOR   *Hoang Quoc Viet*

BOARDS UNDER PREMIER'S OFFICE

AGRICULTURE	Chairman **Hoang Anh**
INDUSTRY	Chairman **Le Thanh Nghi**
FINANCE & COMMERCE	Chairman **Pham Hung**
HOME AFFAIRS	Chairman **Tran Quoc Hoan**
CULTURE and EDUCATION	Chairman *Le Liem*

COUNCIL OF MINISTERS
PREMIER
Pham Van Dong
DEPUTY PREMIER
Pham Hung
Vo Nguyen Giap
Phan Ke Toai
Nguyen Duy Trinh
Le Thanh Nghi

MINISTRIES

AGRICULTURE
Hoang Anh

FOREIGN AFFAIRS
Nguyen Duy Trinh

INTERIOR
Ung Van Khiem

BUILDING
Bui Quang Tao

FOREIGN TRADE
Phan Anh

NATL. DEFENSE
Vo Nguyen Giap

COMMUNICATIONS
& TRANSPORTATION
Phan Trong Tue

HEAVY INDUSTRY
Nguyen Van Tran

PUBLIC HEALTH
Pham Ngoc Thach

CULTURE
Hoang Minh Giam

HOME TRADE
Hoang Quoc Trinh

PUBLIC SECURITY
Tran Quoc Hoan

EDUCATION
Nguyen Van Huyen

LABOR
Nguyen Van Tao

STATE FARMS
Nghiem Xuan Yem

FINANCE
Dang Viet Chau

LIGHT INDUSTRY
Kha Van Can

WATER
CONSERVANCY
Ha Ke Tan

Members and Alternate Members of Political Bureau
Members and Alternate Members of Central Committee

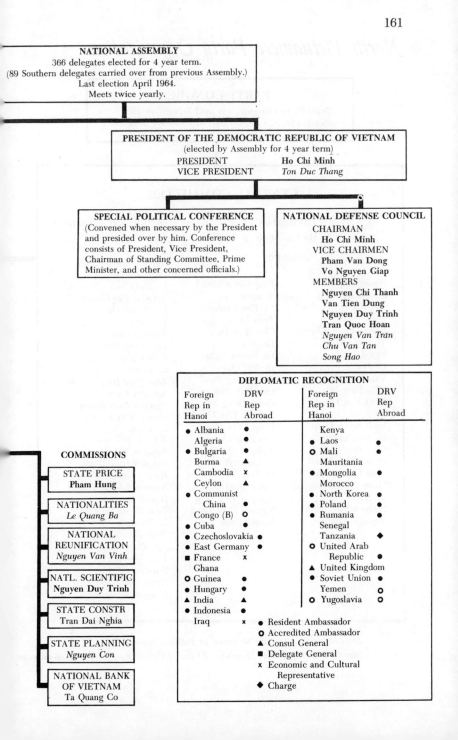

NATIONAL ASSEMBLY
366 delegates elected for 4 year term.
(89 Southern delegates carried over from previous Assembly.)
Last election April 1964.
Meets twice yearly.

PRESIDENT OF THE DEMOCRATIC REPUBLIC OF VIETNAM
(elected by Assembly for 4 year term)
PRESIDENT	**Ho Chi Minh**
VICE PRESIDENT	*Ton Duc Thang*

SPECIAL POLITICAL CONFERENCE
(Convened when necessary by the President
and presided over by him. Conference
consists of President, Vice President,
Chairman of Standing Committee, Prime
Minister, and other concerned officials.)

NATIONAL DEFENSE COUNCIL
CHAIRMAN
  Ho Chi Minh
VICE CHAIRMEN
  Pham Van Dong
  Vo Nguyen Giap
MEMBERS
  Nguyen Chi Thanh
  Van Tien Dung
  Nguyen Duy Trinh
  Tran Quoc Hoan
  Nguyen Van Tran
  Chu Van Tan
  Song Hao

COMMISSIONS

STATE PRICE
Pham Hung

NATIONALITIES
Le Quang Ba

NATIONAL
REUNIFICATION
Nguyen Van Vinh

NATL. SCIENTIFIC
Nguyen Duy Trinh

STATE CONSTR
Tran Dai Nghia

STATE PLANNING
Nguyen Con

NATIONAL BANK
OF VIETNAM
Ta Quang Co

DIPLOMATIC RECOGNITION

Foreign Rep in Hanoi	DRV Rep Abroad	Foreign Rep in Hanoi	DRV Rep Abroad
● Albania	●	Kenya	
Algeria	●	● Laos	●
● Bulgaria	●	○ Mali	●
Burma	▲	Mauritania	
Cambodia	x	● Mongolia	●
Ceylon	▲	Morocco	
● Communist China	●	● North Korea	●
Congo (B)	○	● Poland	●
● Cuba	●	● Rumania	●
● Czechoslovakia	●	Senegal	
● East Germany	●	Tanzania	◆
■ France	x	○ United Arab Republic	●
Ghana		▲ United Kingdom	
○ Guinea	●	● Soviet Union	●
● Hungary	●	Yemen	○
▲ India	▲	○ Yugoslavia	○
● Indonesia	●		
Iraq	x		

  ● Resident Ambassador
  ○ Accredited Ambassador
  ▲ Consul General
  ■ Delegate General
  x Economic and Cultural Representative
  ◆ Charge

North Vietnamese Party Organization

PARTY CONGRESS

(Third Party Congress was held September 1960, attended by 525 regular and 51 alternate delegates.)

CENTRAL COMMITTEE

CHAIRMAN
Ho Chi Minh

MEMBERS

Hoang Anh
Le Quang Ba
Nguyen Luong Bang
Tran Tu Binh
Duong Quoc Chinh
Truong Chinh
Nguyen Con
Le Duan
Van Tien Dung
Tran Huu Duc
Phan Van Dong
Vo Thuc Dong
Vo Nguyen Giap
Ha Huy Giap
Song Hao
Hoang Van Hoan
Tran Quoc Hoan
Pham Hung
To Huu
Nguyen Van Kinh
Nguyen Khang

Ung Van Khiem
Nguyen Lam
Le Van Luong
Tran Luong
Chu Huy Man
Do Muoi
Le Thanh Nghi
Ha Thi Que
Bui Quang Tao
Chu Van Tan
Pham Trong Tue
Nguyen Chi Thanh
Hoang Van Thai
Ton Duc Thang
Nguyen Thi Thap
Le Quoc Than
Le Duc Tho
Xuan Thuy
Nguyen Van Tran
Nguyen Duy Trinh
Hoang Quoc Viet

ALTERNATE MEMBERS

Ly Ban
Nguyen Thanh Binh
Dinh Thi Can
Le Tho Chan
Nguyen Tho Chanh
Le Quang Dao
Tran Do
Nguyen Don
Tran Quy Hai
Tran Quang Huy
Le Hoang
Tran Quy Huy
Nguyen Khai
Nguyen Huu Khieu
Hoang Van Kieu
Le Liem
Ngo Minh Loan
Nguyen Van Loc
Nguyen Huu Mai
Ha Ke Tan
Nguyen Khanh Toan
Hoang Tung
Tran Danh Tuyen
Le Thanh
Dinh Duc Thien
Ngo Thuyen
Tran Van Tra
Bui Cong Trung
Nguyen Van Vinh
Nguyen Trong Vinh

Members and Alternate Members of Political Bureau
Members and Alternate Members of Central Committee

POLITICAL BUREAU
MEMBERS

Ho Chi Minh	Le Duc Tho
Le Duan	Nguyen Chi Thanh
Truong Chinh	Nguyen Duy Trinh
Pham Van Dong	Le Thanh Nghi
Pham Hung	Hoang Van Hoan
Vo Nguyen Giap	

ALTERNATE MEMBERS

Tran Quoc Hoan	Van Tien Dung

SECRETARIAT
FIRST SECRETARY
Le Duan
MEMBERS

Pham Hung	*Hoang Anh*
Le Duc Tho	*To Huu*
Nguyen Chi Thanh	*Le Van Luong*
	Nguyen Van Tran

CENTRAL COMMITTEE DEPARTMENTS

FOREIGN RELATIONS *Xuan Thuy*	MILITARY AFFAIRS
REUNIFICATION *Nguyen Van Vinh*	ORGANIZATION **Le Duc Tho**
PROPAGANDA AND TRAINING *To Huu*	INDUSTRY *Nguyen Huu Mai*
MINORITY AFFAIRS *Le Quang Ba*	RURAL WORK *Nguyen Huu Khieu*
	FINANCE AND TRADE
CONTROL *Nguyen Luang Bang*	

Document # 1

COMMEMORATE THE VICTORY OVER GERMAN FASCISM! CARRY THE STRUGGLE AGAINST U.S. IMPERIALISM THROUGH TO THE END!*

by Lo Jui-ching

FULLY twenty years have elapsed since the great victory over German fascism.

Twenty years have elapsed since the great victory over the bloc of German, Japanese and Italian fascism.

These twenty years have witnessed earth-shaking transformations. As Comrade Mao Tse-tung said, the victory of the anti-fascist World War II "has opened up still wider possibilities for the emancipation of the working class and the oppressed peoples of the world and has opened up still more realistic paths towards it."[1] Since the War, two great historical currents, the socialist revolution and the national-liberation movement, have been rapidly changing the face of the world; they have merged to present a magnificent spectacle— the Four Seas are raging, the Five Continents are rocking. We are filled with boundless confidence in victory as we recall the victory over German, Japanese and Italian fascism twenty years ago, take stock of the excellent situation for the people's revolution in the

Peking Review (May 14, 1965) pp. 7–15.

world today and see the bright prospects of the fight for world peace, national liberation, people's democracy and socialism.

More than twenty years ago, when Hitler swept over the continent of Europe and threw all his forces into the surprise attack on the Soviet Union, believing that she could be "wiped out" in a couple of months, the whole world was heavily overcast for a time as if "the city might crumble under the mass of dark clouds." Many people throughout the world were morbidly afraid of Hitler, paled even at the mention of his name, and they grew pessimistic about the international situation. At the time Hitler's fascist armies were considered to be virtually invincible. Not only were the small European countries unable to withstand them, even the forces of such imperialist powers as Britain and France collapsed at the first encounter or fled pell-mell. In the circumstances, could socialism defeat fascism? Could the socialist system triumph over the capitalist imperialist system? Could the Soviet Union withstand the attacks of Hitler's fascist armies? Could the Soviet army defeat Hitler's fascist army? These were questions of the utmost concern to the people all over the world. This was a grave test for the first socialist state, for the socialist system and for the revolutionary armed forces of the proletariat. This was an issue crucial for the destiny of mankind.

Under the brilliant leadership of the Communist Party of the Soviet Union and the Soviet Supreme Command headed by Comrade Stalin, the Soviet state created by Lenin, a young state which had only recently accomplished socialist industrialization, and its young Red Army of workers and peasants not only stood up to the attack of Hitler's supposedly invincible fascist troops and destroyed the enemy's effectives en masse, but turned to a resolute and timely counter-offensive and pursuit and fought all the way to Berlin, thoroughly smashing Hitler's fascist war machine and scoring the decisive victory in the Anti-Fascist War.

The victory over German fascism was not just an ordinary or regional victory, it was a victory affecting the course of history and the destiny of mankind. It was a triumph for the socialist system. It was a triumph for the Soviet people and the Soviet army. It was a triumph for the Marxist–Leninist leadership of the Communist Party of the Soviet Union headed by Comrade Stalin. It was also a triumph for the people of Germany, of Europe, of Asia and of the whole world in their common struggle.

In their struggle against the fascist brigands, the Soviet people demonstrated iron will and unparalleled heroism. Fearing no sacrifices and defying all difficulties, they made a great contribution to victory in the Anti-Fascist War.

Holding aloft the banner of Lenin and Stalin, the Soviet Red Army fought valiantly in an indomitable revolutionary spirit, advanced wave upon wave and brilliantly performed immortal deeds in playing its glorious role as the main force against fascism.

Following Lenin's behest, Comrade Stalin armed the Soviet people with Marxism–Leninism, and under his leadership, they accomplished socialist industrialization and the collectivization of agriculture before the war, thus building backward Russia into an advanced socialist power. In the face of the powerful onslaught of the fascist Hitlerite forces, he dauntlessly and brilliantly led the Soviet people and army to complete victory in the anti-fascist Patriotic War after an unprecedentedly stubborn struggle. Although Stalin committed certain mistakes, including a number in military affairs, facts showed that he was worthy of the name of a great Marxist–Leninist and of a brilliant commander of the revolutionary armed forces of the proletariat.

The people of the world will always honour the heroic exploits of the Soviet people and army, who reared such heroes as Zoya Kosmodemiyanskaya and Aleksander Matrosov. They will always honour the valiant record of the Communist Party of the Soviet Union headed by Stalin in leading the War.

By spreading countless lies during the past twenty years the imperialists and the modern revisionists have deliberately distorted the history of the anti-fascist Patriotic War, besmirched the heroic stature of the Soviet people and army and grossly slandered the leadership of the C.P.S.U. headed by Stalin. However, the more they do so, the more they prove the correctness of Stalin's leadership and the greatness of the Soviet people and army, united under the banner of Lenin and Stalin. Attempts to distort history can never succeed. Just imagine. If the Soviet people and army had not been led by Stalin but by revisionists such as Khrushchev, and if they had not acted in accordance with the line, policy and method of the Marxist–Leninists represented by Stalin, but with the line, policy and method of the revisionists represented by Khrushchev in the latter's dealings with U.S. imperialism in our day, the outcome could only have been disastrous defeat or capitulation, and who knows how many more hardships the people of the Soviet Union and the world would have had to suffer and how many years Soviet and world history would have been pushed back.

History advances according to its own laws. Alienated from and setting themselves against the people, fascist brigands like Hitler and revisionists like Khrushchev are simply fools on the stage of history, while the socialist cause and the anti-fascist cause to which Stalin and the Soviet people and army under his leadership devoted themselves will shine for ever.

Today, when we commemorate the 20th anniversary of the victory over German fascism and of victory in the whole Anti-Fascist War, we must never forget that U.S. imperialism is playing a role more ferocious than that of Hitler. Immediately upon the conclusion of the Anti-Fascist War, U.S. imperialism stepped into the shoes of German, Japanese and Italian fascism, has worked out and pressed its counter-revolutionary strategy for world hegemony, making the Dollar Empire the greatest international exploiter, the gendarme of the world, the chief bulwark of all the forces of reaction and colonialism, the main source of aggression and war in our times and the sworn enemy of the people of the world.

For the last twenty years, U.S. imperialism has been engaged in frantic arms expansion and war preparations and has launched aggression right and left, and it is preparing to impose another world war on the people. We used to say in the past that fascism means war; today we have all the more reason to say that U.S. imperialism means war. In order to smash the aggression of U.S. imperialism and to frustrate its plot for a new war, it is of great practical importance, nay essential, for the socialist countries and the people of other countries to review the historical experience of the war waged by the people of the world against German, Japanese and Italian fascism.

The historical experience of the Anti-Fascist War teaches us that, so long as imperialism exists, the socialist countries and all revolutionary people must maintain the highest revolutionary vigilance and make effective preparations against the eventuality that imperialism may suddenly impose a war on us.

The danger of war exists so long as imperialism exists. Until imperialism is eliminated and socialism has won victory throughout the world, the victory of socialism in one or a number of countries cannot be regarded as final or complete, nor can the victory of the cause of national independence or national liberation in one or a number of countries.

The truth of this has been repeatedly confirmed by history. The imperialists and reactionaries invariably try by every possible means to suppress and destroy those countries and people who have been victorious in their revolutions. This holds good when the revolutionary forces are weak and continues to hold good when they have grown strong. As Comrade Mao Tse-tung put it, "The principle of the reactionary forces in dealing with the democratic forces of the people is definitely to destroy all they can and to prepare to destroy later whatever they cannot destroy now."[2] This is the way they deal with China as well as the Soviet Union; this is the way they deal with the national independent countries as well as the socialist countries, and this is the way they deal with countries and people fighting for national liberation and carrying on people's revolutionary struggles as well as with countries and people that have achieved victory. This is determined by the class nature of imperialism. After all, imperialism is imperialism, it will never lay down its butcher's knife and suddenly become a Buddha. Khrushchev and other modern revisionists assert that the nature of imperialism has changed as a result of the growing might of the socialist camp. This completely violates Lenin's theory of imperialism and is sheer nonsense.

Today, U.S. imperialism is using its counter-revolutionary dual tactics of war and so-called "peace." While playing up its deceitful talk of peace, it is launching wars of aggression everywhere and accelerating its preparations for new wars. In these circumstances, it is all the more necessary for us to bear in mind the historical experience of the Anti-Fascist War, never cease to maintain high revolutionary vigilance, refuse to be duped by the imperialist peace hoax and guard against any slackening of vigilance and any idea of leaving things to chance. While persevering in their peaceful foreign policy and their economic construction, the socialist countries and the countries that have won national independence must at the same time strengthen their national defences and make adequate preparations against imperialist wars of aggression. It makes a world of difference whether or not one is prepared once a war breaks out. Among all these preparations, political and ideological preparation must be given the first priority. Moreover, these preparations must be made for the most difficult and worst situations that may possibly arise. Preparations must be made not only against any small-scale warfare but also against any medium- or large-scale warfare that imperialism may launch. These preparations must envisage the use by the imperialists of nuclear weapons as well as of conventional weapons. To think and act along these lines is more realistic and more likely to win the initiative, so that come what may, we shall be in a position to cope with the situation successfully and be surer of defeating the enemy.

> The historical experience of the Anti-Fascist War also teaches us that imperialism is perfidious. Under given conditions, it is permissible for socialist countries to enter into negotiations and reach certain agreements with imperialist countries. But in no case should they pin their hopes for the defence of world peace on such negotiations and agreements. They must firmly oppose any Munich policy like that of Chamberlain and Daladier.

The imperialists and all the reactionaries are amoral pragmatists who for all their fine words stop at no crime. When they feel the need, when they are not yet ready to attack you, when they need to put up a smokescreen before launching attacks, and when they need a breathing spell or have to stop after suffering serious defeats in their wars of aggression, they will sit down to negotiate with you and even talk glibly about "peace" and "friendship," sign all kinds of treaties and agreements, and make all sorts of assurances and pledges. But once they think they can swallow you up, when they consider the situation to be in their favour, and when they have sharpened their knives, they will immediately drop this mask and tear all the sacred treaties, solemn agreements and inviolable pledges to shreds. Modern history provides countless instances of this sort. A case in point was the undeclared *blitzkrieg* which Hitler launched against the Soviet Union less than two years after he had concluded a non-aggression treaty with it.

This was how Hitler acted, but doesn't U.S. imperialism act the same way today? Indeed, to say that U.S. imperialism is as perfidious as Hitler doesn't go far enough. For U.S. imperialism is actually many times more insidious and deadly than Hitler. Even with regard to its closest allies and partners, such as Britain and France, and its most faithful lackeys, such as Syngman Rhee and Ngo Dinh Diem, the United States makes use of them when they are useful and kicks them aside when they are no longer needed—sometimes even "slaughtering the donkey after it has done its job at the mill." Such being the way it treats its own partners, is it conceivable that the United States would keep faith with the socialist countries, the national-independent countries and the revolutionary people?

Therefore, in our dealings with the imperialists and reactionaries we must never cherish any illusion about their pledges or lightly believe in their fine words. The socialist nature of our society determines the peaceful nature of our foreign policy. We do not oppose negotiations with imperialist countries which are necessary for the interests of the people and the revolution, for the defence of world peace, and for the exposure of the enemy and the education of the people, but have always taken such negotiations seriously; we do not refuse to sign agreements and treaties which are necessary, and we have always honoured all the agreements and treaties we have signed. But while so acting, we must never forget that no agreements and treaties can stop imperialism when it is bent on war. Whoever pins his hopes for preventing war on treaties and agreements will certainly be badly fooled.

Bullying the weak and fearing the strong are the common characteristics of imperialists and all reactionaries. Whoever wants to ensure his own safety by making concessions to the aggressor and by satisfying his greed at the expense of other people's interests is lifting a rock that will inevitably fall on his own toes. Chamberlain and Daladier rejected the Soviet proposal for an alliance against the fascist war menace and hatched the Munich plot selling out the interests of the Czechoslovak and Polish peoples, in the hope that Hitler would turn the spearhead of his aggression against the Soviet Union. But perceiving their fear of war as a weakness, Hitler struck at them first and caught them unprepared. The three million French troops collapsed in a month and a half, and Great Britain was brought to the verge of subjugation, barely avoiding the tragedy of France thanks to the English Channel. The Munich policy of Chamberlain and Daladier, which inflicted harm on themselves as well as on others, will live in history as a byword of infamy. Today, whoever plots another Munich in the face of the war blackmail of the U.S. imperialists will, like Chamberlain and Daladier, begin by doing harm to others and end by injuring himself. Since the people of the world are awakened, such plots are doomed to failure and such schemers will come to no good end.

The historical experience of the Anti-Fascist War also teaches us that it is imperative to distinguish enemies from friends, make use of contradictions, win over the majority, unite with all the forces that can be united and form the broadest possible united front against the main enemy.

The fascist bloc of Germany, Japan and Italy represented the most rapacious and aggressive imperialism of the time. Their predatory policies seriously menaced the freedom and independence of every nation, not excepting their own partners; that is, the robbers preyed on each other. It follows from the predatory nature of the imperialists that not only will they be opposed by the broadest masses of the people all over the world, but that they are bound to oppose each other and break up.

One of Stalin's major contributions was that he correctly analysed the current situation in the international class struggle, identified the principal contradiction in the world arena and the principal enemy of the world's people and was therefore able to advance the correct slogan of an anti-fascist united front and to rally all the anti-fascist forces in a united front, with the Soviet Union and the world proletariat as its main force. As a result, the imperialist anti-Soviet alliance was shattered with the establishment of an anti-fascist alliance, and the imperialist encirclement of the socialist Soviet Union was broken with the achievement of a counter-encirclement of the fascist forces of aggression by the worldwide forces against aggression; thus a fundamental change was brought about in the strategic situation which became favourable to ourselves and unfavourable to the enemy. This was a vitally important factor in the great victory of the Anti-Fascist War.

Today, U.S. imperialism is not only striving to destroy socialism and grabbing vast regions of Asia, Africa and Latin America, which form the first intermediate zone, it also wants to control the capitalist and imperialist countries of West Europe, North America, Oceania and Japan, which form the second intermediate zone. By its policy of world domination U.S. imperialism is compelling over 90 per cent of the people of the world to rise up against it, inevitably alienating its followers, increasingly isolating itself, and becoming surrounded by enemies. In these circumstances, as Comrade Mao Tse-tung teaches us, the U.S. plans for aggression and war can be frustrated and defeated, provided that we are good at uniting the socialist camp and the people's anti-imperialist forces in all countries as well as at making use of the contradictions within the imperialist camp and forming the broadest possible united front against U.S. imperialism. And if nevertheless U.S. imperialism should venture on a new world war, we will be all the more certain of defeating it completely.

Regarding enemies as friends and friends as enemies, modern revisionists such as Khrushchev unite with the United States in "peaceful co-operation" against the people's revolutions, instead of uniting with all the anti-American forces, making use of the contradictions within the imperialist camp and forming an anti-American united front. This is a gross betrayal of the world proletarian revolution. It is also a gross betrayal of the oppressed nations and peoples. The modern revisionists' actions only help U.S. imperialism to extricate itself from its isolation, inflate its arrogance in aggression and increase the danger of its launching a new war. We must therefore relentlessly oppose such actions.

The historical experience of the Anti-Fascist War also teaches us that the strategy of active defence is the only correct strategy for the socialist countries in fighting against imperialist wars of aggression.

The strategy of active defence applied by the Soviet Supreme Command headed by Stalin was an important factor contributing to victory in the anti-fascist Patriotic War. The Soviet Union applied this strategy, vigorously exposed the aggressive features of fascist Germany, aroused boundless and righteous anger among the Soviet people and army, and won extensive sympathy and support among the people of the world. It was through the application of this strategy that the Soviet army was able to trade space for time, deplete and destroy the enemy's effective forces on a large scale, and compel him to switch from the strategic offensive to the strategic defensive and finally go down in destruction. It was also through the application of this strategy that the Soviet army was able to take full advantage of the superiority inherent in a just war, gather strength in the course of the fighting, turn from the strategic defensive to the strategic offensive and then to pursuit, and, with the support and co-operation of the people of the world, triumph in the anti-fascist Patriotic War.

Khrushchev and his like have done their utmost to denounce this strategy, alleging that it constituted one of Stalin's crimes and was a theory Stalin invented to justify his errors during the early period of the war. This is a gross distortion and slander. If the strategy of active defence adopted by Stalin was wrong, as they assert, one would like to ask: What other strategy should the Soviet Union have adopted? Pre-emptive war? This is obviously incompatible with the nature of the socialist system. It is not necessary, or permissible, for a socialist country to be the first to attack others; it will never fire the first shot. Or should the Soviet Union's strategy have been one of passive defence, of simply waiting to be attacked? This was obviously not to its advantage. Engels affirmed long ago that "passive defence invariably meets with certain defeat, no matter how well armed one is."[3] Or should the strategy of the Soviet Union have been one of surrender to the enemy? This would have been the betrayal of revolution and the people. Whoever wishes to surrender to the enemy will be spurned by the people and branded as a traitor through the ages. Then what is the correct strategy? Of course, it can only be active defence.

Comrade Mao Tse-tung said:

> Active defence is also known as offensive defence, or defence through decisive engagements. Passive defence is also known as purely defensive defence or pure defence. Passive defence is actually a spurious kind of defence, and the only real defence is active defence, defence for the purpose of counter-attacking and taking the offensive.[4]

Operationally, the strategy of active defence should not have the holding or capturing of territory as its main objective. It should be to concentrate superior forces to destroy the enemy's effectives. It was precisely by adopting this strategy in the anti-fascist Patriotic War that the Soviet Union forced Hitler to halt his troops before high mountains and outside fortified cities along the far-flung battle-line stretching from Leningrad, Moscow and Stalingrad to the Caucasus, so that they were caught in an impasse, unable either to advance or to retreat, and suffered tremendous losses. Over 300,000 German fascist crack troops were encircled and annihilated in the Battle of Stalingrad, which marked the turning point of World War II. In the subsequent counter-offensives the effective forces of the aggressor were successively wiped out in large numbers. Such was the brilliant strategy that brought Hitler to his doom. Experience shows that only by energetically wiping out the enemy's effectives is it possible successfully to change the military situation, to defend cities and other places, and finally to defeat the aggressor.

The strategy of active defence does not stop with driving the aggressor out of the country, but requires strategic pursuit to destroy the enemy at his starting point, to destroy him in his nest. As Stalin put it, we must not allow a wounded beast to crawl back to recuperate; we must follow on its heels in hot pursuit and finish it off in its own lair. It was precisely this strategy that was applied by the Soviet Supreme Command headed by Stalin, with the result that the Soviet army's strategic pursuit actively supported the anti-fascist armed uprisings of the peoples of other European countries and helped the East European peoples overthrow their reactionary regimes and win victory in their revolutions. This was a splendid contribution by the Soviet people and army. In any future war against U.S. imperialist aggression, this is the only strategy for the socialist countries to adopt. We seriously warn the U.S. imperialists that they must not expect us to refrain from counter-attacking once they have attacked us. Nothing comes so cheap.

The historical experience of the Anti-Fascist War also teaches us that weapons are an important factor in war but not the decisive factor, and that people and not things are the fundamental factor determining the outcome of war.

Since they are divorced from and antagonistic to the people, imperialists and reactionaries dare not and cannot rely on the masses or on their own troops. In waging war they can only pin their hopes on weapons. They do their best to exaggerate the role of weapons simply because they want to intimidate people, and first of all to disarm the targets of their aggression morally so that their victims lose confidence in their capacity to resist and can be vanquished in a single battle or even without battle. That is the real value of the theory spread by the imperialists and reactionaries that weapons decide everything.

Didn't the theories of the fascist brigands that "air power decides the war" and that "tanks decide the war" inspire fear? The myth created by Goebbels of the invincibility of the German army, together with the scream of the siren-bombs and the activity of its Fifth Columns, spread such terror in capitalist Europe that some countries were morally disarmed even before Hitler attacked them. This was of enormous help to him. But when it came to attacking the socialist Soviet Union, Hitler's planes and tanks were no longer so fearsome or decisive. Why? What was the secret? Was it because the Soviet

Union possessed more and better planes and tanks than Hitlerite Germany? No. The Soviet Union was inferior to Hitlerite Germany in this respect. Then what gave the Soviet army the strength to stand up to and defeat Hitler's fascist army? Truth to tell, there was nothing mysterious about it. It was because the Soviet Union relied on the people, the socialist system, revolutionary political work in the Red Army and the Marxist–Leninist leadership of the Communist Party. In brief, it was by relying on the politically conscious people led by the party of the proletariat that the Soviet Union smashed the fascist military machine. This is a law, this is the truth.

Wasn't this so? What could Hitler's fascist army with all its ferocity and power accomplish in the face of the Soviet army and the broad masses of the Soviet people, who, inspired by the glorious tradition of their October Revolution and armed with Marxist–Leninist ideology, were ready to sacrifice their lives to safeguard their socialist motherland? What could it do in the face of the thousands upon thousands of soldiers who defied death and courageously advanced to engage the enemy in hand-to-hand combat, shouting as their slogans "For the motherland, for Stalin"?

Wasn't this so too? How could Hitler's fascist army, for all its numbers and might, consolidate its occupied areas in the face of the widespread guerrilla warfare and sabotage carried on by the masses behind the enemy lines? What could it do except divert its armed forces? How could it avoid being buffeted on all sides? How could it escape tight encirclement by the people and final defeat?

All these facts show once again that victory in war does not depend on new weapons of one kind or another, or on a particular technical arm. It depends on the close integration of the armed forces and the civilian masses, the joint efforts of the people at the front and in the rear, the co-ordination of the battlefield at the front and the battlefield in the enemy rear, and close co-operation among the different armed services, of which the ground forces, and particularly the infantry, are primary. Without heroic fighting by the ground forces, no new weapons, however powerful, can determine the outcome of battles or achieve the political aim of a war. This is another law or truth governing war. It holds true for other wars as well as for the Anti-Fascist War. It holds true after as well as before the emergence of the atom bomb. It holds true for oppressed peoples engaged in revolutionary struggle as well as for a powerful socialist country such as the Soviet Union.

The historical experience of the Anti-Fascist War also teaches us that all revolutionary wars support each other. Countries which have won victory should support and help the revolutionary struggles of those countries and people that have not yet won victory. The socialist countries should serve as base areas for the world revolution and as the main force in combating imperialist aggression.

By its victory in the anti-fascist Patriotic War the Soviet Union gave support to the people of all countries, helped the East European countries to win liberation and assisted the Chinese people in their War of Resistance Against Japan. At the same time, the anti-fascist struggles of the people of the world, the uprisings of the people of the European countries and their armed struggles against German and Italian fascism, and particularly the great anti-Japanese war with the Chinese people as the main force, to a large extent pinned down, hammered and weakened the military force of the fascist bloc as a whole. Without all these factors, it would have been impossible for the Soviet Union to win such a great victory in the anti-fascist Patriotic War.

From the Marxist–Leninist point of view, a revolutionary war or a war of resistance to aggression waged by a country is at once a struggle in its own national interest and a support for the revolutionary struggles of other countries, a support for those countries that have already won victory and a contribution to the defence of world peace. The countries and peoples engaged in such a war should do their best to tie down and destroy more enemy forces, while the countries that have won the victory, and particularly the socialist countries, should give full play to the spirit of internationalism and regard it as their bounden duty to support the revolutionary struggles of the oppressed peoples. In this mutual support, all countries, large or small, strong or weak, should firmly guard against and resist great-power chauvinism and narrow national egoism. Supporting others means supporting oneself, and therefore no one has the right to assume the airs of a benefactor or liberator. Whether or not a country which has won victory dares to serve as a base area for the world revolution and to support and aid the people's revolution in other countries is the touchstone of whether or not it is really for revolution and whether or not it really opposes imperialism.

Finally, the historical experience of the Anti-Fascist War teaches us that although a war imposed on us by imperialism will cause sacrifices, losses and destruction, it will also educate the people, and that the people will win the war as well as peace and progress.

The German fascists killed countless people and destroyed thousands of cities and villages in the Soviet Union, but the War resulted in victory for the Soviet Union, in the liberation of East Europe and the spread of socialism from one country to a whole camp of countries. The Soviet Union achieved further growth in its socialist construction. It did not become weaker because of the destruction in the War; in the contrary, it grew stronger. After we rose in resistance, fought and won, the war imposed on us by imperialism turned from a bad thing into a good thing, accelerating historical progress and social development. This lesson was confirmed by the Soviet anti-fascist Patriotic War and the revolutionary wars the Chinese people were compelled to fight over decades. It has been further confirmed by the Korean people's war of resistance against U.S. aggression, by the Vietnamese people's war of resistance against French aggression, by the Cuban people's revolutionary war and by Algeria's war of liberation. And there is no doubt that it will be borne out by the wars of liberation being waged at this very moment by the peoples of south Viet Nam, Laos and the Congo (Leopoldville), and by the people's revolutionary wars in other countries.

We are against the launching of wars by the imperialists, but we should not be afraid of war, still less should we oppose revolutionary wars out of fear of war. Of what avail is fear when the imperialists insist on imposing war on us? Can such fear prevent them from launching wars? Can fear eliminate wars? No. History has taught us that fear cannot prevent wars, to say nothing of eliminating them. In order to eliminate wars it is necessary to wage wars of resistance. In order to eliminate counter-revolutionary wars it is necessary to wage revolutionary wars. In order to do away with guns it is necessary to take up guns. It is under compulsion that we have taken up guns; we have waged revolutionary wars not only for the purpose of delivering ourselves from enslavement and oppression, but also for the purpose of eliminating the source of war—imperialism.

The rich historical experience of the Anti-Fascist War was gained at the cost of the blood of the revolutionary people in all countries. It is the common asset of the people of the world and is of immense practical importance for the current struggle against U.S. imperialism.

Hitler, Tojo, Mussolini and the other fascist brigands met their doom long ago. But U.S. imperialism, which since the War has replaced German, Japanese and Italian fascism as the arch-enemy of the people of the world, is now following in these brigands' footsteps, madly pressing ahead with the counter-revolutionary cause which they tried in vain to further and imposing one war of aggression after another on the people of different countries.

Modern revisionists such as Khrushchev say that Hitler would not have attacked the Soviet Union if he had foreseen the outcome of the War. These revisionists say that the chieftains of U.S. imperialism today are quite different from Hitler, that having recognized the strength of socialism they are able to learn the lessons of history, that they have become "sensible" and "peace-loving" and will not run the risk of launching a war as Hitler did. The modern revisionists have woven a fancy fairy tale in a perverse attempt to make people believe that imperialism and socialism can advance hand in hand towards what they call a world "without weapons, without armed forces, without wars."

How can Communists spout such contemptible lies and such non-sense? Everybody knows it was the class nature of German monopoly capital that made Hitler unleash the war. Similarly, it is the class na-ture of U.S. monopoly capital that makes the U.S. imperialists launch wars today. Even before capitalism developed to the stage of monopoly capitalism, Marx cited the following passage in a footnote in *Capital:*

> . . . 100 per cent. [profit] will make it [capital] ready to trample on all human laws; 300 per cent., and there is not a crime at which it will scruple, nor a risk it will not run, even to the chance of its owner being hanged.[5]

The class interests of the monopoly capitalists impel them to embark on mad war adventures in the quest for profit. They are so obsessed with the idea of profit-making that they lose any sense of reality. They invariably underestimate the strength of the people and over-estimate their own, and so again and again they fight "the wrong war, at the wrong place, at the wrong time, and with the wrong enemy."[6] Aren't there plenty of examples in the history books? Napoleon's plan to conquer Europe and the world failed, and Kaiser Wilhelm II followed in his footsteps. Wilhelm failed, and Hitler tried again. Hitler failed, and now U.S. imperialism is following in Hitler's footsteps. They can never learn from the failure of their predecessors. They can only follow each other to the grave until the complete collapse of the imperialist system.

Hitler seemed invincible in his time but he failed in the end. Is U.S. imperialism today more formidable than Hitler was then? Will its fate be any better than Hitler's? Compare the present with the past and you will find a clear answer.

Today, U.S. imperialism is greatly over-extended. The contradiction between its high ambitions, its far-flung battlefronts and remote rear, on the one hand, and its shortage of troops, on the other, is far more serious than in Hitler's case. It is aspiring to destroy the socialist camp, which is a vast expanse of contiguous territories with a total population of one thousand million and many times stronger than the Soviet Union was in Hitler's time. Unlike Hitler, U.S. imperialism is confronted by the solid resistance of unprecedentedly broad national-liberation movements when it wages wars of aggression against the countries of Asia, Africa and Latin America. Its army has frequently been defeated in its wars to suppress the people's revolutions and carry out aggression in other countries. It is an army of pampered soldiers far inferior to Hitler's fascist army. Moreover, U.S. imperialism is facing the disintegration of the aggressive blocs it has so painstakingly pieced together, a situation Hitler did not have to face. In all these respects, it is in a vastly inferior position to that of its predecessor. Comrade Mao Tse-tung pointed out many years ago that U.S. imperialism is only a paper tiger:

> The strength of the United States of America is only superficial and transient. Irreconcilable domestic and international contradictions, like a volcano, menace U.S. imperialism every day. U.S. imperialism is sitting on this volcano.[7]

Since Hitler met with utter defeat in his attack on the Soviet Union when the situation and balance of forces was much more favourable, what can the United States achieve except to hasten its own destruction when waging wars of aggression everywhere under such unfavourable conditions?

Some people may say: After all, U.S. imperialism has the atom bomb and therefore it is more powerful than Hitler. It is true that U.S. imperialism has the atom bomb and Hitler did not, and it is also true that the atom bomb is a weapon of mass destruction. But, as pointed out by Comrade Mao Tse-tung, the atom bomb cannot decide the outcome of war because, "without the struggles waged by the people, atom bombs by themselves would be of no avail,"[8] and "the atom bomb is a paper tiger which the U.S. reactionaries use to scare people."[9] What is more, the United States' monopoly of the atom bomb was broken many years ago. Now other countries have the atom bomb as well as the United States. For the past twenty years, the United States has spent tens of billions of dollars on the mass production of atom and hydrogen bombs, but what use have its atom bombs been, except to frighten those with weak nerves? Its atom bombs could not and did not prevent the great victory of the Chinese people's revolutionary war. They could not and did not prevent the great victory of the Korean people's revolutionary war. They could not and did not prevent the great victory of the Vietnamese people's revolutionary war. They could not and did not prevent the great victory of the Cuban people's revolutionary war. They could not and did not prevent the great victory of the Algerian people's revolutionary war. They have not prevented and will never be able to prevent the growth and triumph of the revolutionary struggles of the peoples of Asia, Africa and Latin America. They have not prevented and will never be able to prevent the growth and triumph of the revolutionary struggles of the peoples of West Europe, Oceania and North America, including the United States.

Although it brandishes atom bombs and shouts about nuclear retaliation, U.S. imperialism is completely helpless before the miracles wrought by rifles, hand-grenades and even such primitive weapons as bows and arrows and knives in the hands of the revolutionary people. This decade is witnessing atomic imperialism playing a superb farce. Isn't it being performed beautifully at this very moment in south Viet Nam? What is there for U.S. imperialism to brag about when this reputed Number One world power, possessing innumerable nuclear missiles, is being battered out of its senses by the 14 million south Vietnamese people, and cannot even protect its own embassy?

The history of the twenty years since the War has fully demonstrated that, with all its nuclear weapons, U.S. imperialism is like a big, hollow worm-eaten tree. The day is drawing nigh when this tree will be uprooted by the worldwide storm of the people's revolution.

However, throughout history all dying reactionary forces have invariably put up final desperate struggles against the forces of revolution. Look at Chiang Kai-shek. He fought the Communists for dozens of years. He lost everything except a handful of bedraggled soldiers with whom he fled to Taiwan, and yet he is daily calling for a counter-offensive against the mainland. Is it conceivable that an imperialist power as big as the United States will lightly leave the stage of history without pitched battles, without repeated trials of strength and without life-and-death struggles? U.S. monopoly capital is still very large. It has a strong industrial base. In twenty years of arms expansion and war preparations since the War, its troops have increased eightfold. Its military bases are to be found in every corner of the world. Out of its armed forces of 2,700,000 men, more than 1,000,000 are stationed abroad for unceasing aggression against the revolutionary people of every country. Clearly, it will never abandon its counter-revolutionary war plans or admit defeat until its counter-revolutionary forces have been destroyed and its last stakes lost. As Comrade Mao Tse-tung pointed out:

> Make trouble, fail, make trouble again, fail again . . . till their doom; that is the logic of the imperialists and all reactionaries the world over in dealing with the people's cause, and they will never go against this logic. This is a Marxist law.[10]

A striking instance of the struggle put up by U.S. imperialism to save itself from defeat is its adventurist expansion of the war of aggression in Viet Nam. Its "special warfare" in south Viet Nam having shamefully failed, it has now invented the theory of the "escalation of the war." It divides the war into several stages and each stage into several steps. In its sequence of steps, it is gradually intensifying and expanding its threat and use of force. A characteristic feature is that, every time it adds a faggot to the fire of its war of aggression, it says a prayer for peace. It is trying to save itself from defeat by a better synchronization of its counter-revolutionary dual tactics of threats and blandishments. In accordance with the theory of "escalation," the United States is leading its war of aggression in south Viet Nam in the direction of a local war of the Korean type. It has already spread the flames of war to north Viet Nam and is preparing to spread them further to China. This is a serious challenge U.S. imperialism has flung down to all the peace-loving countries and peoples.

Today, the heroic Vietnamese people are united as one man under the leadership of the Viet Nam Workers' Party and President Ho Chi Minh and by the vow to "resist U.S. aggression, save the nation, liberate the south, defend the north and reunify the fatherland!" and they are now fighting in the forefront of the struggle against U.S. imperialism. By their courageous action against the U.S. and puppet forces, the south Vietnamese people have already liberated four-fifths of the territory and over two-thirds of the population of south Viet Nam, and are daily approaching final victory in their war of liberation. The north Vietnamese people, who are determined to fight and win, are waging a heroic battle against the U.S. imperialist bombing raids and have dealt one heavy blow after another to the aggressors. The valiant fight of the Vietnamese people is tying down more and more of the armed forces of U.S. imperialism, upsetting its counter-revolutionary global strategy, supporting the revolutionary struggles of the people of all other countries, giving a brilliant example to the people the world over and making a great contribution to the defence of peace in Asia and the whole world.

All revolutionary people rejoice at the great victories of the Vietnamese people, and a tremendous mass campaign to aid Viet Nam in resisting U.S. aggression is mounting throughout the world. The revolutionary people of all countries are dealing blows to U.S. imperialism and its lackeys in various ways. The heroic people of the Congo (Leopoldville), Laos, Korea, Indonesia, Cambodia, Japan, Cuba, Venezuela, the Dominican Republic and the Arab countries, and all other countries and peoples who are combating U.S. imperialism and its lackeys, have each made their contribution to the frustration of the U.S. imperialist policies of aggression and war and to the sacred cause of defending world peace.

The Chinese people resolutely support the Vietnamese people's struggle to resist U.S. aggression and save the nation and the struggle of the people of all other countries against U.S. imperialism. We not only fully support these struggles politically and morally and help them materially to the limit of our capabilities, but are also prepared to send our men to fight together with the people of Viet Nam when they need us. This attitude of ours is firm and unshakable. We will go on supporting and aiding the Vietnamese people, whether or not U.S. imperialism bombs our country and whether or not it enlarges the war. We are not frightened by the U.S. imperialists' bombing threats or their clamour for enlarging the war. Our opposition to U.S. imperialism has always been clear-cut. Our principle is: We will not attack unless we are attacked; if we are attacked, we will certainly counter-attack. We shall wipe out anybody who dares to attack us. On whatever scale the United States attacks us, we will reply on the same scale. We always mean what we say. We are fully prepared for war. The Chinese people and the Chinese People's Liberation Army are fully prepared. If U.S. imperialism should insist on imposing war on us, together with the people of the whole world we will resolutely crush its counter-revolutionary war by a revolutionary war and do our part in thoroughly destroying U.S. imperialism, the arch-criminal of contemporary aggression and war!

In commemorating the great victory over German fascism and the great victory of the war against fascism as a whole, we pay high tribute to and express our full confidence in the great Soviet people and the great Soviet army, who grew up nurtured by the brilliant thinking of Lenin and Stalin, who have a glorious revolutionary tradition, who stood the test of the war against fascism and triumphed. We are deeply confident that we will be united on the basis of Marxism–Leninism and proletarian internationalism, will fight shoulder to shoulder against our common enemy, U.S. imperialism, and advance together with the people of the world towards final victory in wars against aggression and towards the new era of lasting peace for mankind!

(Published in "Hongqi," No. 5, 1965.)

NOTES—APPENDIX FOUR—DOCUMENT # I

[1] Mao Tse-tung, "Revolutionary Forces of the World Unite, Fight Against Imperialist Aggression!", *Selected Works,* Eng. ed., Foreign Languages Press, Peking, 1961, Vol. IV, p. 284.

[2] Mao Tse-tung, "Some Points in Appraisal of the Present International Situation," *Selected Works,* Eng. ed., F.L.P., Peking, 1961, Vol. IV, pp. 87–88.

[3] Frederick Engels, "The History of the Rifle," *Works of Marx and Engels,* Ger. ed., Dietz Verlag, Berlin, 1961, Vol. 15, p. 218.

[4] Mao Tse-tung, "Problems of Strategy in China's Revolutionary War," *Selected Works,* Eng. ed., F.L.P., Peking, 1964, Vol. I, p. 207.

[5] Karl Marx, *Capital,* Eng. ed., F.L.P.H., Moscow, 1954, Vol. I, p. 760.

[6] Testimony by Omar Bradley, Chairman of the U.S. Joint Chiefs of Staff, before the Senate Joint Armed Services and Foreign Relations Committees, May 1951.

[7] Mao Tse-tung, "The Present Situation and Our Tasks," *Selected Works,* Eng. ed., F.L.P., Peking, 1961, Vol. IV, p. 172.

[8] Mao Tse-tung, "The Situation and Our Policy After the Victory in the War of Resistance Against Japan," *Selected Works,* Eng. ed., F.L.P., Peking, 1961, Vol. IV, p. 21.

[9] Mao Tse-tung, "Talk with the American Correspondent Anna Louise Strong," *Selected Works,* Eng. ed., F.L.P., Peking, 1961, Vol. IV, p. 100.

[10] Mao Tse-tung, "Cast Away Illusions, Prepare for Struggle," *Selected Works,* Eng. ed., F.L.P., Peking, 1961, Vol. IV, p. 428.

Document # 2

THE HISTORICAL EXPERIENCE OF THE
WAR AGAINST FASCISM*

by the Editorial Department of "Renmin Ribao"

TWENTY years have passed since the great war against fascism ended in victory.

The Anti-Fascist War was a gigantic struggle between the anti-fascist forces of the world, of which the main force was the socialist Soviet Union, and the three fascist powers, Germany, Italy and Japan. It was a just war and a war on a scale unprecedented in history. It ended with the triumph of the anti-fascist forces and the rout of German, Italian and Japanese fascism. First came the collapse of Italian fascism, and then German imperialism and Japanese imperialism surrendered unconditionally, on May 8 and September 2, 1945, respectively.

On the eve of final victory in the Anti-Fascist War, Comrade Mao Tse-tung made the following appraisal and forecast of the world situation in accordance with fundamental Marxist–Leninist principles:

> Contrary to the predictions of the Chinese and foreign reactionaries, the forces of fascist aggression will undoubtedly be overthrown and the people's democratic forces will undoubtedly triumph. The world will unquestionably take the road of progress and not the road of reaction.[1]

*Peking Review (May 14, 1965) pp. 15–22.

He added, "War has educated the people and it is the people who will win the war, win the peace and win progress."[2]

The course of events fully corroborated Comrade Mao Tse-tung's scientific predictions. The victory of the Anti-Fascist War marked another great turning point in history, following on the October Revolution. It opened a new page in history.

The victorious Anti-Fascist War dealt a severe blow to international imperialism. While the Great October Revolution made the first breach in the front of world imperialism, the victorious Anti-Fascist War destroyed a large section of it. The rise of fascism and its embarkation on world war represented the last-ditch struggles of the most reactionary forces of imperialism. The jack-booted fascist hordes overran Europe, Asia and Africa, wreaking havoc over a large part of the globe, but this did not save them from extinction. The outcome of the war was the overthrow of three imperialist powers, Germany, Italy and Japan, and the serious weakening of two others, Britain and France. By starting the world war, imperialism moved much nearer to its grave.

The victory of the Anti-Fascist War substantially consolidated and extended the great achievements of the October Socialist Revolution. The world forces of socialism expanded. Tempered in the war, the first socialist state, the Soviet Union, grew stronger. In the new historical conditions resulting from the victorious Anti-Fascist War, a number of socialist countries were born in Europe and in Asia. Together with the Soviet Union, these countries formed the powerful socialist camp, which confronted the decaying camp of imperialism. Comrade Mao Tse-tung said:

> With the victory of the Great October Socialist Revolution in the Soviet Union, a world situation appeared where victory for the people became a foregone conclusion; and now with the founding of the People's Republic of China and the other People's Democracies, the situation has developed and become consolidated.[3]

Victory in the Anti-Fascist War ushered in a new stage in the revolutionary struggle of the oppressed peoples and nations. The roar of the guns awoke the oppressed peoples and nations in every corner of the world. Great revolutionary storms rose in Asia, Africa and Latin America. After World War I imperialist rule in the colonies and semi-colonies enjoyed a period of relative stability, but there has been no such relative stability since World War II. The unceasing anti-imperialist revolutionary struggles of the people have been shaking and destroying the foundations of imperialist rule. Imperialism has lost its stable rear area once and for all.

In summarizing the great historic significance of the victory in the Anti-Fascist War, Comrade Mao Tse-tung said:

> If the October Revolution opened up wide possibilities for the emancipation of the working class and the oppressed peoples of the world and opened up realistic paths towards it, then the victory of the antifascist Second World War has opened up still wider possibilities for the emancipation of the working class and the oppressed peoples of the world and has opened up still more realistic paths towards it.[4]

The victory of the Anti-Fascist War was a victory of socialism, the most advanced social system in history, a victory of the people in all countries who united to win freedom and liberation, and a victory of Marxism–Leninism. The history of the War gave fresh and conclusive proof that the fundamental principles of Marxism–Leninism are universally applicable and hold for all time and that a guiding line, policy, strategy or tactics based on these principles is invincible.

There is a whole series of important differences of principle between Marxist–Leninists and the modern revisionists on the question of how to assess the Anti-Fascist War and on the lessons to be drawn from it. Basing themselves on historical materialism, the Marxist–Leninists respect the facts of history, ascertain the laws inherent in them and thus draw the correct conclusions. On the other hand, in order to adulterate Marxism–Leninism, the Khrushchev revisionists, the representatives of modern revisionism, have been deliberately distorting history ever since the 20th Congress of the C.P.S.U., obscuring facts and concocting conclusions that are extremely harmful.

In the first place, the history of the Anti-Fascist War shows that the socialist system has a tremendous vitality that can stand the severest tests and that a state of the dictatorship of the proletariat is invincible.

The main contest in the Anti-Fascist War was between the Soviet Union, the only socialist state at the time, and fascist Germany, then the most powerful imperialist state. After occupying almost the whole of capitalist Europe, the German fascists mobilized immense resources and manpower and made war on the Soviet Union. It was a severe test for the young Soviet state. It was a decisive battle between the two systems, imperialism and socialism.

Instead of being crushed by Hitler's war machine, the first socialist state, created by Lenin, achieved a great historic victory. Headed by Stalin, the C.P.S.U. held high the fighting banner of Leninism and led the Soviet people and the heroic Soviet army, reared in the glorious tradition of the October Revolution, in overcoming innumerable difficulties and in eventually defeating the Hitler gang which had mustered the military and economic strength of more than a dozen European countries. The Soviet people and army successfully defended their own country and opened the way for the East European peoples to liberate themselves from the enslavement of the Hitler brigands. The Soviet people proved themselves worthy of the name of a great people, and the Soviet army proved itself worthy of the name of a great army. Time will never dim their glorious exploits.

The heroic deeds of the Soviet people and army are indissolubly linked with the incomparable superiority of the Soviet socialist system and the great strength of the dictatorship of the proletariat. It was the socialist system and the dictatorship of the proletariat that guaranteed victory for the Soviet people and army. Only this system and this dictatorship could have stood firm under the surprise attack of the most ferocious imperialist power and trained such an army and such a people who fought the fascist brigands resolutely until final victory. Only this system and this dictatorship could have accomplished the industrialization of the Soviet state and the collectivization of its agriculture in so short a period and thus built up sufficient economic and military strength to defeat the Hitler thugs. As Stalin put it, "Our victory signifies, first of all, that our Soviet *social* system was victorious, that the Soviet social system successfully passed the test of fire in the war and proved that it is fully viable." He also said, "The war proved that the Soviet social system is a genuine people's system, which grew up from the ranks of the people and enjoys their powerful support. . . ."[5]

The victory of the Soviet people and army are indissolubly linked with Stalin's leadership. In the hour of crisis for the Soviet state after the outbreak of the War, it was Stalin who shouldered the heavy responsibility of leading the Party and the state and it was he who welded together the multi-national Soviet people into a force of invincible steel for their life-and-death struggle against the fascist brigands. As supreme commander of the Soviet armed forces, Stalin directed the entire war and all its major campaigns, from its outbreak to final victory. At the critical moment when Hitler's gangster forces stood at the very gates of Moscow, it was Stalin's supremely confident and determined voice that the people of the Soviet Union and the whole world heard, saying, "Annihilate to a man all the German occupationists who penetrated our country."[6] And when the War entered the stage of counter-offensive, it was Stalin's great call that all the officers and men of the Soviet armed forces heard, saying, "The wounded beast must be pursued close on its heels and finished off in its own lair."[7] The name of Stalin inspired the Soviet people and army throughout the War. Although he made certain mistakes, Stalin was a great Marxist–Leninist and proved himself a great commander. His outstanding contribution to victory in the Anti-Fascist War can never be erased.

All these conclusions have long been established and accepted by the whole world. Nonetheless, Khrushchev and his disciples brazenly distort the history of the Soviet people's war against fascism. They worked out their anti-Marxist–Leninist revisionist line at the 20th Congress of the C.P.S.U. Khrushchev's report on the work of the Central Committee and the secret report he delivered at the Congress were typical revisionist products. A striking expression of their revisionist line was the complete negation of Stalin. They completely blackened the socialist system and the dictatorship of the proletariat, slanderously depicted the great Soviet people as pessimistic and degenerate philistines, and vilified the heroic Soviet army as a cowardly mob.

According to Khrushchev, before the War Stalin took a "carefree attitude" towards the enemy's plans for aggression and "everything was ignored"; when the War broke out he lost heart and "relinquished leadership," thinking that "all was finished"; and during the whole course of the War he simply "planned operations on a globe." In short, according to Khrushchev, Stalin was not a great commander but an "idiot."

While pouring endless abuse on Stalin, these falsifiers of history lauded Khrushchev to the skies. They said that during the War Khrushchev "always stood where the difficulties were greatest" and on many occasions made "more reasonable decisions" than those of the Supreme Command. Khrushchev was not only "the soul of the Stalingraders" but the leader in many "decisive battles." Lieutenant-

General Khrushchev thus became Commander-in-Chief of the Soviet Patriotic War.

The Khrushchev revisionists' vehement denunciation of Stalin and lavish praise of Khrushchev were very important steps for opposing Marxism–Leninism and promoting revisionism. They tried hard to belittle or obliterate Stalin's role in the Anti-Fascist War in order to destroy his prestige among the people of the Soviet Union and the world as a great Marxist–Leninist and in order to adulterate Marxism–Leninism. Actually, in smearing Stalin, they smeared the socialist system, the dictatorship of the proletariat and the C.P.S.U. itself, and thus paved the way for changing the dictatorship of the proletariat into a "state of the whole people" and the proletarian party into a "party of the entire people." They dressed up that clown Khrushchev as the "hero" of the Anti-Fascist War so as to build up his prestige and to enable Khrushchev revisionism to supplant Marxism–Leninism. But after all, gold remains gold in the furnace of history and dross remains dross. The Khrushchev revisionists have already met with failure in their attempt to tamper with history and in their strenuous efforts to negate Stalin and to oppose Marxism–Leninism, and total failure is awaiting them.

In the second place, the history of the Anti-Fascist War shows that imperialism is the source of wars in modern times, that the aggressive nature of imperialism will not change and that to defend world peace it is necessary to wage a tit-for-tat struggle against imperialism.

World War II was the culmination of a series of wars of aggression which were launched and gradually extended in the 1930s by the three fascist powers, Germany, Italy and Japan. It was the result of the imperialist policies of aggression and war. These fascist countries were the three most aggressive imperialist powers. They did not scruple to launch wars of aggression to extricate themselves from their political and economic crises and to plunder more and more countries more and more ruthlessly.

At that time two diametrically opposed policies towards fascist aggression held the world stage. For a long period the British, French and U.S. imperialists and their partners followed a policy of appeasement towards German, Italian and Japanese fascism, indulging the evil-doers and conniving at their crimes. They tacitly consented to the aggression of Japanese imperialism against China. They allowed Mussolini to commit aggression against Abyssinia (Ethiopia). They encouraged the German and Italian fascists in their armed intervention in Spain. They connived at Hitler's annexation of Austria and the Sudetenland of Czechoslovakia. Instead of buying peace, all this served to whet the fascists' appetite for further aggression and to bring on the world war. By their policy of appeasement the British, French and U.S. imperialists lifted a rock only to drop it on their own toes, and history meted out due punishment to them.

But the people of the world pursued another policy, that of dealing resolute counter-blows to fascist aggression. The people of the Soviet Union, China and many other countries firmly opposed the British, French and U.S. imperialist policy of appeasement, courageously shouldered the heavy responsibility of fighting fascism and eventually won not only the war but also the peace.

Summing up the experience of the Chinese people and the people of the whole world in their struggles against imperialists and all reactionaries, as well as the experience of the Anti-Fascist War, Comrade Mao Tse-tung has categorically stated that the nature of imperialism will never change, that we must never cherish illusions about the imperialists but must wage a tit-for-tat struggle against them. He said that "the imperialists will never lay down their butcher knives. . . . they will never become Buddhas, till their doom" and that "it is impossible to persuade the imperialists and the Chinese reactionaries to show kindness of heart and turn from their evil ways. The only course is to organize forces and struggle against them."[8] Developments in the twenty years since the War have proved the correctness of this policy of struggling against imperialism and all reactionaries, as pointed out by Comrade Mao Tse-tung.

In the period since the War, U.S. imperialism has taken the place of German, Italian and Japanese fascism and become the most aggressive imperialist power. U.S. imperialism is the main force of aggression and war. It harbours the vain hope of subjugating the whole world, and it is the sworn enemy of the people of all countries. It encroaches everywhere and launches wars of aggression one after another. The Truman, Eisenhower, Kennedy and Johnson Administrations have all been patterned from the same mould, they have all been faithful executors of the U.S. monopoly capitalist policies of aggression and war. From their own experience the people of the world have come to understand with increasing clarity that peace can never be won by begging for it from imperialism, and that, on the contrary, it can be effectively preserved only by waging resolute struggles against imperialism, and especially against U.S. imperialism. The victory of the Chinese people's revolutionary war, the victory of Korea's war of resistance against U.S. aggression, the victory of the Cuban people's revolutionary war and the victories won in anti-U.S. struggles in many other countries have all served to puncture the arrogance of the U.S. imperialist aggressors and were all effective in defending world peace. It is now plain that the only way the people of the world can smash the U.S. imperialists' plans for aggression and war and prevent another world war is to hit the U.S. aggressors hard on every front of the struggle against U.S. imperialism.

Imperialism always uses the counter-revolutionary dual tactics of armed aggression and fraudulent peace, sometimes alternately, sometimes simultaneously, against the revolutionary people of any country. The people in their turn must make skilful use of revolutionary dual tactics in struggling against imperialism. The signing of the Soviet–German non-aggression treaty on the eve of the Anti-Fascist War and the conclusion of the Korean armistice agreement and of the two Geneva agreements after the War all show that so long as the basic interests of the people are not violated, it is perfectly permissible and even necessary to conduct negotiations with the imperialists and reach certain agreements with them on appropriate occasions. However, a tit-for-tat struggle is necessary when negotiating with the imperialists. It is absolutely impossible to gain through talks what is not won on the battlefield. Even when certain agreements are reached and signed with the imperialists, they never keep their word and they may tear up the agreements at any time. Whoever pins his hopes of preventing war and safeguarding peace on negotiations with the imperialists, or goes so far as to accommodate himself to imperialism at the expense of the basic interests of the people, will come to grief in the face of reality.

The Khrushchev revisionists completely ignore this important historical lesson of the Anti-Fascist War. They eagerly preach that the nature of imperialism has changed and they have tampered with the fundamental Marxist–Leninist thesis that imperialism is the source of war in modern times. In their opinion, world wars are not a product of the imperialist system or of the predatory nature of imperialism, but are a result of momentary impulse or loss of reason on the part of certain individuals. They used to describe Eisenhower and Kennedy as "peace-loving," and now they have spoken of the

Johnson Administration as being "moderate" and "sensible." In their relations with U.S. imperialism, they practise capitulationism, spread the idea of "mutual concessions," "mutual compromise," "mutual conciliation" and "mutual accommodation," and try to subordinate the revolutionary struggles of the people in various countries to their general line of "peaceful coexistence" and "Soviet–U.S. co-operation for the settlement of world problems." Again and again they have betrayed the interests of the revolutionary people—in the Caribbean crisis, in the matter of the Congo, the German peace treaty and West Berlin, and the partial ban on nuclear tests.

Khrushchev's successors are more cunning in their ways, they utter fine-sounding words and play various tricks; nevertheless, they cling to the revisionist line laid down at the 20th Congress of the C.P.S.U., carry out Khrushchev's old policies and still want the revolutionary peoples to submit to what they call "Soviet–U.S. co-operation." They even want to organize a "U.N. force" in collaboration with U.S. imperialism and play the world gendarme to hold down the oppressed peoples and nations. They are colluding with the U.S. aggressors and plotting to sell out the basic interests of the people of Viet Nam and of all other countries, including the Soviet Union. The Khrushchev revisionists are out-and-out appeasers. Their line does not safeguard world peace, but aids and abets U.S. imperialism in committing unbridled aggression and unleashing war. This line is inevitably being discredited as the people throughout the world become more and more awakened.

In the third place, the history of the Anti-Fascist War shows that a people's war is sure of victory, that it is entirely possible to defeat the imperialist aggressors, that imperialism is a paper tiger, which is outwardly strong but actually weak, and that the atom bomb is also a paper tiger and it is people and not weapons, of whatever kind, that decide the outcome of war.

In the early period of the War, the three fascist countries, Germany, Italy and Japan, arrogantly threw their weight around, and quite spectacularly so for a time. They set their whole war machine in motion and they had great superiority in military strength. They dominated almost the whole of capitalist Europe, occupied half of Asia and invaded Africa, treading 800 million people beneath their heels. But that was only a transitory phenomenon. It was the people and not the fascists with their military superiority who proved really powerful. The reason was that the fascists were waging an unjust war of aggression, that they were the enemies of the people of every country, including their own, and that their temporary victories were therefore built on sand and were without any solid foundation. The war that the people of the world were fighting was a just war against aggression and in defence of their motherlands. The potential strength of the people is inexhaustible. Given correct leadership in accordance with a correct line, the people will gradually grow stronger and become powerful in struggle, gradually change the balance of forces, and in the end they will defeat the fascist aggressors. The just people's war is bound to triumph; the unjust imperialist war is bound to go down in defeat.

In 1946 Comrade Mao Tse-tung advanced his celebrated thesis that imperialism and all reactionaries are paper tigers, and he did so after summing up the experience of the revolutionary struggles of the Chinese people and of the people of the world as well as the historical experience of the Anti-Fascist War. He said:

> All reactionaries are paper tigers. In appearance, the reactionaries are terrifying, but in reality they are not so powerful. From a long-term point of view, it is not the reactionaries but the people who are really powerful.[9]

He added:

> Wasn't Hitler once considered very strong? But history proved that he was a paper tiger. So was Mussolini, so was Japanese imperialism. On the contrary, the strength of the Soviet Union and of the people in all countries who loved democracy and freedom proved much greater than had been foreseen.[10]

Sharply criticizing the theory that "weapons decide everything," Comrade Mao Tse-tung pointed out that it was "a mechanical approach to the question of war and a subjective and one-sided view." He said:

> Our view is opposed to this; we see not only weapons but also people. Weapons are an important factor in war, but not the decisive factor; it is people, not things, that are decisive. The contest of strength is not only a contest of military and economic power, but also a contest of human power and morale.[11]

He declared emphatically:

> The atom bomb is a paper tiger which the U.S. reactionaries use to scare people. It looks terrible, but in fact it isn't. Of course, the atom

bomb is a weapon of mass slaughter, but the outcome of a war is decided by the people, not by one or two new types of weapon.[12]

The twenty years since the War have demonstrated the incontrovertible truth of Comrade Mao Tse-tung's theses that imperialism and all reactionaries are paper tigers and that the relationship between man and weapons must be correctly handled, theses that have stood the test of practice. Despite its possession of nuclear weapons, U.S. imperialism was unable to prevent the victory of the Chinese revolution, of Korea's war of resistance against U.S. aggression, of the Cuban revolution or of the revolutionary struggles in many other regions, and it will definitely not be able to prevent the Vietnamese people from achieving victory. The nuclear weapons of the U.S. imperialists may scare the faint-hearted but can never intimidate revolutionary people. However savagely the U.S. imperialists suppress the people's revolutionary struggles, the flames of the people's revolution can never be quenched. Is there not a most convincing proof in the surging national-democratic revolutionary movement in Asia, Africa and Latin America and in the fact that the people's struggle against U.S. imperialism is growing in breadth and depth in all countries?

The Khrushchev revisionists completely ignore this important historical lesson of the Anti-Fascist War. They have lost confidence in the struggle against imperialism, they have never had faith in the great strength of the people, in the ability of the people of all countries to win victory in their revolutionary struggles. They believe one hundred per cent in the theory that "weapons decide everything." All they see is the nuclear weapons in the hands of the U.S. imperialists, and they tremble with fear. They play up the horrors of war and preach the philosophy of survival—"What is the use of principles if one's head is chopped off?"—in order to intimidate the people and to oppose and, indeed, sabotage the people's revolutionary struggles in all countries. They have degenerated into willing propagandists for the U.S. imperialists' policy of nuclear blackmail.

In the fourth place, the history of the Anti-Fascist War shows that, in order to defeat the imperialist aggressors, it is imperative to rely upon the unity of the people's revolutionary forces in all countries, win over to our side all the forces that can be won over, form the broadest possible international united front, and concentrate our blows on the main enemy of the people of the world.

The victory won in the Anti-Fascist War was a victory of the broad international united front against fascism. As far back as June 23, 1941, the day after the outbreak of the Soviet–German war, Comrade Mao Tse-tung clearly pointed out:

> For Communists throughout the world the task now is to mobilize the people of all countries and organize an international united front to fight fascism and defend the Soviet Union, defend China, and defend the freedom and independence of all nations. In the present period, every effort must be concentrated on combating fascist enslavement.[13]

At that time, the German, Italian and Japanese fascists constituted the gravest menace to mankind; they started aggressive wars and formed the centre of world reaction. To oppose fascist aggression and enslavement was the common fighting task of the people of all countries. The people were the basic force combating fascism. It was because all the different peoples supported each other and fought shoulder to shoulder that the Anti-Fascist War was won.

The Soviet Union, which was the only socialist country at the time, was the main force in annihilating the German fascists and played the decisive role in defeating fascism. The Chinese people waged their revolutionary war against Japanese imperialism, for a very long time on their own, and made a most significant contribution to victory in the Anti-Fascist War. Likewise, the people of many countries in Europe, Asia, Africa, Oceania and America made their own contribution to the Anti-Fascist War. The people of the countries occupied by German, Italian and Japanese fascism either persisted in guerrilla warfare and underground struggles at home, or organized themselves into armies abroad which later fought their way back to their own countries. In the latter period of the War, the people in some countries successfully staged armed uprisings and liberated large tracts of their territory, or sent troops to join in the pursuit of the fascist hordes and to support the people's liberation struggle in other countries after their own countries had been freed. In Germany, Italy and Japan, the masses of the people also resisted fascist rule at home in various ways, up to and including armed struggle, and supported the struggle of other peoples suffering from fascist aggression and enslavement. All these struggles contributed to victory in the Anti-Fascist War and each occupies a place of honour in the history of the War. The Khrushchev revisionists, however, try at one stroke to write off the role played by the people of all other countries in the Anti-Fascist War, arrogantly declaring that the Soviet Union was "the only force smashing the German fascist machine." By this they try to promote their great-power chauvinism and demand that all countries which were helped by the Soviet army should obey their orders, submit to their control and bullying, and put up with their exploitation.

The history of the Anti-Fascist War teaches us that the imperialist countries do not form a monolithic bloc. Owing to the uneven development of capitalism, the German, Italian and Japanese fascists struck first at the spheres of influence of Britain, France and the United States. Although in the early stages of the War the British, French and U.S. imperialists first followed the appeasers' policy of conniving at aggression, and then for a time after the outbreak of the Soviet–German war followed the policy of "sitting on top of the mountain to watch the tigers fight," there were irreconcilable contradictions between them and the German, Italian and Japanese fascists. They finally joined the anti-fascist ranks for their own interests.

Obviously, it would have been impossible to win the War without the unity of all the forces that could be united against fascism and without a broad, worldwide united anti-fascist front.

Since the War U.S. imperialism has become the principal enemy of the people of the world. It is now the world's biggest monopoly capitalist power and the chief prop of every reactionary force. The armed interventions and wars of aggression it is launching one after another in different parts of the world are a grave menace to world peace. U.S. imperialism today is taking the same path as that travelled by German, Italian and Japanese fascism over twenty years ago.

U.S. imperialism is indulging in unscrupulous military threats and war provocations against the socialist countries and brazenly suppressing the revolutionary struggles of the oppressed peoples and nations. This demands the formation of a close-knit militant alliance by the socialist countries and all the oppressed peoples and nations against U.S. imperialism and its lackeys.

At the same time, U.S. imperialism is intensifying its control over and bullying of all its allies in the political, economic and military spheres. There are irreconcilable contradictions between the United

States and its allies, who, in their own interests, are likely to take action against U.S. imperialism on one issue or another sooner or later.

It is therefore the common task of the people of the whole world to unite all the forces that can be united, direct the spearhead of their struggle against U.S. imperialism and concentrate their forces on combating the main enemy.

In view of this situation, Comrade Mao Tse-tung has issued a great call for the formation of an international united front against U.S. imperialism and its lackeys. He said:

> The people of the countries in the socialist camp should unite, the people of the countries in Asia, Africa and Latin America should unite, the people of the continents of the world should unite, all peace-loving countries and all countries that are subject to U.S. aggression, control, interference and bullying should unite, and should form the broadest united front to oppose the U.S. imperialist policies of aggression and war and to safeguard world peace.[14]

This international united front is now growing and expanding. Making enemies all over the world, U.S. imperialism is inevitably meeting with resistance everywhere. It is becoming increasingly isolated and is besieged ring on ring by the people of the world.

The Khrushchev revisionists competely ignore this important historical lesson of the Anti-Fascist War. They have betrayed proletarian internationalism, and have been treating enemies as friends and vice versa. Instead of uniting with all possible forces against U.S. imperialism, they are bent on aligning themselves with U.S. imperialism against the people of the world and on realizing U.S.–Soviet world hegemony. Obstinately persisting in their schismatic line, they undermine the unity of the socialist camp and the international communist movement and regard the fraternal countries and Parties which adhere to Marxism–Leninism as their enemies. Despite the U.S. imperialist expansion of the war of aggression in Viet Nam and the acute need for unity against the enemy, they held the Moscow meeting in March, which was a grave step to split the international communist movement.

The successors to Khrushchev are now talking loudly about "unity against the enemy" and "concerted action." This is nothing but a swindle. We would like to ask: Who exactly is the enemy you wish to confront? Is it U.S. imperialism or the revolutionary people of the world? What is the purpose of the concerted action you demand?

Is it to combat U.S. imperialism, or to surrender to it? What is the basis of the unity you demand? Is it Marxism–Leninism, or Khrushchev revisionism?

How can you expect "concerted action" with the Marxist–Leninists and the masses of the people in all countries, who constitute over 90 per cent of the world's population, when you persist in the revisionist line laid down at the 20th and 22nd Congresses and embodied in the Programme of the C.P.S.U., and when you persist in the line of "Soviet–U.S. co-operation for the domination of the world"? Do you want us to join you and work for revisionism and submit to your line of "Soviet–U.S. co-operation for the domination of the world"? To speak frankly, that will never happen.

In short, to assess the history of the Anti-Fascist War correctly and to draw the necessary lessons from it is not merely a matter of assessing history, it is also of profound practical significance. Here the difference between the Khrushchev revisionists and ourselves is in essence a difference over whether or not to oppose imperialism, whether or not to make revolution and whether to have genuine unity or sham unity, and, in the last analysis, it is the difference between loyalty to Marxism–Leninism and its betrayal.

The great Lenin told us that "a struggle against imperialism that is not closely linked up with the struggle against opportunism is an idle phrase, or a fraud."[15] The postwar practice of revolutionary struggle by the people of various countries has proved that one must follow the Marxist–Leninist line if one wants to expand the forces of revolution, promote the revolutionary cause and defend world peace. If, instead, one acts in accordance with the Khrushchev revisionist line, the inevitable result is to weaken the forces of revolution, ruin the revolutionary cause and endanger world peace. We must thoroughly expose the true face of Khrushchev revisionism, eliminate its influence and carry the struggle against it through to the end in order to promote the revolutionary struggles of the oppressed peoples and nations, smash the U.S. imperialist plans for aggression and war and defend world peace, and in order to expand the united front against U.S. imperialism and its lackeys.

Today, the whole world is faced with the grave danger of the extension of the war of aggression in Viet Nam by U.S. imperialism. The Viet Nam question is the focal point in the present worldwide struggle between the revolutionary forces of the people and the forces of counter-revolution, between the forces of peace and the forces of war. The heroic patriotic struggle of the 30 million people of Viet Nam against U.S. aggression is not only a struggle to defend and reunify their fatherland, but also a struggle to safeguard world peace. It is the bounden international duty of all revolutionary forces and all peace-loving countries and people to support and aid the Vietnamese people in their struggle.

More recently, U.S. imperialism has dispatched large numbers of troops to invade the Dominican Republic in its attempt to suppress the struggle of the Dominican people to overthrow the traitorous dictatorial rule in their own country. This constitutes not only a wanton interference in the internal affairs of the Dominican Republic, but also an act of provocation to the people of Latin America and to the people of the whole world who have the sacred right to safeguard their own national independence and win democracy and freedom.

U.S. imperialism is still carrying on intervention and aggression in Laos, Cambodia, south Korea and Japan. In collusion with British imperialism, it has created "Malaysia" and is committing aggression against Indonesia. It is trying to put down the revolutionary movement of the people of the Congo (Leopoldville) by armed force. It is using Israel to menace the Arab countries. It is continuing its disruptive and subversive activities against Cuba. It is fostering West German militarism and attempting to grab West Berlin and subvert the German Democratic Republic. It is also perpetrating many other crimes in other countries in Asia, Africa, Latin America, Oceania and Europe. It is also a bounden international duty of all revolutionary forces and all peace-loving countries and peoples to give firm support to the struggles against U.S. imperialism waged by the people in these countries. If the U.S. aggressors are allowed to do whatever they please and the modern revisionists are allowed to conspire with them and sell out the interests of the peoples, that will only whet the appetite of the U.S. imperialists for aggression and encourage them to spread the flames of war. Conversely, if all revolutionary people and all peace-loving countries and peoples unite and act in a determined struggle against U.S. imperialism, they will be able to smash its plans to extend its war of aggression.

The most pressing task facing the people of the world today is to broaden the united front against U.S. imperialism and its lackeys, unfold an unprecedentedly powerful mass movement on a world scale, and compel the U.S. aggressors to get out of Viet Nam, out of the Dominican Republic, out of Asia, Africa and Latin America, out of Europe and Oceania, out of all the places they have invaded.

The world situation is now fundamentally different from what it was before the Anti-Fascist War.

The revolutionary forces of the people of the world are now stronger than ever before. Whereas there was then only one socialist state, the Soviet Union, there is now a socialist camp consisting of a number of socialist countries. Wide expanses of Asia, Africa and Latin America have ceased to be the rear areas of imperialism and instead have become the frontlines in the struggle against imperialism. Moreover, the working class and the working people in Western Europe, North America and Oceania are experiencing a new awakening.

The Marxist–Leninist ranks are now stronger than ever before. Steeled in the struggle against modern revisionism, the international communist movement has vastly increased its fighting capacity. Long-tested Marxist–Leninist nuclei of leadership have appeared in many Communist Parties. The forces of Marxism–Leninism are developing even within those Communist Parties that are temporarily dominated by revisionism.

International imperialism has become far weaker. U.S. imperialism is having an increasingly hard time. It is sitting on a volcano which rumbles again and again. The contradictions among the imperialists are growing sharper and their camp is in the process of disintegrating.

The true face of the Khrushchev revisionists as accomplices of the imperialists has been more and more clearly exposed. Their revisionist line is already bankrupt. Everywhere the revisionists are just a handful of people. Even these are jostling each other and parting company. So far from being able to save the lives of the imperialists, the revisionists find that their own thrones are tottering.

In the present world situation, the United States is in a much worse strategic position than was Hitler in his day. It is much more difficult for the United States to unleash a world war. At the same time, the forces defending world peace are much stronger than twenty years ago. The possibility of averting a world war has enormously increased. Through their common struggle the revolutionary people and the peace-loving countries and people can frustrate the U.S. imperialist plans for aggression and war. The people's cause of world peace, national liberation, people's democracy and socialism is sure to win still greater victories. If, following in Hitler's footsteps, U.S. imperialism dares to impose a world war on the people, it will inevitably come to the same ignominious end as Hitler.

Comrade Mao Tse-tung pointed out long ago:

> The First World War was followed by the birth of the Soviet Union with a population of 200 million. The Second World War was followed by the emergence of the socialist camp with a combined population of 900 million. If the imperialists insist on launching a third world war, it is certain that several hundred million more will turn to socialism, and then there will not be much room left on earth for the imperialists; it is also likely that the whole structure of imperialism will utterly collapse.[16]

The just cause of the people of the world is bound to triumph! U.S. imperialism is bound to fail!

Marxism–Leninism is bound to triumph! Revisionism is bound to fail!

(Published on May 9, 1965.)

NOTES—APPENDIX FOUR—DOCUMENT #2

[1] Mao Tse-tung, "On Coalition Government," *Selected Works,* Vol. III.

[2] Ibid.

[3] Mao Tse-tung, "Opening Speech at the Third Session of the First National Committee of the Chinese People's Political Consultative Conference," *Renmin Ribao,* October 24, 1951.

[4] Mao Tse-tung, "Revolutionary Forces of the World Unite, Fight Against Imperialist Aggression!", *Selected Works,* Eng. ed., Foreign Languages Press, Peking, 1961, Vol. IV, p. 284.

[5] J. V. Stalin, Speech Delivered at an Election Meeting in the Stalin Election District, Moscow, February 9, 1946.

[6] J. V. Stalin, "The Twenty-fourth Anniversary of the October Revolution," *The Great Patriotic War of the Soviet Union,* Eng. ed., International Publishers, New York, 1945, pp. 33–34.

[7] J. V. Stalin, "May Day, 1944," *The Great Patriotic War of the Soviet Union,* Eng. ed., International Publishers, New York, 1945, p. 125.

[8] Mao Tse-tung, "Cast Away Illusions, Prepare for Struggle," *Selected Works,* Eng. ed., F.L.P., Peking, 1961, Vol. IV.

[9] Mao Tse-tung, "Talk with the American Correspondent Anna Louise Strong," *Selected Works,* Eng. ed., F.L.P., Peking, 1961, Vol. IV, p. 100.

[10] Ibid., pp. 100–101.

[11] Mao Tse-tung, "On Protracted War," *Selected Works,* Vol. II.

[12] Mao Tse-tung, "Talk with the American Correspondent Anna Louise Strong," *Selected Works,* Eng. ed., F.L.P., Peking, 1961, Vol. IV, p. 100.

[13] Mao Tse-tung, "On the International United Front Against Fascism," *Selected Works,* Vol. III.

[14] Mao Tse-tung, *Statement Expressing the Chinese People's Firm Support for the Panamanian People's Just, Patriotic Struggle,* Eng. ed., F.L.P., Peking, 1964, p. 3.

[15] V. I. Lenin, "The War Program of the Proletarian Revolution," *Selected Works,* Eng. ed., F.L.P.H., Moscow, 1946, Vol. I, p. 746.

[16] Mao Tse-tung, *On the Correct Handling of Contradictions Among the People.*

Document # 3

Foreign Ministry Spokesman's Statement

MALINOVSKY IS A LIAR*

May 3, 1966

ACCORDING to a report of the Hungarian Telegraph Agency, U.S.S.R. Minister of National Defence Malinovsky said in a speech in Hungary on April 21 that the aid for the Vietnamese people's struggle could be still more efficient should the Chinese leaders not hamper these efforts, and that as the Soviet Union did not border on the Democratic Republic of Vietnam, its aid for the Vietnamese brothers could only reach them through Chinese territory. In this connection, a spokesman of the Chinese Ministry of Foreign Affairs makes the following statement:

Malinovsky is a liar. China has never hampered the transit of Soviet aid materials to Vietnam. All military aid materials which Vietnam asked for and which the Soviet Union asked China to forward have been transported to Vietnam by China with priority, at high speed and free of charge. From February 1965 when the Soviet Union asked for the sending of its aid materials to Vietnam through China up to the end of 1965, China transported a total of 43,000 odd tons of Soviet military aid supplies to Vietnam. The Vietnamese Government is well aware of this. And so is the Soviet

°*Peking Review* (May 3, 1966) pp. 25–26.

Government. The facts are all there, and nobody can succeed in distorting them.

Both in quantity and quality, the aid the Soviet Union gives to Vietnam is far from commensurate with its strength. It should have been easy for a big power like the Soviet Union to provide Vietnam with several hundred thousand tons of military supplies. But it has only given a few tens of thousands of tons, a deplorably meagre amount. It must be further pointed out that most of the Soviet supplies consisted of old weapons of its own armed forces, which had been replaced and which even included some that were worn-out and of no use at all. True, the Soviet Union has also given Vietnam some weapons of comparatively new types, but even these are already outmoded. As for those of truly good quality, the Soviet Union either does not supply them or is unwilling to supply them in large quantities. This state of affairs is definitely not due to any hindrance on the part of China. How can the blame be laid at the door of China when the Soviet Union is simply unwilling to supply good things in large quantities? Take, for instance, the first quarter of this year. For this period the Soviet Union asked us to earmark a transport capacity of 1,730 wagons. We agreed and readied the wagons. However, the actual Soviet delivery was only 556 wagon-loads. Such was the fact. How can anyone who is not off his head talk about China hampering Soviet aid to Vietnam?

As is well known, in Khrushchev's days the Soviet Union refused to aid Vietnam. The new leaders of the Soviet Union put up the signboard of aiding Vietnam when they took over. Some people think that the leading group of the Soviet Union has really changed, but the change in fact is only in method and tactics. **Both Khrushchev's no aid for Vietnam and the new Soviet leaders' aid for Vietnam are aimed at controlling the Vietnam situation and bringing the Vietnamese people's struggle against U.S. aggression and for national salvation into the orbit of "U.S.–Soviet collaboration."** Therefore, the new leaders of the Soviet Union hastily began to engineer so-called peace talks behind the back of Vietnam to meet the needs of U.S. imperialism, even before the first batch of their promised aid materials arrived in Vietnam last year.

The Soviet leading group knows that to serve U.S. imperialism it must first of all sow discord between China and Vietnam and undermine the unity of the Chinese and Vietnamese peoples against U.S. imperialism. In the past year or more, the Soviet Union has been making use of the question of its aid to Vietnam to attack China. Its aid to Vietnam has been scanty, but the rumours it spread slandering China have been numerous. For a time the method used by the Soviet leading group in serving the United States has indeed become a little more covert owing to the constant exposures by China and by all Marxist–Leninists of the world, but its behind-the-scenes activities have never stopped.

At its 23rd Congress, the leading group of the C.P.S.U. assumed a posture for unity against imperialism, and not a few people unaware of the truth thought that it was sincere. Now, everybody can see that this was mere pretence. In reality, **at the 23rd Congress the leading group of the C.P.S.U. still employed the dual tactics of sham opposition but real capitulation to imperialism, sham revolution but real betrayal, and sham unity but real split.** The Hungarian delegate sang the loudest in the anti-Chinese chorus at the 23rd Congress, and quite logically it was in Hungary that shortly afterwards **Malinovsky, a member of the Soviet leading group, personally divulged the hidden anti-Chinese theme of that Congress.**

As a soldier, Malinovsky ought to know that besides ground and air communications there are sea routes to link various countries in the world. It is utterly groundless to say that aid cannot be rendered in the absence of a common boundary. The Soviet Union has no common boundary with Cuba which lies far away, yet it could ship rocket-nuclear weapons to and back from Cuba. It is not even that far from Vietnam, why can't it ship even conventional weapons there? Again, the Soviet Union has no common boundary with India, yet it could ship large quantities of military materials there by sea to help the Indian reactionaries attack China. Why then can't it ship aid materials by sea to help the Vietnamese people fight the United States? It is sheer nonsense to play on the existence or absence of a common boundary. **The heart of the matter is that the Soviet revisionist leading group has already degenerated into an accomplice of U.S. imperialism. Its so-called aid to Vietnam is a sham. Its real aim is to oppose China, Vietnam and all people persevering in revolution. What it hankers after is "world domination through U.S.-Soviet collaboration."**

Document # 4

EXPOSE THE BIG CONSPIRACY OF "INDUCEMENT TO PEACE TALKS BY A SUSPENSION OF BOMBINGS"*

U.S. IMPERIALISM and the Soviet revisionist leading group have become more unashamedly outspoken in their collusion to market their "peace talks" conspiracy on the Vietnam question, with the current U.N. General Assembly session as the centre of their intrigues.

On September 22, Arthur G. Goldberg, U.S. delegate to the U.N., put forward the United States' so-called "3-point proposal" at the U.N. General Assembly session. Around this time, A. A. Gromyko and N. T. Fedorenko had long talks or lunched together with Lyndon Johnson and Dean Rusk. They professed to each other their belief that the Soviet Union and the United States were "getting closer and closer together." The two parties were fraternizing like real brothers. Under the Soviet and American lead, their followers got busy. The result was a big crop of assorted "peace talks" plans. The British Labour government gave out a so-called "6-point plan"; the Vatican issued a so-called "peace" appeal; U.N. Secretary-General U Thant reiterated his "3-point" plan; and India and Yugoslavia also ran here and there peddling the "peace talks" swindle. Everything points to a new and large-scale "peace offensive" over the Vietnam question by U.S. imperialism and Soviet revisionism.

Peking Review (October 14, 1966) pp. 28–30.

What U.S. imperialism and Soviet revisionism are up to in their "peace offensive" this time can be seen clearly if we only make an analysis of the U.S. "3-point proposal."

The first point in the U.S. proposal is that the United States may "first cease its bombing of north Vietnam" on the condition that the Vietnamese people "take corresponding and timely steps to reduce or bring to an end" their "military activities."

Divested of its wrappings, this point boils down to one word—deception. The only way to restore peace in Vietnam is to immediately withdraw all the U.S. armed forces and its followers' armed forces from Vietnam. It is not a question of temporarily stopping the bombing of the northern part of Vietnam. When Johnson began his massive bombing of north Vietnam in February last year, he aimed at forcing and inducing the Vietnamese people to accept "peace talks." His tactics were to alternately use bombings and a cessation of bombings. The bombing was to "force peace talks" while a cessation was to "induce peace talks." If the "bombing to force peace talks" had no effect, "cessation of bombings to induce peace talks" was tried. The bombing-cessation trick has been played twice in the last year or so. Now the United States is having another try at cessation. People have long seen through these worn-out tactics.

It must be pointed out that while the bombing is blatant war blackmail, in no less sense is its cessation war blackmail. While the United States was handing out its "3-point proposal," the U.S. imperialists were frenziedly rushing more troops to south Vietnam and planning a new "dry season offensive." It was revealed that the Johnson Administration has already made plans to land U.S. troops near the provisional military demarcation line. This means, the U.S. imperialists' intention is: if they can deceive, they will deceive; if not they will go in for fighting in a big way.

The second point of the U.S. proposal is that "the United States stands ready to withdraw its forces as others withdraw theirs" and that it is "willing to agree to a time schedule" for the "withdrawal from south Vietnam of all external forces."

What absurdity, indeed! The only "external forces" in Vietnam are the troops of U.S. imperialism and its accomplices. This aggressor army should have long cleared out of Vietnam; there is no room for bargaining on this point. As long as one U.S. soldier remains on Vietnamese soil, the 31 million Vietnamese people have every right to carry on the anti-U.S. national revolutionary war in any manner they choose. To describe the people's forces of south Vietnam as "external forces" is a vicious slander of the heroic Vietnamese people and a pretext of the American aggressors to try to hang on in Vietnam.

The third point of the U.S. proposal is that "the place of the Viet Cong in the negotiations" will not be "an insurmountable problem."

Many people who do not know the truth of the matter regard this as an American "concession." In truth it is a most dangerous hoax. The United States does not recognize the South Vietnam National Front for Liberation as the sole legal representative of the south Vietnamese people. All the United States has said is that the N.F.L. may have a chair at the conference table laid by the Americans and sit together with the U.S. puppets from Saigon. Here U.S. imperialism is trying to copy the old trick of the triumvirate in Laos, in order to gain what it cannot gain on the battlefield through a so-called coalition government.

It must be pointed out that the seemingly neutral "3-point" plan of U.N. Secretary-General U Thant is in fact a wholly American product. A comparison of U Thant's "3-point" plan with that of the Americans makes things even clearer. The first point in U Thant's plan is "cessation of the bombing of north Vietnam" while the first point in the American proposal is "cease its bombing of north Vietnam." The only point of difference is the United States states more explicitly the conditions for the cessation of bombings while U Thant buries his conditions in his so-called second point on the reduction of "military activities" by both sides. It certainly cannot be said that U Thant is fairer than the United States; he is just as sinister. U Thant's reduction of "military activities" by both sides is a twin version of the American second point on troop withdrawal by both sides. U Thant's third point is "the participation of the National Liberation Front in any peaceful settlement" while the third point in the U.S. proposal says that "the place of the Viet Cong in the negotiations" is not "an insurmountable problem." See, aren't U Thant's "3-point" plan and the U.S. "3-point proposal" exactly the same?

Whether it be the U.S. "3-point proposal," or U Thant's "3-point" plan, or the other assorted "peace talks" propositions, the substance of them all is to use the cessation of bombing north Vietnam as a bait to induce the Vietnamese people to cease their struggle and accept "peace talks" and to provide the U.S. aggressors with the right to hang on in south Vietnam. This of course the heroic Vietnamese people cannot accept. As President Ho Chi Minh pointed out in his Appeal: "Let the United States end its war of aggression in Vietnam, withdraw from this country all U.S. and satellite troops, and peace will return here at once. Vietnam's stand is clear: it is the four points of the Government of the Democratic Republic of Vietnam and the five points of the South Vietnam National Front for Liberation. There is no alternative!"

The criminal purpose of U.S. imperialism and Soviet revisionism and their followers in busily enacting the "peace talks" conspiracy in the United Nations is to exploit the worry among the majority of the member nations over the expansion of the Vietnam war in the service of their "peace talks" swindle. Furthermore, they are attempting to link the Vietnam question with the United Nations to create an established fact for illegal U.N. intervention in the Vietnam question. This big conspiracy must be exposed. The Government of the Democratic Republic of Vietnam and the South Vietnam National Front for Liberation have stated clearly and repeatedly that the United Nations has no right to meddle in the Vietnam question. All countries with a sense of justice should resolutely support the Vietnamese people's just stand and resolutely oppose U.S. imperialism and Soviet revisionism's use of the United Nations to intervene in the Vietnam question.

On the Vietnam question, the issue of right and wrong is very clear. The United States is the aggressor, and Vietnam is the victim of aggression. The U.S. aggression against Vietnam must be roundly condemned, and the U.S. aggressor troops must be withdrawn from Vietnam immediately and completely. On this question of principle, there must absolutely be no compromise. The Afro–Asian countries with their sufferings from imperialist and colonialist aggression still fresh in memory should never compromise. All countries upholding justice should never compromise. It is quite natural for the majority of the countries attending the U.N. General Assembly session to show concern over the serious situation generated by the U.S. aggression against Vietnam. But to prevent this legitimate concern from being exploited by U.S. imperialism and Soviet revisionism, it is necessary to adamantly expose the U.S. and Soviet big conspiracy to use the United Nations to intervene in the Vietnam question. It is also necessary outside the U.N. to strongly condemn in every possible way the heinous crime of U.S. imperialist aggression in Vietnam. There should be unanimous demand that the aggressor troops of the United States and its accomplices must immediately be pulled out of the sacred soil of the Vietnamese people lock, stock and barrel. Without this, appealing for peace without differentiating right from wrong, echoing the U.S. deception of "inducing peace talks by a cessation of bombing" and letting the U.S. intrigue of using the U.N. prevail, will only end in rendering service to the U.S. and the Soviet revisionist "peace talks" conspiracy and in encouraging the United States to widen still further its aggressive war in Vietnam and pose a greater menace to the independence of the people of all countries and world peace.

Comrade Mao Tse-tung pointed out the impossibility of persuading the imperialists "to show kindness of heart and turn from their evil ways. The only course is to organize forces and struggle against them." Today, the 31 million Vietnamese people, in response to President Ho Chi Minh's Appeal, are organizing their own forces to wage a heroic struggle against the U.S. aggressors. The great Vietnamese people are invincible. U.S. imperialism is doomed to final defeat no matter what "peace talks" trickery it may resort to or what military adventure it may plot.

("Renmin Ribao" editorial, October 10.)

Document # 5

REFUTATION OF THE NEW LEADERS OF THE CPSU
ON "UNITED ACTION"

by the Editorial Departments of *Jen-min Jih-pao* and *Hung Ch'i*
(November 11, 1965)

Excerpt [*Peking Review*, Vol. VIII, No. 46 (November 12, 1965),
pp. 10–21, at pp. 12–21]°

The Khrushchev Revisionists Have Undermined
the Common Basis of Unity

The essence of the Khrushchev revisionist theory and line, which
the new leaders of the CPSU are persisting in and developing further,
is to protect imperialist rule in the capitalist world and restore
capitalism in the socialist world.

Between the Marxist–Leninists and the Khrushchev revisionists
there is a difference of fundamental line, a major difference between
what is right and what is wrong. In the circumstances, how can there
be "a common ideology" and "a common programme" between the
Marxist–Leninists and the Khrushchev revisionists? How can there
be a common basis for unity? In the circumstances, the relation between the Khrushchev revisionists and ourselves is certainly not one

°As quoted in *Sino–Soviet Relations, 1964–1965*, William E. Griffith (Cambridge, Massachusetts: Massachusetts Institute of Technology Press, 1967), pp. 455–470.

in which "what binds us together is much stronger than what divides us," as alleged by the new leaders of the CPSU; on all the fundamental issues of the present epoch the relation is one of sharp opposition; there are things that divide us and nothing that unites us, things that are antagonistic and nothing that is common.

Since there is such a difference of fundamental line, the achievement of unity requires either that we discard Marxism–Leninism and follow their revisionism, or that they renounce revisionism and return to the path of Marxism–Leninism. These are the only alternatives. It is impermissible and indeed utterly wrong if we take an equivocal or vague position on such a sharp question.

Are we expected to follow the new leaders of the CPSU in order to achieve unity under their revisionist programme? Wouldn't that mean that we must join them in betraying Marxism–Leninism, in putting down the people's revolutions in various countries and in acting as accomplices of the imperialists? It goes without saying that we will never do so.

Are we expected to look on and remain completely silent without criticizing, exposing and opposing the new leaders of the CPSU, while they are betraying all the fundamental principles of Marxism–Leninism, striving for Soviet–U.S. collaboration to dominate the world and opposing the people's revolutions in various countries? Wouldn't that mean that we must also abandon Marxism–Leninism, act as their ally in opposing the people's revolutions and become the accomplice of imperialism? It goes without saying that we will never do that either.

If the new leaders of the CPSU really want unity with the Marxist–Leninists, they must change their revisionist line and honestly admit their mistakes. They must publicly and solemnly admit before the Communists and the people of the world that their Khrushchev revisionism, great-power chauvinism and splittism are wrong, publicly admit that the revisionist line and programme decided upon at the 20th and the 22nd Congresses of the CPSU are wrong, and publicly guarantee not to repeat the errors of Khrushchev revisionism. Is it possible that they will do all this?

The antagonism between Marxism–Leninism and Khrushchev revisionism is a class antagonism between the proletariat and the bourgeoisie; it is the antagonism between the socialist and the capitalist roads and between the line of opposing imperialism and that of surrendering to it. It is an irreconcilable antagonism.

As Lenin said, "Unity is a great thing and a great slogan. But what the workers' cause needs is the *unity of Marxists,* not unity between Marxists, and opponents and distorters of Marxism." [13]

United Action Is Impossible with Those Who Transpose Enemies and Friends

The new leaders of the CPSU argue that even if there are differences of theory and line, these can be put aside and that "united action" should be taken and "unity against the enemy" achieved in practical struggle against imperialism.

The sharpest difference of theory and line between Marxism–Leninism and Khrushchev revisionism concerns precisely the question of handling our relations with enemies and friends, in other words, the question of whether to oppose or unite with imperialism, and above all the question of whether to oppose or unite with U.S. imperialism. This difference is decisive for all the most important practical actions in the international class struggle. How can it possibly be put aside in favour of an unprincipled unity that does not distinguish between enemies and friends?

The reactionary nature of Khrushchev revisionism is expressed in concentrated form in the line of Soviet–U.S. collaboration for the domination of the world. The Khrushchev clique completely transposed enemies and friends; it regarded U.S. imperialism, the arch enemy of the people of the world, as its closest friend, and the Marxist–Leninists of the world, including those of the Soviet Union, as its principal enemy.

It was precisely on this question that Khrushchev revealed himself as a renegade. It was on this question that the Marxist–Leninists of the whole world waged the sharpest struggle against the Khrushchev revisionists. And it was on this question that the Khrushchev revisionists were spurned by the revolutionary people of the world.

How have the new leaders of the CPSU acted on this question? Have they changed the line of Soviet–U.S. collaboration for world domination? Have they stopped transposing enemies and friends? Have they changed from being a force allied with U.S. imperialism to one opposing it?

The facts show they have not.

Let us consider the facts:

ONE. Immediately after taking office, the new leaders of the

CPSU extolled Johnson as "sensible" and "moderate." They have continued to proclaim that the Soviet Union and the United States are two super-powers on which the fate of the world depends, that "there are sufficiently broad areas for co-operation" between them, and that "there are still many unutilized potentialities." [14] Even after the rabid expansion by U.S. imperialism of its war of aggression in Viet Nam, they have kept on stressing their desire for the "development and improvement of relations with the United States of America." At times they find it necessary to talk about a tendency towards a "freeze" in Soviet–U.S. relations, but behind the scenes they are stepping up their secret diplomacy and their deals with the United States.

TWO. The signing of the partial nuclear test ban treaty by the Soviet Union, the United States and Britain was an important landmark in Khrushchev's alliance with the United States against China. Not only have the new leaders of the CPSU accepted this legacy, but with this treaty as a basis they are actively plotting new deals with the United States for the "prevention of nuclear proliferation" and similar so-called "disarmament" measures in an effort to maintain the monopoly of the two nuclear overlords, the Soviet Union and the United States, against China and all other independent countries.

THREE. U.S. imperialism has been using the United Nations as a tool for opposing the revolutions of the people of the world. Catering to U.S. imperialism, Khrushchev used the United Nations as a stock exchange for the domination of the world by two great powers, the Soviet Union and the United States. The new leaders of the CPSU have continued this reactionary policy. They have again brought up Khrushchev's proposal for a standing U.N. armed force. They voted in the United Nations for a "ceasefire" and for the realization of "national reconciliation" in the Congo (L), and they also voted for the "ceasefire" in the Dominican Republic. Wherever the people rise up in armed struggle against U.S. imperialism or win victories in such struggle, and wherever U.S. imperialism suffers defeats and finds itself in a predicament, the new leaders of the CPSU hurriedly come forward to help it out. Together with the U.S. imperialists, they are using the United Nations to attack, weaken and divide the forces opposing imperialism, colonialism and neo-colonialism, and to save, strengthen and extend U.S. imperialist positions. They serve as a fire-brigade for U.S. imperialism trying to stamp out the flames of revolution.

On April 7 this year, together with his proposal for "unconditional discussions" on the question of Viet Nam, Johnson publicized the scheme for "the international development of Southeast Asia" in order to undermine the struggle against U.S. imperialism waged by the people of Viet Nam and the other Southeast Asian countries and to step up economic infiltration, and he expressed the hope that the Soviet Union would join in. The United States regards the establishment of the "Asian Development Bank" as a means of putting this scheme into practice. In response to Johnson's call, the new leaders of the CPSU went so far as to send a delegation to Bangkok in October to sit together with delegations from the United States, Japan, and such puppet cliques as the Chiang Kai-shek gang, south Korea and "Malaysia" and take an active part in preparing for the establishment of the "Asian Development Bank." Such is the ardour of the new leaders of the CPSU for united action with U.S. imperialism.

FOUR. The new leaders of the CPSU have taken over and expanded the enterprises of the firm of Kennedy, Nehru and Khrushchev which Khrushchev worked hard to establish. They have carried further their alliance against China with the Indian reactionaries who are controlled by the U.S. imperialists. During Shastri's visit to the Soviet Union, they granted India aid to the tune of U.S. $900 million in one go, which is more than all the loans Khrushchev extended to India in nine years. They have speeded up their plans for military aid to India and are working hand in glove with the United States to help India's arms expansion, so that the Indian reactionaries are able to use Soviet-made weapons against China and other neighbouring countries.

Recently, during India's armed aggression against Pakistan and also in connection with the Sino–Indian boundary question, the new leaders of the CPSU revealed in all its ugliness their support of the aggressor and their alliance with the United States and India against China. The Soviet Union and the United States joined in an anti-China chorus both inside and outside the United Nations. In September 1965, in statements on the armed conflict between India and Pakistan, TASS attacked China by insinuation, and *Pravda* even openly sided with India against China on the Sino–Indian boundary question. People will recall that it was precisely with a TASS statement on the Sino–Indian boundary question that Khrushchev started his public attacks on China in September 1959. But his attacks pale into insignificance in comparison with those of the present leaders of the CPSU. They have discarded even the small fig-leaf Khrushchev used in order to feign neutrality. Small wonder that the U.S. imperialists are gleefully hailing a "new era" in U.S.–Soviet co-operation.

The new leaders of the CPSU are able to deceive people because they sometimes make a few verbal attacks on U.S. imperialism. Why do they have to do this? The answer is that this meets the need of the U.S. imperialists as well as the revisionists themselves. The Khrushchev revisionists have to give the appearance of opposing the United States in order to render effective help to U.S. imperialism, hoodwink the masses and sabotage revolution. Otherwise, they could not play this deceptive role, and that would not be to the advantage of U.S. imperialism. Minor attacks in words but major help in deeds— such is the way the new leaders of the CPSU serve U.S. imperialism.

Some people ask, why is it that the Marxist–Leninists and the revolutionary people cannot take united action with the new leaders of the CPSU, yet can unite with personages from the upper strata in the nationalist countries, and strive for united action with them in the anti-imperialist struggle, and can even exploit the contradictions among the imperialist countries in the struggle against the United States?

The reason is that in the contemporary world opposition to or alliance with U.S. imperialism constitutes the hallmark for deciding whether or not a political force can be included in the united front against the United States.

In Asia, Africa and Latin America, with the exception of the lackeys of imperialism, personages from the upper strata in many nationalist countries desire in varying degrees to oppose imperialism, colonialism and neo-colonialism headed by the United States. We should co-operate with them in the anti-imperialist struggle.

In the imperialist countries which are in sharp contradiction with the United States, some monopoly capitalists follow the U.S. imperialists, but there are also others who desire in varying degrees to oppose the United States. In the struggle against the United States, the people of the world can take united action with the latter on some questions and to a certain degree.

The crux of the matter is that, so far from opposing U.S. imperialism, the new leaders of the CPSU are allying themselves and collaborating with it to dominate the world. They have thus set themselves in opposition to the united front against U.S. imperialism. If they really opposed U.S. imperialism and did so by actual deeds we would readily take united action with them. But their so-called opposition to U.S. imperialism is only verbal and not genuine. We must tell them the truth: So long as their line of Soviet–U.S. collaboration against world revolution remains unchanged, and so long as they do not abandon their alliance with U.S. imperialism and reaction, we absolutely refuse tc take any "united action" with them. We absolutely refuse to serve as ι. pawn in their secret diplomacy with U.S. imperialism or help them cover up their assistance to U.S. imperialism in suppressing the peoples' revolution in various countries.

The New Leaders of the CPSU Are Taking United Action with the United States on the Question of Viet Nam

The new leaders of the CPSU never weary of saying that, however serious the differences between them, Communists must take "united action" on the question of Viet Nam at this urgent juncture in the Vietnamese people's struggle against the United States.

Since the new leaders of the CPSU have destroyed the basis of international proletarian unity, and since they transpose enemies and friends and persist in the line of Soviet–U.S. collaboration for world domination, is it still possible for the Marxist–Leninist parties to take united action with them on the question of Viet Nam?

At a time when the U.S. imperialists are committing rabid aggression against Viet Nam, all Communist Parties and socialist countries should as a matter of course take a unanimous stand and firmly support the Vietnamese people's just struggle to smash this aggression. The point is that the stand taken by the revisionist leadership of the CPSU on the question of Viet Nam is inseparable from their revisionist programme and line, and is contrary to the principled stand required of a Marxist–Leninist party.

When Khrushchev was in power, the revisionist leadership of the CPSU openly sided with U.S. imperialism and opposed and undermined the revolutionary struggle of the Vietnamese people against U.S. aggression. They alleged that "any small 'local war' might spark off the conflagration of a world war." [15] Using this absurd argument to frighten and intimidate all peoples engaged in revolutionary armed struggle, they openly refused to support and aid the Vietnamese people in their anti-U.S. struggle. When the struggles of the Vietnamese and the Laotian peoples against U.S.

imperialism grew acute, their policy on the question of Indo-China was one of "disengagement." In July 1964, they indicated the desire of the Soviet Government to resign from its post as one of the two co-chairmen of the Geneva conference. Soon afterwards, when the U.S. imperialists engineered the Bac Bo Gulf incident, Khrushchev went so far as to concoct the slander that the incident was provoked by China.

The situation in Viet Nam developed directly contrary to the wishes of the Khrushchev revisionists. The Vietnamese people won victory after victory in their revolutionary anti-U.S. struggle, while the U.S. aggressors grew hard pressed. The new leaders of the CPSU came to realize that it was no longer advisable to copy Khrushchev's policy of "disengagement" in its totality. So they switched to the policy of involvement, that is, of getting their hand in.

The policy of involvement and the policy of disengagement are essentially the same. Both are products of Khrushchev revisionism and both are designed to meet the needs of U.S. imperialism.

The U.S. imperialists urgently need to extinguish the roaring flames of the Vietnamese people's revolution. And so do the Khrushchev revisionists because they want to carry out their line of Soviet–U.S. collaboration for world domination. When Khrushchev was following the policy of "disengagement," he was acting in close co-ordination with John F. Kennedy. And now that the new leaders of the CPSU are following the policy of involvement, they are similarly acting in tacit agreement and close collaboration with Lyndon B. Johnson.

Please consider the following facts:

In January 1965 the U.S. imperialists asked the Soviet Government to use its influence to have the Government of the Democratic Republic of Viet Nam accept two conditions: (1) stop supporting south Viet Nam, and first of all stop supplying it with guns; and (2) stop the attacks on cities in south Viet Nam. Faithfully obeying the orders of the U.S. imperialists, the new leaders of the CPSU officially transmitted to the Democratic Republic of Viet Nam these preposterous demands, which were aimed at forcing the Vietnamese people into unconditional surrender.

The new leaders of the CPSU have been busy running errands for the U.S. aggressors, who are anxious to find a way out of their predicament in Viet Nam. When Kosygin, Chairman of the Council of Ministers of the USSR, passed through Peking on his visit to Viet Nam in February 1965 and exchanged views with Chinese leaders, he stressed the need to help the United States "find a way out of Viet Nam." This was firmly rebutted by the Chinese leaders. We expressed the hope that the new leaders of the CPSU would support the struggle of the Vietnamese people and not make a deal with the United States on the question of Viet Nam. Kosygin expressed agreement with our views and stated that they would "not bargain with others on this issue." However, the new leaders of the CPSU soon went back on their promise.

Johnson wanted to play his fraudulent game of "unconditional discussions." So the new leaders of the CPSU put forward the idea of "unconditional negotiations." On February 16 this year, the day after Kosygin's return to Moscow, the Soviet Government officially put before Viet Nam and China a proposal to convene a new international conference on Indo-China without prior conditions, which in fact was advocacy of "unconditional negotiations" on the Viet Nam question. On February 23, disregarding the stand which the Vietnamese Government had taken against this proposal and without waiting for a reply from China, the new leaders of the CPSU discussed the question of calling the above-mentioned international conference with the President of France through the Soviet Ambassador to France.

Johnson's fraud of "unconditional discussions" met with a stern rebuff from the Government of the Democratic Republic of Viet Nam. The new leaders of the CPSU then began publicly to insinuate that negotiations could be held if only the United States stopped its bombing of north Niet Nam. They engaged in vigorous activities in the international field with a view to putting this project into effect. In communications to certain fraternal Parties, they said explicitly that they favoured negotiations with the United States on condition it stopped bombing north Viet Nam. They also said that ways and means should be sought to settle the Viet Nam question through negotiations. And sure enough, not long afterwards Johnson came out with the manœuvre of "the temporary suspension of bombing."

After these plots of "unconditional negotiations" and of "stopping the bombing and holding negotiations" were foiled, the new leaders of the CPSU began to collaborate with the Indian reactionaries and the Tito clique—both lackeys of U.S. imperialism—as brokers on the question of Viet Nam. In their prescription for this question there was only mention of the cessation of U.S. bombing of north Viet

Nam, only abstract talk about the implementation of the Geneva agreements but no mention of the fact that the crucial point in the implementation of these agreements is the complete withdrawal of the U.S. aggressor troops from Viet Nam. In addition, the new leaders of the CPSU have been engaged in secret diplomatic activities. In a nutshell, their purpose is to help the United States to bring about "peace talks" by deception, "peace talks" which could go on indefinitely and also allow the United States to hang on in south Viet Nam indefinitely.

To curry favour with U.S. imperialism, the new leaders of the CPSU went to the length of brutally suppressing demonstrations in the Soviet Union opposing U.S. imperialism and supporting Viet Nam which were held by students from Viet Nam, China and other Asian, African and Latin American countries.

Particularly noteworthy is the fact that last April the new leaders of the CPSU let Khrushchev emerge from limbo to talk with Western correspondents. In that interview, he advocated "peaceful co-existence" and attacked the Vietnamese people's struggle against U.S. aggression, alleging that "trouble starts with small things like Viet Nam and ends with disaster." [16] This was not accidental. It shows that, like Khrushchev, the new leaders of the CPSU are afraid that the so-called "minor trouble," that is, the question of Viet Nam, may spoil their fond dreams of Soviet–U.S. collaboration.

The new leaders of the CPSU are doing exactly what Khrushchev did before them, namely, pulling the Viet Nam question into the orbit of Soviet–U.S. collaboration. Since they are co-operating so closely with the U.S. imperialists in united action, it is of course impossible for Marxist–Leninists to join in and take "united action" with them.

At bottom, the new leaders of the CPSU are clamouring for "united action" on the Viet Nam question because this slogan is highly deceptive and is apt to create the illusion that it is still possible to have "unity against U.S. imperialism" with the new leaders of the CPSU who are intent on Soviet–U.S. collaboration for world domination. They do so in order to worm their way into the anti-U.S. front and carry out their policy of involvement in the service of U.S. imperialism.

Look at the trick of "aid" to Viet Nam the new leaders of the CPSU are playing and you will understand the real nature of their policy of involvement more clearly.

We have invariably held that it is the bounden proletarian-internationalist duty of all countries in the socialist camp to aid the fraternal Vietnamese people. The Vietnamese people who are standing in the forefront of the struggle against U.S. imperialism have every right and reason to demand and receive aid from every socialist country. China is helping the Vietnamese people to the best of her ability. We have stated on many occasions that if the Soviet Union genuinely wants to help the Vietnamese people in their struggle against U.S. aggression, the greater and more practical the aid the better. But what have the new leaders of the CPSU done? Whether in quantity or quality, their aid to Viet Nam is far from commensurate with the strength of the Soviet Union. They have ulterior motives in giving a certain amount of aid—they are trying to hoodwink the people at home and abroad, to keep the situation in Viet Nam under their control, to gain a say on the Viet Nam question and to strike a bargain with U.S. imperialism on it.

The U.S. imperialists appreciate the trick being played by the new leaders of the CPSU. They know full well that it is to their advantage for the new leaders of the CPSU to get involved in the Viet Nam question. Far from objecting to "aid" in Viet Nam from the new leaders of the CPSU, they welcome it. The U.S. authorities have made it clear that Soviet involvement in the Viet Nam question is preferable to Soviet non-involvement. It has been pointed out in a U.S. magazine that "eventually, an arrangement might be contrived involving the stationing of Soviet troops in north Viet Nam . . . while American troops remain in south Viet Nam," and that "one of the paradoxical advantages of more direct Soviet military involvement would be the establishment of a direct American–Soviet bargaining relationship in this area."[17] In fact, the new leaders of the CPSU have disclosed the details of their so-called "aid" to Viet Nam to the Americans through various channels. On this matter, too, they are taking united action with the U.S. imperialists.

Furthermore, the new leaders of the CPSU have been using their "aid" to Viet Nam as a pretext for wantonly vilifying China, and have been assiduously spreading the lie that "China obstructed the transit of Soviet military equipment for Viet Nam." The truth is that we have always honoured our agreements and done our utmost speedily to transport to Viet Nam all military *matériel* in transit which was furnished by the Soviet Union with the concurrence of the Vietnamese comrades. By these fabrications and slanders, the new leaders of the CPSU have supplied further proof that they stop at nothing in order to ally themselves with the United States against China.

Marxist–Leninists must penetrate the appearance of things to get at their essence. Having carefully observed the actions of the new leaders of the CPSU on the question of Viet Nam over the past year, we can only reach the following conclusion: In calling so vehemently for "united action" on the Viet Nam question and trying by every means to bring about a summit conference of the Soviet Union, Viet Nam and China and an international meeting of the socialist countries and the fraternal Parties, the new leaders of the CPSU have no other purpose in mind than to deceive the world, to tie the fraternal countries to the chariot of Soviet–U.S. collaboration for world domination, to use the question of Viet Nam as an important counter in their bargaining with the United States, and to isolate and attack the Chinese Communist Party and all the other fraternal Parties which uphold Marxism–Leninism.

Things could not be clearer. If we were to take united action on the question of Viet Nam with the new leaders of the CPSU who are pursuing the Khrushchev revisionist line, wouldn't we be helping them to deceive the people of the world? Wouldn't we be helping them to bring the question of Viet Nam within the orbit of Soviet–U.S. collaboration? Wouldn't we be joining them in betraying the revolutionary cause of the Vietnamese people? Wouldn't we be joining them in attacking the Chinese Communist Party and all the other Marxist–Leninist parties? Wouldn't we be joining them in serving as accomplices of U.S. imperialism? Of course, we shall do nothing of the sort.

"United Action," So Called, Is a Means of Promoting Splittism

The clamour raised by the new leaders of the CPSU for "united action" is an attempt both to conceal and to carry on their great-power chauvinism and splittism under the cover of hypocritical words. They claim to have "made a number of major moves" to promote unity and improve the relations between fraternal Parties and Soviet–Chinese relations. Let us look at the steps they have actually taken.

The March Moscow meeting which will remain for ever infamous was convened by the new leaders of the CPSU under the slogan of "united action." Khrushchev revisionism and splittism had in effect divided the international communist movement, and the March meeting, which the new leaders of the CPSU called regardless of all consequences, was an extremely grave step to bring about an open split. Since that meeting, they have taken a number of other steps in continuation of this divisive line.

The new leaders of the CPSU have condi ted a feverish campaign against the Chinese Communist Party throughout their Party and among the entire Soviet People. They have organized meetings in offices, schools, factories and villages to hear anti-Chinese speeches, wantonly attacking and vilifying China. Some of these speeches were made in the presence of Chinese comrades. They have been busy sending emissaries to many countries for the sole purpose of engaging in anti-Chinese activity and of spreading all sorts of anti-Chinese slanders. In international organizations and international activities they stop at nothing in pushing their anti-Chinese schemes.

The new leaders of the CPSU are continuing Khrushchev's anti-Albanian policy. Although in Japan they have met with serious set-backs in their criminal effort to support Yoshio Shiga and other renegades from the Japanese Communist Party in collusion with the U.S. imperialists and the Japanese reactionaries, they remain unreconciled and are continuing their counter-revolutionary sabotage and subversion against the Japanese Communist Party. They are also continuing their attacks on the Indonesian Communist Party, the Communist Party of New Zealand and other fraternal Parties which uphold Marxism–Leninism, and are carrying on various kinds of sabotage and subversion against them.

While continuing the practice of subjecting other Communist Parties and socialist countries to pressure, sabotage and subversion, the new leaders of the CPSU are also employing the more insidious stratagems of trying to woo them, buy them over, deceive them and sow dissension among them. They take the Chinese Communist Party, which firmly opposes Khrushchev revisionism, as the main target of their concentrated attacks, and they are trying to isolate it.

In the international mass organizations, the new leaders of the CPSU, using the slogan of "united action," continue to push their capitulationist line of not opposing the United States and not supporting revolution and their work of splitting anti-imperialist unity. They repeat Khrushchev's despicable stock tricks at the meetings of these international organizations, rely on behind-the-scene manipulation as well as open trouble-making and even resort to such ludicrous tactics as banging tables and stamping their feet.

In the name of "united action" the revisionist leadership of the CPSU is vainly trying to recover its position as the "father party," so that it may continue to wield the baton and compel the other Communist Parties and socialist countries to do this today and that tomorrow. Actually, however, its former power and prestige are gone beyond recall. Today, the new leaders of the CPSU and their followers are drawn together by self-interest, each seeking his own ends. The baton of the new leaders is less and less effective.

Facts have shown that if the Communists of a particular country accept the hodge-podge of revisionism, great-power chauvinism and splittism of the leaders of the CPSU, the country's revolutionary cause is impaired and undermined, its Communist Party becomes corrupted, goes downhill and degenerates, and both the country and Party find themselves beset with difficulties and at the mercy of others. On the other hand, those who firmly resist and oppose this hodge-podge find themselves in a quite different and much better position. This is as true today as it was before.

One of the purposes of the new leaders of the CPSU in advocating "united action" is to stop the open polemics. They want to gag the Marxist–Leninists and prevent the latter from exposing and criticizing them, so as to be free to carry out Khrushchev revisionism.

How can such a thing be possible? The present great debate has most vividly and clearly revealed what is decadent and dying and what represents the direction of future development and victory in the international communist movement. Khrushchev revisionism has been refuted down to the last point, and this poisonous weed has been converted into good fertilizer on the fields of world revolution. Truth becomes clearer through debate; the more the polemics, the higher the level of revolutionary consciousness and the greater the degree of revolutionary vigour. We shall certainly carry the debate to the finish and draw a clear line between what is right and what is wrong on the major problems. Failure to do so would be extremely harmful to the revolutionary cause of the people of the world and to the cause of opposing imperialism and defending world peace.

Another purpose of the new leaders of the CPSU in advocating "united action" is to stop what they call "factional activities" by the Marxist–Leninist parties. They want to strangle the Marxist–Leninist forces which are fighting to rebuild revolutionary proletarian parties or establish new ones, and to prevent the Chinese Communist Party and other Marxist–Leninist parties from supporting these new-born revolutionary forces.

In many countries, the Marxist–Leninists have broken with the revisionist cliques and either rebuilt Marxist–Leninist parties and organizations or founded new ones. This is the inevitable outcome of the practice of revisionism, great-power chauvinism and splittism by the leaders of the CPSU; it is the inevitable outcome of the struggle between the Marxist–Leninists and the revisionists in those countries and of the regrouping of the revolutionary forces under conditions of deepening class struggle both internationally and domestically.

Bowing to the baton of Khrushchev revisionism the leading groups in the Communist Parties of those countries have forbidden their members to do what the imperialists and reactionaries fear most, and only allowed them to do what is to the liking of the imperialists and reactionaries or is at least tolerable to them. Whoever acts differently is attacked, disciplined or expelled. Such being the case, the staunch Marxist–Leninists in those Parties are left with no alternative but to break with the revisionist leading groups, and the founding and growth of genuine revolutionary Marxist–Leninist parties and organizations become inevitable.

Revolution, the fight against imperialism and the fight against revisionism all have right on their side. Beyond all doubt, it is perfectly right to discard these decaying old revisionist groups and build new revolutionary parties.

We resolutely support all the forces in the world that persevere in Marxism–Leninism and revolution. It is our lofty proletarian-internationalist duty to strengthen our united action with all the Marxist–Leninist forces in the world.

"United Action," So Called, Is a Slogan to Deceive the Soviet People

The new leaders of the CPSU claim that the socialist countries have "a socio-economic system of the same type" and share the "common goal of building socialism and communism." This is one more reason they cite in their clamour for "united action."

This is throwing dust in people's eyes. Following in Khrushchev's footsteps, the new leaders of the CPSU are bringing about the further degeneration of the Soviet Union towards capitalism in the name of realizing "communism." Like Khrushchev, they use the slogan of "the state of the whole people" to abolish the dictatorship of the proletariat in the Soviet Union, thus making the Soviet state degenerate into an instrument for the rule of the privileged bourgeois stratum over the Soviet people. Like Khrushchev, they use the slogan of "the party of the entire people" to alter the proletarian character of the Communist Party of the Soviet Union and turn it into a party serving the interests of the privileged bourgeois stratum.

In their appraisal of Stalin, the new leaders of the CPSU pretend to be somewhat different from Khrushchev. But this is only an attempt to allay the resentment of the broad masses of the people and Party members in the Soviet Union. Far from criticizing Khrushchev's mistake in completely negating Stalin, they have followed him in describing the period of Stalin's leadership as "the period of the personality cult." They have sponsored the publication of numerous articles and literary and other works which keep on besmirching all aspects of the great Marxist–Leninist Stalin, the dictatorship of the proletariat and the socialist system.

Taking advantage of the state power they wield, the new leaders of the CPSU have centred their efforts on undermining the economic base of socialism, socialist ownership by the whole people and socialist collective ownership, and on setting up and developing a new system of exploitation and fostering and supporting the new bourgeoisie, thus accelerating the restoration of capitalism.

The report on the problems of industry by Kosygin, Chairman of the Council of Ministers of the USSR, at the recent plenary session of the Central Committee of the CPSU and the resolution which it adopted marked a big step along the road of the restoration of capitalism in the Soviet economy.

Through a Party resolution and government decrees, the new leaders of the CPSU have confirmed the experiments initiated in the Khrushchev period as a result of which socialist enterprises owned by the whole people degenerate into enterprises of a capitalist nature, and they have spread these experiments throughout the country. The key feature of the "new system" of industrial management they have instituted is to enforce the capitalist principle of profit and to make profit-seeking the basic motive force of production in the enterprises through the "enhancement of economic incentives." In the name of widening the enterprises' right to self-management, they have scrapped a series of important quotas formerly set by the state for the enterprises in accordance with the plan, substituting capitalist free competition for socialist planned economy. They have vested in the managers the power to hire and fire workers, fix the level of wages and bonuses and freely dispose of large funds, thus turning them into virtual masters of the enterprises, who are able to bully and oppress the workers and usurp the fruits of their labour at will. In reality, this means restoring capitalism, replacing socialist ownership by the whole people with ownership by the privileged bourgeois stratum, and converting the socialist enterprises in the Soviet Union step by step into capitalist enterprises of a special type. This is by no means a "new creation"; it has been copied and developed from the old "experience" of the Tito clique in restoring capitalism in Yugoslavia.

It is elementary Marxism–Leninism that the system of management comes within the sphere of the relations of production and is an expression of the system of ownership. Under the guise of reforming the system of management, the new leaders of the CPSU have undermined the very foundation of the system of ownership by the whole people. This is exactly what the Tito clique of Yugoslavia did. Having a guilty conscience, the new leaders of the CPSU cry out that those who talk about the "bourgeois transformation" of the Soviet economy are "bourgeois ideologists" and "our enemies." [18] This is what the Tito clique said too. Such protestations are like the sign, "There is no silver buried here," put up by the man in the legend over the place where he hid his money.

In the countryside, too, the new leaders of the CPSU are accelerating the growth of capitalism, developing the private economy, enlarging the private plots, increasing the number of privately raised cattle, expanding the free market and encouraging free trading. They are using a variety of economic and administrative measures to encourage and foster the growth of a new kulak economy, sabotaging and disintegrating all aspects of the socialist collective economy.

Khrushchev wrought alarming havoc in Soviet agriculture. After taking office, the new leaders of the CPSU boasted that they had worked out "a scientifically based programme for an immediate and sharp rise in agricultural production." [19] But a year later, Soviet agriculture still remains in a mess, creating untold difficulties in the lives of the Soviet people. The new leaders of the CPSU are now laying the entire blame on the fallen Khrushchev. In fact, these serious troubles are precisely the outcome of their own intensified application of Khrushchev revisionism.

Facts show that the replacement of Khrushchev by these new leaders has been merely a change of personalities in the revisionist dynasty—just as all reactionary ruling classes have to change horses in order to maintain their rule. Although Khrushchev himself has fallen, the leading group of the CPSU is still the same old Khrushchev crowd; organizationally, it remains basically unchanged, and whether ideologically, politically, theoretically or in the realm of policy, theirs is still the same old Khrushchev revisionist stuff.

As Lenin pointed out, "opportunism is no chance occurrence, sin, slip, or treachery on the part of individuals, but a social product of an entire period of history."[20] It is inevitable that Khrushchev revisionism will exist as long as the social basis and the class roots which gave birth to it remain and as long as the privileged bourgeois stratum exists.

Because they are the political representatives of the privileged bourgeois stratum in the Soviet Union, just as Khrushchev was, the new leaders of the CPSU pursue domestic and foreign policies which are not proletarian but bourgeois, not socialist but capitalist. Like Khrushchev, they are in a position of antagonism to the Soviet people, who constitute more than 90 per cent of the Soviet population, and they are encountering ever stronger dissatisfaction and opposition on the part of the Soviet people.

When the new leaders of the CPSU loudly assert that the socialist countries have a "socio-economic system of the same type," they do so with the aim of covering up their restoration of capitalism in the Soviet Union, of preventing us from unmasking them, and of setting the Soviet people against China.

In our view, when a revisionist clique emerges and a capitalist come-back occurs in a socialist country, all the Marxist–Leninists in the world are duty-bound to expose and struggle against these things; this is the only correct and principled stand. The only way to serve the fundamental interests of the great Soviet people and to give them genuine support is resolutely to expose the fact that the revisionist leadership of the CPSU is restoring capitalism in the USSR.

If we should cease exposing and combating the domestic and external revisionist policies of the new leaders of the CPSU, if we should abandon our principled stand and take so-called "united action" with them, that would suit them very well. It would help them to hoodwink the Soviet people. It would hinder rather than support the Soviet people's struggle to defend the fruits of their socialist revolution; it would hinder rather than support the Soviet people's struggle against Khrushchev revisionism without Khrushchev.

Comrade Mao Tse-tung has often said to comrades from fraternal Parties that if China's leadership is usurped by revisionists in the future, the Marxist–Leninists of all countries should likewise resolutely expose and fight them, and help the working class and the masses of China to combat such revisionism. Taking the same stand, we consider it our bounden proletarian-internationalist duty firmly to expose the revisionist leadership of the CPSU to draw a clear line between ourselves and them, and to persist in the struggle against Khrushchev revisionism.

Persevere in the Struggle Against Khrushchev Revisionism

A fierce struggle is going on between the revolutionary people of the world on the one hand and the imperialists headed by the United States and their lackeys on the other. The characteristic of the present world situation is that with the daily deepening of the international class struggle, a process of great upheaval, great division and great reorganization is taking place. The revolutionary movement of the people of the world is surging vigorously forward. Imperialism and all other decadent reactionary forces are putting up a wild death-bed fight. Drastic divisions and realignments of political forces are taking place on a world scale.

The revolutionary forces of the people of the world have surpassed the reactionary forces of imperialism. The advances of the revolutionary movement of the people of the world is the main current in the present situation. The people's revolutionary struggles in all countries will certainly triumph, while imperialism, reaction and modern revisionism will step by step descend to their doom. This is the inevitable trend of world history which no decadent reactionary force can change. But imperialism and reaction will not fall unless you strike them down, and modern revisionism, too, will not collapse unless you fight it. Before being overthrown and eliminated, they will invariably collaborate and, using different tactics, do all they can to hurl desperate attacks on the revolutionary forces. Thus, along with the growth and deepening of the revolutionary movement, there is an adverse counter-revolutionary current. The course of international development is unavoidably filled with contradictions and conflicts; there are bound to be zigzags and reversals. In all countries the people's revolutionary struggles necessarily advance in the form of waves.

As the struggle against the United States reaches a crucial phase, U.S. imperialism needs the services of Khrushchev revisionism all the more acutely. Hence it is inevitable that the struggle against Khrushchev revisionism must sharpen.

In the course of combating Khrushchev revisionism, there is bound to be a certain unevenness in the degree of people's understanding of the struggle. This kind of phenomenon becomes particularly conspicuous when the struggle becomes sharp. That is both natural and inevitable. Lenin said that when astonishingly abrupt changes took place, people "who were suddenly confronted with extremely important problems could not long remain on this level. They could not continue without a respite, without a return to elementary questions, without a new training which would help them 'digest' lessons of unparalleled richness and make it possible for incomparably wider masses again to march forward, but now far more firmly, more consciously, more confidently and more steadfastly." [21] Just such a situation exists at present.

As the struggle against Khrushchev revisionism becomes sharper and deeper, a new process of division will inevitably occur in the revolutionary ranks, and some people will inevitably drop out. But at the same time hundreds of millions of revolutionary people will stream in.

Faced with a complex situation of this kind, Marxist–Leninists must never abandon or slur over principles, but must take a clear stand, uphold revolutionary principles and persevere in the struggle against Khrushchev revisionism. Only in this way can the unity of the revolutionary forces be strengthened and expanded.

At present, the task facing all the Marxist–Leninist parties is to draw a clear line of demarcation both politically and organizationally between themselves and the revisionists, who are serving U.S. imperialism, and to liquidate Khrushchev revisionism in order to welcome the high tide of revolutionary struggle against U.S. imperialism and its lackeys.

In the final analysis, in all parts of the world including the Soviet

Union, the masses of the people, who constitute the overwhelming majority of the population, and the overwhelming majority of Communists and cadres want revolution and are upholding or will uphold Marxism–Leninism. They are steadily awakening and joining the ranks of the struggle against imperialism and revisionism. It is certain that over 90 per cent of the world's population will become more closely united in the fight against imperialism, reaction and modern revisionism.

All the Communist Parties and all the socialist countries will eventually unite on the basis of Marxism–Leninism and proletarian internationalism and take united action in the struggle against imperialism. As Lenin told the old-line revisionists, the proletariat will sooner or later unite and eventually win on a world scale, "only it is moving and will move, is proceeding and will proceed, against you, it will be a victory over you." [22]

Unless the new leaders of the CPSU stop practising Khrushchevism without Khrushchev, admit and correct their mistakes and genuinely return to the revolutionary path of Marxism–Leninism, it is absolutely out of the question to expect the Marxist–Leninists to abandon the struggle against Khrushchev revisionism.

> *With power and to spare, we must not cease the pursuit*
> *Or halt in mid-course for the sake of idle laurels.*

This couplet summarizes an extremely important historical lesson. The Marxist–Leninists and all the other revolutionary people of the world must continue their victorious pursuit and carry the struggle against Khrushchev revisionism through to the end!

NOTES—APPENDIX FOUR—DOCUMENT #5

[13] V. I. Lenin, "Unity," *Collected Works*, Eng. ed., Progress Publishers, Moscow, 1964, Vol. XX, p. 232.

[14] A. A. Gromyko, Speech at the Plenary Session of the 19th General Assembly of the United Nations, December 7, 1964.

[15] N. S. Khrushchev, Talk at a Press Conference in Vienna, July 8, 1960.

[16] "Mr. K. Speaks," *Daily Express*, April 6, 1965.

[17] Zbigniew Brzezinski, "Peace, Morality and Vietnam," *The New Leader*, April 12, 1965.

[18] A. N. Kosygin, "On Improving Industrial Management, Perfecting Planning, and Enhancing Economic Incentives in Industrial Production," *Moscow News*, Supplement, October 2, 1965.

[19] "In Lenin's Way, with Scientific Accuracy," editorial in *Sovietskaya Russia*, March 28, 1965.

[20] V. I. Lenin, "The Collapse of the Second International," *Collected Works*, Eng. ed., Progress Publishers, Moscow, 1964, Vol. XXI, p. 247.

[21] V. I. Lenin, "Certain Features of the Historical Development of Marxism," *Collected Works*, Eng. ed., F.L.P.H., Moscow, 1963, Vol. XVII, p. 42.

[22] V. I. Lenin, "Imperialism and the Split in Socialism," *Collected Works*, Eng. ed., Progress Publishers (Moscow, 1964), Vol. XXIII, p. 111.

Document #6

STATEMENT
OF THE SOUTH VIETNAM NATIONAL LIBERATION FRONT*

AMERICAN imperialist aggression against South Vietnam and inter-ference in its internal affairs have now continued for more than ten years. More American troops and supplies, including missile units, Marines, B-57 strategic bombers, and mercenaries from South Korea, Taiwan, the Philippines, Australia, Malaysia, etc., have been brought to South Vietnam.

In their fury, the Americans have ordered their air force and that of their satellites to attack North Vietnam and Laos. Faced with complete defeat in South Vietnam, U.S. imperialism has discarded its disguise and stands exposed as an outright colonialist aggressor. The U.S. imperialists are not only extending their criminal war in South Vietnam, but are endeavouring to spread it to the rest of Indo-China and the whole of Southeast Asia.

The Saigon puppet regime, paid servant of the United States, is guilty of the most heinous crimes. These despicable traitors, these boot-lickers of American imperialism, have brought the enemy into our country. They have brought to South Vietnam armed forces of the United States and its satellites to kill our compatriots, occupy and ravage our sacred soil and enslave our people.

°*New Times* (March 27, 1965) pp. 36–40.

The Vietnamese, the peoples of all Indo-China and Southeast Asia, supporters of peace and justice in every part of the world, have raised their voice in angry protest against this criminal unprovoked aggression of the United States imperialists.

In the present extremely grave situation, the South Vietnam National Liberation Front considers it necessary to proclaim anew its firm and unswerving determination to resist the U.S. imperialists and fight for the salvation of our country.

1. The U.S. imperialists are sabotaging the Geneva agreements; they are the most arrant warmongers and aggressors, they are the sworn enemies of the Vietnamese people.

The world knows that in their valorous war of resistance, the Vietnamese defeated the French colonialists. The U.S. imperialists interfered in this war on the side of the French. They gave the French colonialists $2,600 million, hundreds of thousands of tons of arms, and 200 military advisers to crush Vietnam's struggle for independence and freedom. But our people stood firm in their determination to die in battle rather than live in slavery. And by dint of heroic effort, with the full support of the peoples of the world, they were victorious: they freed half of our beloved country from enemy oppression and made possible the 1954 international Geneva agreements, which solemnly proclaimed the sovereignty, independence and territorial integrity of Vietnam, Laos and Cambodia, re-established peace in this area and laid the foundations for Vietnam's peaceful reunion.

The Vietnamese fully appreciate the value of the Geneva agreements. Now as always, they faithfully observe them, and are resolved to fight for their full implementation, in strict conformity with their spirit and letter. In contrast, the U.S. imperialists and their South Vietnam flunkeys have openly and flagrantly violated the Geneva agreements and have, in effect, denounced them. For throughout these past eleven years they have been waging a savage war of aggression in an effort to suppress and enslave our people, turn the country into a U.S. colony and war base, and perpetuate the division of Vietnam.

No sooner were the Geneva agreements signed than the U.S. imperialists began to draw their stooges into the Seato military alliance and unlawfully placed South Vietnam under its "protection." To all practical purposes, this placed South Vietnam under

American control. Since then the United States has been increasingly and flagrantly interfering in the affairs of South Vietnam. In the period from the end of 1954 to 1959, the U.S. imperialists and the puppet Diem regime carried out numerous punitive operations (in Truong Tan Buu, Thoai Ngoc Hau and other areas) against peaceful populations, murdering former Resistance fighters, members of religious sects—in short everyone who did not approve of Diem's policy.

Immediately after the ceasefire, blood was being shed on the streets of Saigon, in Duy-xyen, Huong-dien, Cho Duoc, Vinh-trinh and many other areas. In an attempt to activize and expand these punitive operations, the Diem regime, on orders from the U.S. imperialists, promulgated Law 10/59, a fascist-type law that banned all political associations and provided for the prosecution of any individual opposed to the Americans and the Diem clique, and therefore branded as a "Communist." Guillotines were set up throughout the country as more and more death sentences were passed. The Americans and their henchmen killed or jailed hundreds of thousands of South Vietnamese patriots for advocating peace and demanding observance of the Geneva agreements and convocation of a consultative conference on general elections to reunite the country. Some were sentenced simply for "disobedience."

These criminal actions of the U.S. imperialists and their hirelings have kindled the flames of wrath in Vietnam and aroused a storm of indignation throughout the world.

Public opinion in Vietnam, Asia and the world has condemned these crimes. Everywhere there has been a vocal demand for an immediate end to the aggression and stringent observance of the 1954 Geneva agreements. But the U.S. imperialists have been extending their dirty war.

Eleven years of aggressive colonial war in South Vietnam have cost the U.S. government $4,000 million in "aid." More than 80 per cent of the money has gone to finance military operations. The rulers of America attach especial importance to the aggressive war in South Vietnam. President Johnson (like the late President Kennedy), the National Security Council, the Defence and State Departments, the Central Intelligence Agency keenly follow events in South Vietnam. Representatives of the White House and the Pentagon and U.S. generals in the Pacific area meet every month in Honolulu to discuss plans for more intervention in South Vietnam.

To place the war under their direct control, the U.S. imperialists have set up, in addition to the Military Assistance Advisory Group, their own military command in Saigon, headed by General Harkins. More recently they have set up a joint American–Vietnamese command, which in reality is a military agency of the United States enjoying sweeping powers and directly accountable to the U.S. President and the U.S. Defence Department. Practically all top American officials, including Ministers and Generals, have been to South Vietnam on inspection missions and to work out plans for expanding the aggression. More, the U.S. government has sent some of its top military men, among them Generals O'Daniel, Collins, McGarr, Williams and Harkins, to direct operations against the Vietnamese patriots. Some time ago, Washington dispatched to Saigon Maxwell Taylor, former Chairman of the Joint Chiefs of Staff, together with a group of senior officers, among them Westmoreland and Throckmorton.

The U.S. imperialists are employing every type of modern weapon, stopping short only at nuclear bombs, to intimidate and destroy the South Vietnamese, in an attempt to impose their overlordship and convert the country into a U.S. colony and war base.

In these eleven years, the U.S. imperialists and their henchmen have carried out more than 160,000 punitive operations, killed about 170,000 persons, wounded or maimed nearly 800,000, threw into jail over 400,000, raped tens of thousands of women, including nuns and elderly women, tortured or buried alive more than 50,000 persons, destroyed numerous villages, drove more than 5,000,000 into the 8,000 concentration camps, hypocritically designated as "prosperity zones," "resettlement centres," and "strategic hamlets," used poisonous chemicals in many areas, destroying hundreds of thousands of acres of crops and orchard, and poisoning tens of thousands of people. The record also shows that they have destroyed thousands of pagodas, churches and shrines and killed tens of thousands of their congregations. Under the iron heel of the American aggressors and their servitors, our beautiful country has been turned into a tortured and devastated land. The barbarous fascist regime set up by the U.S. imperialists and their lackeys has surpassed the brutality of the nazis and of the darkest days of the Middle Ages.

These facts and figures—and more could be cited—are ample proof of the brutality and heinous crimes of the U.S. imperialists and the South Vietnamese traitors, they show the vile role the Saigon clique plays. The United States and its lackeys have not only violated the ceasefire agreement and the final declaration of the 1954 Geneva conference; they have cynically discarded these international agreements and the decisions of the Bandung conference. They have trampled underfoot all the accepted standards of international law and decency. Such are the facts, and they are irrefutable.

To disguise their aggression and rapine, the U.S. imperialists are resorting to demagogy, which, however, has failed to mislead world public opinion. Washington's recently published White Paper has absolutely no substantiation in fact. It is a case of the thief crying "Hold Thief." But, at the same time, it sheds a revealing light on America's intention to expand and intensify the aggression. The real situation in Vietnam is that the U.S. imperialists are waging a criminal war of aggression and are flagrantly sabotaging the Geneva agreements. They are the most dangerous war instigators and aggressors, the sworn enemies of the people of Vietnam, Indo-China and the world.

2. The heroic South Vietnamese are determined to expel the U.S. imperialists, liberate their country and create an independent, democratic, peaceful and neutral state advancing towards national reunification.

The people of South Vietnam have always cherished peace, but they will not remain passive, will not allow the American aggressor and his accomplices to go on torturing their country. They are prepared to die rather than become slaves. The courageous 14 million people of South Vietnam have risen in a life-and-death struggle to crush the American aggressors and the South Vietnamese traitors, liberate the country and assure it independence, democracy, peace and neutrality. Theirs is a patriotic war, and it fully accords with the elementary and fundamental principles of international law, with the right of nations to self-determination, with their right to wage a patriotic defensive war against foreign aggression. And in this sacred war of liberation, the people of South Vietnam employ every type of weapon against the enemy. The biggest purveyor of arms for the South Vietnamese patriots is U.S. imperialism, which has sustained one heavy defeat after another.

Having begun the war practically unarmed, the people of South Vietnam have overcome immense difficulties and have scored important victories.

The South Vietnamese are firmly convinced that, by their own efforts and with the sincere support of the peoples of the world, they can win complete victory. The U.S. imperialists and their flunkeys are in a hopeless predicament. They will be driven out by the powerful wave of the South Vietnamese revolution, but they will make desperate attempts to hold on. In their blind fury, the U.S. imperialists are rushing headlong into an extremely dangerous military gamble.

They have brought in more weapons and more men—ground, naval and air units—and mercenaries from South Korea and other satellite countries. Their air force is attacking the Democratic Republic of Vietnam and the Kingdom of Laos. This is not an indication of strength. On the contrary, it is evidence of the impotent malice of a ferocious enemy no longer guided by reason. His fury will scare no one. The present escalation of the aggressive war is in itself evidence that America's imperialist plans have failed, that the policy of colonial aggression which it has pursued in South Vietnam over the past eleven years, and the so-called "special war," have proved a complete failure.

The Americans are bogged down in their "special war." They will be bogged down still more if they try to extend the war to the entire area. If they decide to escalate the war to North Vietnam, Indo-China and other areas, their defeat will be all the quicker and all the more ignominious.

The South Vietnam National Liberation Front declares: America's plan of bringing in more American and satellite naval, ground and air forces, of launching more attacks on North Vietnam and Laos, is meant to create a "position of strength," from which it intends to compel the National Liberation Front and the people of South Vietnam to sell their country cheap at the conference table. This is no more than wishful thinking by political madmen and military adventurers. The South Vietnamese people say to the imperialists and their agents: The only solution now is for you to quit South Vietnam. If you persist in continuing this insensate war, your defeat will be all the greater and all the more inglorious. On behalf of 14 million courageous South Vietnamese, the National Liberation Front solemnly declares: The South Vietnamese people and its armed forces are determined not to lay down arms until their basic aims are achieved. These aims are independence, democracy, peace and neutrality.

The people of South Vietnam are resolved to continue to deal crushing blows at the U.S. aggressors and their understrappers. Our people never doubt that victory will ultimately be theirs. There is no point in negotiating with the U.S. imperialists until they withdraw all their troops from South Vietnam, all their military equipment, also the troops and military equipment of their satellites, and dismantle all their war bases. There can be no negotiations as long as the traitors continue to sacrifice to the U.S. imperialists our people's sacred right to independence and democracy, and as long as the National Liberation Front—the sole genuine spokesman of our 14 million population—is denied a decisive voice.

3. The people and heroic Liberation Army of South Vietnam are determined to perform their sacred duty to the end and drive out the U.S. imperialists in order to liberate South Vietnam and defend North Vietnam.

Vietnam is one country and the Vietnamese are one nation. North and South Vietnam are one family. This feeling of unity is higher than the mountains and deeper than the seas; it is just as natural as the rising of the Sun in the East. It is a feeling no force on earth can shake. In the present extremely tense situation, when our people are waging a life and death struggle against the U.S. imperialists and their hirelings, the heart aches when the arm bleeds. And it is only natural and logical that the people of North Vietnam should be determined to fulfil their duty to their brothers and sisters in the South.

On behalf of the 14 million South Vietnamese, the National Liberation Front conveys to our 17 million brothers and sisters in the North a message of deep confidence and makes this pledge: The people and heroic Liberation Army of South Vietnam will fulfil their sacred duty; they will expel the U.S. imperialists, liberate the South and defend the North in order to reunite our Fatherland.

In a desperate attempt to extricate themselves from their critical position and ward off inevitable defeat in South Vietnam, the U.S. imperialists and their lackeys have sent planes and warships to bomb North Vietnam. They have been given a fitting rebuff by the army and people of North Vietnam: more than 50 U.S. jet planes have been shot down. The army and people of South Vietnam rejoice in these brilliant exploits of their brothers in the North.

The heart aches when the arm bleeds. The army and people of

the South are prepared to defend the North, and they will make the American aggressors and their agents feel the full power of their wrath. Every blow the American imperialists deal the North will be met by a double and triple blow from the army and people of the South.

In February, when the aggressors and Saigon traitors attacked the North, the Liberation Army dealt smashing blows at the enemy's major bases and his main forces. Enemy casualties amounted to 20,706 (including nearly 600 Americans killed, wounded or taken prisoner). The Liberation Army captured 4,144 weapons of various types and downed, damaged or destroyed 111 enemy planes.

The South Vietnam National Liberation Front warns the U.S. imperialists and the Vietnamese traitors: You could not subject the 14 million population of South Vietnam, and you will never bring the 30 million people of Vietnam to their knees. Escalation of the war and more reckless operations will not help you; they will only hasten your utter defeat.

In another attempt to find a way out of the stalemate in South Vietnam, the U.S. imperialists and their lackeys have sent their air force to attack the liberated areas of Laos, have repeatedly violated the frontier of Cambodia, have bombed and used poisonous chemicals against the people of Cambodia. The armies and peoples of Laos and Cambodia have administered the aggressors and their mercenaries a fitting rebuff.

The South Vietnamese express their admiration of the indomitable and heroic spirit of the peoples of these two countries. They are determined to stand side by side with them in the struggle against the common enemy, U.S. imperialism and its lackeys. The people and Liberation Army of South Vietnam are unbending in their resolve to crush the American aggressors and their agents in South Vietnam, which they are using as an operational base for aggression against Laos and Cambodia.

The South Vietnamese welcome the success of the recent Indo-China Solidarity Conference, which voiced the people's opposition to the U.S. imperialists.

The National Liberation Front and people of South Vietnam warn the U.S. imperialists and their agents that, should they venture to spread their aggressive war to the whole of Vietnam and Indo-China, the 30 million people of Vietnam will be joined by the colossal might of the hundreds of millions of Indo-China and Asia. They will constitute a force capable of moving mountains, a force that will destroy and bury the U.S. imperialists and their lackeys.

4. The South Vietnamese are deeply grateful for the sincere support of the peoples of the entire world, of everyone who cherishes peace and justice. They are prepared to accept any assistance, including arms and other military equipment, from their friends on the five continents.

Our just patriotic war has the sympathy, support and approval of all the world's nations, of everyone who stands for peace and justice. We are receiving not only moral, but also material support. The South Vietnamese people and their spokesman, the National Liberation Front, have every right to accept this valuable assistance, which they warmly welcome.

The National Liberation Front will continue to rely chiefly on its own forces and potentialities, but it is prepared to accept any assistance, moral and material, including arms and other military equipment, from all the socialist countries, from nationalist countries, from international organizations, and from the peace-loving peoples of the world. The National Liberation Front naturally reserves the right to purchase weapons and military supplies in order to strengthen its forces in this defensive war.

The international conference for solidarity with the people of Vietnam against U.S. imperialist aggression and for the defence of peace, which met towards the end of last year and was attended by representatives of more than 50 countries and 16 international organizations, supported our urgent and justified demands. If the U.S. imperialists continue to send more of their own and satellite forces to South Vietnam, if they persist in spreading the war to North Vietnam and Laos, the National Liberation Front will appeal to the peoples of various countries to send volunteers, civilian and military, to join our people in the battle against the common foe.

If the U.S. imperialists continue to sow death and devastation in South Vietnam, the National Liberation Front will, if necessary, call on the sons and daughters of South Vietnam who under the Geneva agreement were resettled in the North, and who for ten long years have lived away from their homes, to return and join the struggle to destroy the enemy and save their country and families.

There is a Vietnamese saying: "It takes sharp nails to peel a thick-skinned orange." The U.S. imperialists and their lackeys will not escape the wrath of the Vietnamese and all peace-loving peoples. They will be held responsible for all the grievous consequences of their aggression.

Speaking for the 14 million South Vietnamese, the Central Committee of the National Liberation Front wishes again to express its heartfelt gratitude to the socialist countries, the nationalist countries, international organizations and peace-loving peoples of the world, to all who cherish peace and justice and sincerely support our just patriotic war of resistance. More than ever before we deem it our internationalist duty to make every sacrifice and exert all our energies to promote the great world-wide struggle in defence of independence, democracy, peace and social progress in Indo-China and Southeast Asia and all other areas, and make our contribution to the great battle to defeat aggressive American imperialism.

5. United, our people will continue their heroic advance, resolved to fight and rout the American aggressors and the South Vietnamese traitors. Very important victories have already been scored in that struggle.

The U.S. imperialists and their lackeys only seem so formidable, inside they are very weak, are beset by consternation and are isolated more than ever before. True to their watchword: "Better die in battle than live in slavery" our people will crush this cruel and inhuman foe.

The National Liberation Front and the people of South Vietnam are fighting in a righteous cause. Their material strength and organization are rapidly growing. They continue to score impressive victories and their successes will mount the better and harder they fight. This will further increase their forces and result in even greater victories.

We are worthy successors to the glory of Dien Bien Phu. We have raised aloft the heroic banner of our people, we are continuing the tradition of 4,000 years of struggle against the invader. The National Liberation Front and our people are waging their valorous struggle in the very favourable conditions of this era, when the oppressed nations of Asia, Africa and Latin America are rising to achieve freedom. The socialist countries and the world democratic forces represent a cardinal factor in mankind's onward march, in the struggle to eliminate imperialism and colonialism in all their diverse manifestations. And should the U.S. imperialists and their lackeys recklessly spread the war to the whole of Indo-China, the peoples of that area and of Southeast Asia will rise to a man and throw them into the ocean.

Our people and their sole genuine spokesman, the National Liberation Front, are sure of final victory.

The Central Committee of the National Liberation Front calls on the 14 million courageous South Vietnamese and on their armed forces to continue the fight on all fronts with greater courage and military dexterity in order to achieve the following:

Monolithic unity of the entire people;

Arming of the entire people to expel the American marauders and the South Vietnamese traitors;

The Liberation Army and the popular armed detachments must fight continuously and with the utmost energy, dealing telling blows, giving the U.S. aggressors and their underlings no respite and destroying more of the enemy's manpower;

In the rural areas the people must continue to destroy all remaining "strategic hamlets," break down enemy control, expand the liberated areas, unite liberated villages and towns into solid districts and turn them into operational bases, fight the enemy, wherever he appears, with the utmost determination, and defend their homes and fields against enemy incursions;

The people in Saigon, Hue, Da Nang, and other towns must vigorously develop their revolutionary organizations, continue to stage street demonstrations, activate their struggle on all issues, demand an end to the U.S. aggressive war and expose the South Vietnamese traitors, who are helping the aggressors and betraying our country and people;

Everyone, cadre personnel, soldiers and officers, must continue to advance under the banner of liberation and bend all their energies to drive out the American aggressors and their henchmen and save our country and our families.

Even if we have to fight ten, twenty or more years, even if we have to endure still greater hardship and privation, we are prepared to fight to the end, until not even the shadow of an American soldier remains on our soil.

The Vietnamese have a long and proud history—the heroic history of a heroic people, and they have written a new glorious page in the past ten years of battle against the U.S. aggressors.

We have scored many victories, we shall score many more. The U.S. imperialists and their agents stagger from one setback to another. This is proof that we are invincible and that the U.S. aggressors and their agents are becoming weaker, not stronger. We were able successfully to oppose them for ten long years; now the conditions for our victory are even more favourable. If the American aggressors and their lackeys suffered defeat in the past ten years, then it is only natural that they should become weaker, and will sustain even heavier defeats. If they dare to extend the war to North Vietnam their defeat will be all the more ignominious.

We are confident that victory will be ours. We are determined to fight, to deliver stronger, more telling blows at the American marauders and their helpers. We are determined to liberate the South, defend the North and reunite the Fatherland.

Central Committee,
South Vietnam
National Liberation Front

March 22, 1965

THE VIETNAMESE PEOPLE
ON THE ROAD TO VICTORY*

by Lieutenant-General Nguyen Van Vinh

New Features of the War

AMERICAN "special warfare" in South Vietnam has basically failed after having been experimented for more than three years with different strategies and tactics, new weapons and techniques and most cruel methods: its main props, the puppet troops and administration, have seriously disintegrated; the "strategic hamlet" system considered as its backbone has been wiped out in the main: the helicopter and amphibious car tactics regarded as more mobile and more manœuvrable than guerilla tactics have gone bankrupt; the towns and other temporarily occupied areas, described by the aggressors as their safest rear, have been encircled, narrowed down and are in confusion in face of the unremitting political struggle waged by millions of urban and rural people; the neo-colonialist character of U.S. imperialism has been laid bare before the world

---

*PUBLISHER'S NOTE: *The Vietnamese People On The Road To Victory* is a full translation of an article by Lieutenant-General Nguyen Van Vinh published in the *Hoc Tap* (Studies), theoretical and political review of the Vietnam Workers' Party. General Nguyen Van Vinh is Deputy Chief of Staff of the Vietnam People's Army.—*Foreign Languages Publishing House,* Hanoi—1966.

people; the enemy's efforts to stem and isolate the South Vietnamese people's struggle, and carry out sabotage activities in North Vietnam with commandos sent from the South, have met a bitter fiasco.

Very clearly, with the collapse of Ngo Dinh Diem's nepotic regime, American neo-colonialism has headed more rapidly towards complete bankruptcy, while the recall of Maxwell Taylor proved that U.S. "special warfare" has been fundamentally foiled. As for the South Vietnamese people's revolutionary forces led by the National Front for Liberation, they have grown very quickly and checked all strategies and tactics and most ruthless war methods of the American imperialists and their flunkeys; they have broken the enemy's grip and proudly stood on the international arena with millions and millions of peace- and justice-loving people behind them.

Stubborn in their aggressive policy, the American imperialists act like a losing gambler who puts down one stake after another. In 1965 they successively introduced tens of thousands of U.S. combat troops into South Vietnam in an attempt to prevent the disintegration of the puppet army and administration and win back the initiative. At the same time, they speeded up air warfare against North Vietnam. In April 1965, they spread a smokescreen of "peace discussions". By so doing they thought they would soon be able to force on our army and people a cease-fire under their own terms in both North and South Vietnam.

However, reality has fallen short of their dark design; *the South Vietnamese army and people have gained major successes in all fields.* They speeded up the destruction and disintegration of the puppet troops and administration right at the time when the U.S. imperialists carried out their military build up to save the puppet forces. In 1965 about two hundred thousand puppet troops were destroyed and disintegrated, including forty-three battalions and four motorized squadrons completely wiped out, while the puppet administration also seriously disintegrated. As for the U.S. expeditionary corps including naval, ground and air forces and many of the American army's best units, they have been unable not only to fulfil their political task which is to prevent the disintegration of the puppet troops and administration, but they themselves have also suffered heavy losses, all arms and services of the U.S.A. and their satellites have sustained bitter defeats. The Third Marine

Division lost over eight companies at the Vantuong battle and in engagements in the coastal bases guarded by it. The Paratroop Brigade lost one battalion at Datcuoc, two companies at Bencat and in zone D. The 101st paratroop brigade lost more than a company at Thuanninh near Ankhe, the First Airmobile Cavalry Division, the much cherished creation of McNamara and the "trump card" thrown by the U.S. imperialists into the High Plateaux theatre to win back the initiative of operations there, was dealt heavy blows by the iron-like fighters of the Liberation army, the famous victors of Pleime who annihilated an important part of it around Chupong. The First Infantry Division formed in the First World War and dubbed "Red One", which had been thrown into the jungle of Thudaumot province in the hope of destroying the Liberation armed forces there, lost several of its battalions at Baubang and Nhamat.

All enemy important military bases along the coast, in the jungle or even in the towns have been subjected to the attacks of the Liberation armed forces who slipped right into their centres or encircled them by a guerilla belt. They have thus caused heavy human and material losses to the enemy and, consequently, increased his many difficulties in logistics in South Vietnam.

Along with the serious setbacks in the South Vietnam theatre, *sabotage warfare mainly by air force against North Vietnam has also met with heavy failures.* The myth of the terrific strength of the U.S. Air Force cultivated by American psychological warfare has been shattered by the realities of the people's war in North Vietnam. Over nine hundred up-to-date planes of all descriptions were shot down by various kinds of weapons. The U.S. imperialists think that air warfare against North Vietnam can intimidate our people in both zones and weaken their solidarity and mutual assistance in their fight. But they are mistaken: their adventurous and silly action has aroused still more hatred among our people and strengthened their unshakable determination to liberate the South, defend the North and advance towards national reunification.

While the true meaning of the U.S. imperialists' hypocritical "peace offensive" is laid barer with every passing day, the correct stand of the Democratic Republic of Vietnam and the South Vietnam National Front for Liberation on the Vietnam problem has been raised aloft like a radiant torch. *All those who cherish independence, democracy, peace and socialism all over the world, including the progressive people in the United States, support our stand and energetically protest against the aggressive war,* which drives the American imperialists into further embarrassment and unprecedented isolation.

Since the introduction of some hundred thousand U.S. and satellite combat troops into South Vietnam and the intensification of the sabotage air warfare against North Vietnam, the scale and aspects of the war have changed. *In the South "special warfare" has shifted to a local war* while keeping certain of its features. This is because the aggressors are not free to go beyond any limit and throw into the war as many troops as they like. They are bound to maintain the role of the puppet troops and administration, and their domination in South Vietnam continues to be exercised along a neo-colonialist line.

The changes in the scope and aspects of the war stem mainly from the changes in the forces used by the U.S. imperialists to speed up the war. If in "special warfare" they chiefly relied on the puppet forces, now they have to count on two big strategic forces, namely, the American troops (including those of the U.S. satellites) and the puppet troops. The latter are not only a military prop for U.S. imperialism, but also a political prop for the U.S. troops. As for the expeditionary force, it has now become the backbone of the puppet troops and at the same time, forms the strategic mobile force for the aggressive war.

In spite of the changes mentioned above, *the nature and political goals of the Americans' war remains the same:* it still is a neo-colonialist war of aggression aimed at realizing American neo-colonialism in South Vietnam. Though the aggressors have increased tenfold the number of their troops in a year, they have been for several years incapable of carrying out their scheme, that is, to find out ways and means to prevent the disintegration of the puppet troops and administration, control and concentrate the population in one form or another, win back the initiative and reoccupy a number of areas, thin out and destroy the revolutionary forces, stem and isolate the South Vietnamese people's liberation war.

In short, the war situation in Vietnam at the present stage may be featured as follows: the American "special warfare" strategy in South Vietnam has been fundamentally frustrated, the massive introduction of American and satellite troops has changed the scope and aspects of and the forces engaged in, the war, the American aggressors have extended sabotage air warfare in North Vietnam and started a diplomatic offensive with "unconditional discussions", but under the counter-blows of the army and people of North and South Vietnam the U.S. imperialists have sustained bitter defeats on all military, political and diplomatic fields.

Our People Will Certainly Win

The U.S. imperialists dispose of large material resources and a big war potential. Despite heavy defeats, they do not yet give up their design of invading the southern part of our country. This is a reality. In the near future, they may introduce many more forces, bringing the number of their own troops and those of their satellites to three hundred thousand or more. *This is a possibility.* But there does exist another possibility, namely, in whatever circumstance the army and people of both North and South Vietnam will vanquish the U.S. aggressors.

Some time ago when the American imperialists were waging "special warfare" in the South, we affirmed that it was entirely possible for our people to emerge victorious in this type of warfare. This was based on a theoretical study, taking into account the perspective of the situation. Now it is clear to everyone that what we affirmed then has become reality. *The American imperialists' strategy of "special warfare" in South Vietnam has ended in failure.* We also foresaw the eventuality of the American aggressors bringing more troops into South Vietnam, enlarging the scope of the war, and also envisaged the possibility that the Liberation Army and people of South Vietnam would check whatever type of warfare the enemy engaged in. Nevertheless in dealing with this possibility apart from certain concrete facts that served as a basis for our analysis (among others, our experiences in the victorious resistance war against the French imperialists and in countering various American tactical innovations with the use of air power and some new weapons used in their "special warfare" in South Vietnam) we based our belief in certain victory under such circumstances, on theoretical grounds. For at that time, the Liberation Army and people of South Vietnam had not yet engaged in direct combat with U.S. ground units in the South, neither had our army and people been in action against the U.S. Air Force in the North. At present, it is obvious that there are enough real facts to show the possibility of our certain victory over whatever form of warfare adopted by the American imperialists.

Apart from theoretical arguments, we have an abundance of very real facts from the victorious struggle of nearly one year against U.S. ground forces and other arms and services in the South and against the war of destruction launched by the U.S. Air Force in the North.

There is no question but that our people will win because we have absolute political and moral superiority, correct leadership, the unity of the entire people, the invincible people's war and also the sympathy and powerful support of people throughout the world. As for the American imperialists, they will lose no matter how stubborn and ferocious they prove. Apart from such oft-cited fundamental factors as the unjust nature of the war they have imposed on us, the characteristics of the present epoch, and the unfavourable—for them—world relation of forces, the following direct causes point to their inevitable defeat in Vietnam.

First, even the Americans put 300,000 or more troops into South Vietnam *it will be impossible for them to transform the existing relation of forces to the point where they can change the situation in their favour.*

Indeed, even if American reinforcements including those of their satellites, arrive in hundreds of thousands, this will not prevent the local puppet troops from being worn down, wiped out or disintegrated in the same proportions while the Liberation armed forces, taking advantage of favourable conditions will rapidly reinforce their ranks. Thus there will be no favourable change for the Americans in the facts of the past year. The massive landing of American troops has in no way basically changed the relation of forces between them and the puppets on the one hand, and the Liberation armed forces on the other. In general this has remained unchanged but where changes have taken place, they have been in favour of the National Front for Liberation and not the U.S. imperialists.

Here it is worthwhile clarifying our conception of how to estimate the relation of forces between the enemy and ourselves. In general, the forces that a country can deploy in a war include the following factors. The number and morale of effectives that can be sent to the front lines, the means in material deployed to support the pursuit of the war, including the quantity and quality of the arms available for the front, the support for the war from non-belligerent countries. If we only count the economic war potential, the arms and technique utilized, then it is clear that the enemy is stronger than we are in South Vietnam. In this field we have to fight a stronger enemy with a small force. But if we consider all the elements which constitute the forces that both sides are able to throw into the war, in the South of our country as well as in the whole of Vietnam, we can conclude that *we are the stronger.* The American imperialists can only mobilize a part of their forces for the war in Vietnam. Because their unjust war of aggression is not supported by the American and world people, because it is being waged thousands of miles from the United States and they are obliged to cope with hostile situation in many other parts of the world. The Saigon puppet army and administration have been seriously weakened. The troops of satellite countries that Washington has managed to have sent to Vietnam through all sorts of intrigues, corruption and pressures, are very limited. All the three forces have no ideal for which to fight. The Americans having no alternative but to wage a war according to outmoded bourgeois military concepts, counting on arms and technique to try and deal rapid blows and snatch a quick military victory.

On our side, because we wage a just war, a self-defence war on our own soil, we not only have armed forces at our disposal but also millions of patriots taking part in the war in a thousand different ways. Our armed forces include regular troops, regional troops and guerilla units—an armed force absolutely superior to the enemy in numbers and quality.

We can very rapidly replenish and develop our revolutionary armed forces from the immense manpower reserves of our population. Our fighters are not only capable of handling modern weapons, but also of employing rudimentary ones able to cause numerous losses to the enemy in self-defence fighting in the villages. It is on this basis that our compatriots in the South wage an invincible people's war which their adversaries are incapable of countering. In addition they enjoy unstinted aid from the population of the North and increasing support from the socialist camp and peace- and justice-loving people throughout the world, including the American people.

From an analysis of the forces and war concepts of the belligerents, it is clear that even if the aggressive troops of the Americans and their satellites reach up to 300,000 and more it will still be impossible for them to regain the initiative, to reoccupy lost terrain, or to change the situation in a sense favourable for them. On the contrary their losses will be heavier than ever.

What will happen to the relation of forces if the aggressive forces of the Americans and their satellites reach up to 400,000 or 500,000 men, that is equal to the U.S. and so-called U.N. troops sent to Korea over ten years ago?

In Korea when the U.S. and U.N. troops reached a ceiling of nearly half a million men, the American imperialists were not obliged to divert a large part of their forces to secure their rear areas. They were free to commit their whole expeditionary corps and South Korean forces to confront the Korean–Chinese forces along the 38th parallel. It is completely different in South Vietnam today where the political and armed forces of the revolution are very powerful. An eventual 400/500,000 men from the American expeditionary corps would be powerless, even to bar the rising tide of the revolutionary movement. How could the Yankees envisage a massive concentration of forces on a front aimed at North Vietnam and Laos to try and encircle and isolate the patriotic war of our compatriots in the South? If we consider the possibility of the American imperialists launching a ground war of aggression against North Vietnam, we see that the relation of forces will again be completely different. North Vietnam has solid defences at its disposal and the socialist countries are ready to come to its aid. If the American imperialists undertake aggression against North Vietnam, under these conditions and at a time when their reserves are piling up in South Vietnam, no matter what size the forces thrown into the bottomless abyss of such a conflict, they could not avoid final defeat by the immense forces of their adversaries in this region.

Second, the American imperialists and their traitor valets are incapable of "pacifying" South Vietnam. That is one of the realities of the war. In any aggressive war when the aggressor has wiped out his adversary or forced him to retreat, seized the area and installed his power, then the region is immediately transformed into his rear. Willy-nilly, the human and material resources of the region become in the whole, or at least very largely, a source for replacing his losses. In numerous regions of our country however, during the resistance against the French colonialists and still more so in South Vietnam at present, despite their forces and savage measures of repression, our adversaries have never found a quiet corner to establish a foothold. From the "pacification" of the whole of South Vietnam under the Staley–Taylor plan to the "pacification by priority sectors" as planned by McNamara, Cabot Lodge and Taylor, all their efforts have failed, even though they have employed whole divisions for a year or two to "pacify" at any price some districts, even two or three villages at the gates of Saigon–Cholon, or in the outskirts of American bases. The guerillas and Liberation armed forces of Saigon–Cholon are not content to operate only in the perimeter of the enemy's nerve-centres, but they carry out sudden and devastating blows even right in the centre of these towns and solidly defended bases. At the same time the population of the controlled areas wage fierce struggle against the measures introduced by the puppets, against taxation, impositions, fines and forced relocation, and above all against the forcible recruiting of young people into the puppet army. The enemy is not free to exploit the human and material resources even in the areas he controls and can neither eat nor sleep in peace in his resting-places.

This is so because the people of South Vietnam have high political consciousness, deep patriotism, great hatred for the enemy, they are not afraid of sacrifices or hardships and they are not duped by the enemy's deceitful tricks and ballyhoo. The Liberation armed forces, born of the South Vietnamese patriotic movement, know their enemy perfectly, and under all circumstances they enjoy the protection of the people. This is why they are capable of striking by night as well as by day, not only in the outskirts but right in the centre of the towns, at the very headquarters from which the war and massacre of the population is directed, such as the American Embassy, the Central Commissariat of Police in Saigon, etc.

Military history shows that no belligerent can be considered winning if he does not have a secure rear, if he is unable to pacify the inhabited areas which he has seized and exploited the human and material resources there for his war needs. In South Vietnam we have the following situation existing over wide areas and for many years. Our enemies cannot succeed in pacifying their rear areas and in maintaining a grip on the population in the regions they control. Because of this, their defeat is inevitable.

Third, the army and people of South Vietnam are perfectly capable of wiping out and bringing about the disintegration of the major part of the puppet army and administration.

Despite the presence of numerous troops of the U.S.A. and its satellites on South Vietnamese soil, a fact that has changed the scope and form of the war, the role of the South Vietnamese puppet army and administration, remains very important. They constitute a military and political prop for the American imperialists. They cover up to a certain extent the face of the colonialist aggressors, fight as mercenaries and thus reduce the manpower losses of the American expeditionary corps. Thus the annihilation and disintegration of the major part of the puppet army (and the puppet administration) is of very important strategic significance.

Will the army and people of South Vietnam succeed in this task? The facts have abundantly answered to this question. If the regime of Ngo Dinh Diem collapsed, this was because the puppet troops and the administrative apparatus had been cut to pieces in a very large part of the rural areas. If the tactics of America's "special warfare" basically failed, this was the result of the collapse of a great part of the puppet administration and the decimation, the annihilation or serious weakening of the puppet army, trained and commanded by American advisers with the active support of American air power, artillery and tanks.

In 1965 alone, about one third of the puppet infantry battalions were completely wiped out. Of the ten puppet divisions, five (the 2nd, 22nd, 5th, 25th and 27th) were defeated on several occasions with heavy losses. About half of the battalions of each of these divisions were wiped out. The five other divisions also received repeated heavy blows. More than half of the 12 battalions of parachutists and marines which constitute the strategic reserve of the Saigon army, were completely wiped out. The enemy has tried to replace his losses by transferring part of lower-grade units and this is precisely why not only are all echelons below strength but the quality of the troops is very uneven and their combat efficiency low. As for the provincial, district and village security forces, they have suffered very heavy losses and are reduced to trying to defend provincial capitals and district centres. Here and there they try to extend their activities, but for the main part they content themselves with digging in behind their fortifications.

Today the problem is posed in these terms: can the arrival of American troops ensure the continued existence of the puppet army?

The arrival of American troops certainly strengthened the latter's forces. In certain cases and in certain places, American troops gave them support, mainly in air power. But over all, the fate of the puppet army remains basically unchanged.

Today, American troops have arrived in the battlefields of the mountain areas—that graveyard of the puppets, it is precisely since their arrival to help the puppets in the mountain that the latter have been wiped out faster than ever. In 1964, before this development, less than 10 battalions were wiped out in the whole theatre of operations in South Vietnam. In 1965, with the massive landing of American troops, almost 40 puppet battalions have been wiped out in the mountain regions alone. There have been cases in which American troops did not come to the help of the puppets, but it was the latter who had to come to the help of the former, as in the battle of Pleime.

In the plains, the arrival of American troops has not brought any appreciable change for the puppets. Theirs is still the task of protecting the "strategic hamlets" that still remain, ensuring the defence of villages in the controlled zones and protecting district and provincial centres. No matter what their numbers, the American troops are incapable of replacing the puppets in these tasks. Also the ever sparser strong points in the network of puppet positions are not only incapable of protecting the puppet regime in Saigon, but they cannot even prevent the continuing defection from their own forces before the combined military-political offensives of the South Vietnamese people and troops. Even if the American forces reach 250,000 or 300,000 or more, they will never be able to hold more than a few dozen provincial and district centres°. The 200 district and provincial centres which remain in their hands will always have to be entrusted to temporary occupation by the puppet army.

Fourth, the army and people of South Vietnam as well as the army and people of Vietnam as a whole are perfectly capable of defeating the American army of aggression.

That is a new problem. But in Vietnam at the present time, in affirming that we will defeat the American troops, we base ourselves on what we have already done and what we will do. Apart from the reasons for victory cited above, we can make a more concrete analysis of our capabilities to defeat all American arms and services.

°The American expeditionary corps at present includes over 220,000 men. It occupies only a dozen provincial and district centres of South Vietnam.

Including the effectives of the 7th Fleet, slightly more than 270,000 American troops* are actually engaged in Vietnam, the greater part operating in the South, only part of the air force in the North.

American naval forces engaged in Vietnam are only worthy of note as floating airfields, comprising the 5 aircraft carriers of the 7th Fleet from which about 400 fighter planes take off to raid South and North Vietnam. The other activities of the 7th Fleet—patrolling along the coast, supporting U.S. ground forces operating in the coastal regions, helping to land reinforcements, supplies, etc.—are only an indirect support, nothing decisive. That is why in a war mainly fought on solid ground, where we benefit from the backing of millions of patriots enabling us to hold on to our mountains, forests, plains and towns, when we are able to live and fight with all the resources that exist in our country without needing supplies or reinforcements from the other side of the ocean, an enemy fleet no matter how powerful, can never undertake any decisive action against us.

U.S. air-power at present constitutes an appreciable support in fire-power and rapid transport of troops in South Vietnam. We must however make a correct appreciation of the value of each category of planes.

As to B.52 strategic bombers, there are now two divisions of the Pacific Strategic Air Command engaged in South Vietnam and they have carried out more than a hundred bombing raids. However, if one compares the number of raids and the quantity of bombs dropped with the damage caused, one must conclude that these planes are the least efficient of the American air force, those that hit their targets the least often and which cause the least number of dead and wounded for the South Vietnam armed forces. The raids which our enemies classify as for "extermination" undertaken with the B.52's, would only be effective against big cities with high concentrations of industry and population, not equipped with modern defensive weapons. However, if they are sent against the towns of North Vietnam these planes, because of their big size and reduced speed, will be the easiest to knock down. In South Vietnam, because of the low density of the rural population—which has the tendency these days to spread out more thinly all the time—and because of

---

* The Seventh Fleet has more than 70,000 men; the U.S. troops in South Vietnam amount to over 200,000.

the wise distribution of the Liberation armed forces, plus the well-tested defensive measures against planes taken by the troops and the population, the use of B.52's, though very costly, has little effect.°

The other types of aviation operating in Vietnam in 1965, consists of about 2,870 planes. Most of them are used in South Vietnam of which about 1,070 helicopters, 1,090 combat planes and 710 of other types.

The main role of the *combat planes* is to carry out isolated bombing raids or give close support to infantry engaged in ground operations. They have committed numerous crimes against the unarmed population of South Vietnam, but their capacity for harm is reduced every day thanks to the progressive improvement of people's defence measures. Against the Liberation armed forces they can only more or less influence combat methods and the length of an engagement, the timing of an attack and disengagement, the manner of gaining mastery of the terrain and mopping up the battlefield without ever preventing them from engaging in large-scale actions to annihilate the enemy by entire battalions or regiments. We can recall that the 10,000 tons of bombs dropped on the Duongminh-chau zone and the 3,000 tons on Boiloi (in Tayninh province) in recent months, resulted in nothing more than "the death of a few persons" (according to the report presented following a control operation by the enemy). The American combat planes and artillery in the battles of Bagia, Vantuong, Thuanninh and above all at Pleime, proved absolutely incapable of saving the American and puppet troops from very serious defeats, to such a point that the enemy "began to doubt the efficiency of air power and artillery" and was astounded at the "endurance and demoniacal combat spirit" of the Liberation troops.

To fight against enemy air-power, apart from protection measures taken by the population and troops, and the political struggle to force the enemy to halt the bombing raids and compensate the victims, crushing blows have rained down on the U.S. Air Force. In 1965 alone, over 900 planes were destroyed in South Vietnam, a great part of them on their own bases. If one adds up the American losses in pilots, technical personnel and planes and compares them with those inflicted on our South Vietnamese people by enemy

°One hour of flight by a B.52 costs $1,053 compared to about $50 for a tactical plane.

planes, then one sees that in many respects the enemy losses are far heavier in this kind of warfare.

In North Vietnam, the enemy bombers and fighters have caused certain losses in men and material and they have interfered with our communications and transport to a certain extent. However as we had foreseen, and as confirmed by the events of last year, the enemy's air-power can neither gain him the victory nor can it sabotage our largely agricultural economy, nor affect our regional industries and handicrafts, nor bring our communications and transport to a halt.

Helicopters play an important role in increasing the mobility of enemy infantry. They only play a limited role in other missions as transports for material, evacuation of wounded, firing platforms, etc. As for the efficacity of helicoptered transport of puppet troops, the fiasco of "helicopter tactics" in American "special warfare" is a sufficient reply to the question.

As for *American ground troops* landed by tens of thousands in South Vietnam, we must appreciate them at their true value in order to face up to them correctly.

It is clear that the massive despatch of U.S. troops to South Vietnam will tend to prolong the war and make it still more fierce, it will result in more difficulties and losses for the South Vietnamese people. But from another viewpoint it is an excellent occasion for us to wipe out large numbers of the enemy's effectives.

In fact, in hurling themselves into the arena to help their puppets, the American troops will only be wiped out themselves. The more their effectives are thrown in, the more the American people will realize the realities of the situation, the more their opposition to Washington's policy of aggression grows in resoluteness, the more the American imperialists' will of aggression will be crushed and they will thus have to accept defeat.

The war history of the U.S.A. testifies to the fact that usually, it is only at the moment of a favourable evolution of affairs that the Americans decide on armed intervention. In the First World War, they waited until the Germans were on the point of being beaten to commit their troops. In the Second World War, it was only after the decisive victories of the Soviet Red Army had brought about the imminent collapse of Hitler's troops that they decided to open a second front in Western Europe. At the same time they hastened to use the A-bomb for prestige reasons when they saw that the Soviet Red Army and the Chinese People's Liberation Army were on the point of wiping out the whole of Japanese troops in Manchuria and North Korea. Over ten years ago in Korea, and more recently in the Congo and the Dominican Republic, the American troops were used either to halt a situation critical for the American imperialists or to bring about changes to their advantage.

Used to subjective calculations, they believed by sending a few hundreds of thousands of troops to South Vietnam and by intensifying their air raids against the D.R.V. that they could bring about changes in their favour, force the South Vietnam Liberation troops on to the defensive, oblige them to go back to isolated guerilla activities and compel the people in the two zones of North and South Vietnam to capitulate. But the circumstances of the massive commitment of American troops in South Vietnam are completely different to the cases cited above. This has not taken place at a moment when the South Vietnamese troops are weak, but at the moment when the puppet army and administration have started serious disintegration, when the setback to "special warfare"—pushed to its highest stage—has been fundamentally completed, when the invincible South Vietnamese people and their armed forces are solidly deploying their forces all over the country, when the revolutionary movement is developing with a vigour hitherto unknown from Quangtri to Camau, in the countryside as in the towns. This is precisely the reason why the Pentagon, from the moment of the arrival of U.S. troops in South Vietnam, has had to order the greater part of these forces to defensive positions.

Apart from the 3rd Brigade of the U.S. 25th Infantry Division, just recently sent to Pleiku, still intact as it has not yet dared to make a single sortie, all other units of the U.S.A. and those of its satellites, have suffered very heavy blows, regardless of their specialty or type of arms. Almost twenty big battles waged by the American troops since their commitment to South Vietnam have proved that the Liberation troops are perfectly capable of beating them.

The latter have employed the most varied tactics and combat methods (sudden attacks against U.S. military bases, active defence at Vantuong, surprise battle at Thuanninh, assault at Nuithanh and Baubang, ambush at Datcuoc, attacking a post and intercepting reinforcements at Pleime, Dongduong, etc.). They have engaged in com-

bat by night and by day, during the rainy season and the dry season, battles of a few hours or continuous month-long actions, actions
in the mountains and forests as well as in the plains and towns, with
the size of units involved varying according to the circumstances.
The brilliant victories of the Liberation armed forces have proved
that the troops and population of South Vietnam are perfectly
capable of defeating American troops under any circumstances
whatsoever.

One can better appreciate this in an evaluation of some American
ground units.

The 1st Airmobile Cavalry Division, a new-type unit, the best
equipped and the most mobile, was beaten at Pleime, where it fled,
abandoning its dead, by the Liberation troops moving simply on
foot. From this, it is clear that if the "helicopter tactics" worked
out years ago could not save the puppet troops, that of the U.S.
1st Airmobile Cavalry Division has shown itself just as incapable
of saving American troops who have come from afar to the forests
and mountains of South Vietnam, the topography of which they are
not acquainted with, and whose combat spirit is in no way superior
to that of the puppets.

The most modern equipment cannot secure for them mobility
equal to that of the South Vietnamese troops and people nor prepare them for the degree of combativity of the latter who are
fighting for a revolutionary ideal, who are in constant readiness to
fight on the spot, who are present everywhere by an immense network of regional and guerilla troops, possessed of strong points
worthy of battle-hardened regular troops, ready to pounce on the
enemy at any moment. That is the real situation, illustrated by
the reality of the South Vietnam theatre of operations.

The U.S. First Infantry Division, trained for conventional operations without any ideal for which to fight, highly motorized but
in fact no more mobile than the puppets when it comes to moving,
operating in a country and terrain with which they are unfamiliar,
with deplorably low morale, has shown itself incapable of standing
up to the invincible Liberation armed forces. In the recent battles
at Baubang and Nhamat, the units of the 1st Infantry Division taking part were sliced into sections in the first minutes by the assault
teams of the Liberation forces and were wiped out within a few
hours.

Rocking on its heels after several crushing defeats, this division is still asking itself what it has to do to avoid being outmanœuvred and to avoid further defeats. It hesitates between several alternatives: Keep to the defensive and dig in in fortified bases, only carry out sorties when conditions are such that they can be absolutely certain of not being defeated, avoid in any attack to get engaged with a force of equal size, keep a respectable distance from the Liberation forces in case of an engagement so they can call on planes and artillery. Unfortunately for the 1st Division, the Liberation forces have the habit of hitting the enemy under all conditions, whether he is on the defensive or goes over to the attack. They know how to fight in the appropriate manner according to the size of the enemy's force, "grabbing him by the belt" to deal him blows and prevent him from keeping at a distance. This spirit and style of fighting is summed up in the following slogan: "Seek out the Yankees to Wipe Them Out, Pursue the Puppets To Hit Them".

The U.S. *Parachute Brigades* have hardly had occasion to use their parachute tactics having understood after their misadventure at Thuanninh that they can only be successful against an easily impressionate adversary whose rear is not very secure. In South Vietnam however, wherever they descend from the sky, they find a hostile terrain. They are received everywhere by guerillas, by spiked trenches and by regular troops who hit them in force before they get into action, pinning them to the ground to wipe them out. This is why parachute operations, scarcely before they have been tried out in Vietnam, have already become an outdated tactics. The U.S. parachute units, at present, rarely jump—they have got used to being transported by helicopters or to using their own legs for an occasional surprise attack. The parachutists are even less effective in combat than the other American specialized units.

The U.S. *Marines* were sent to South Vietnam as one whole division plus one brigade. Today they are only employed to guard military bases along the coast. According to American military practice their mission should be to effect landings and for rapid assaults against islands and coastlines, securing the latter for infantry landings. In South Vietnam however, the whole of the coastline is a theatre of operations for the guerillas. After their defeat at Vantuong, the marines were reduced to guarding the bases along the coastline and to patrol the immediate surrounding areas. And yet, it is very rare for them to acquit themselves well of this mission. All the bases that they have been entrusted to protect have been attacked from inside, held in the pincers of the guerillas and brought under fire by snipers from outside. From time to time the marines launch attacks of a defensive nature outside their bases but each time they have suffered heavy losses.

The so-called logistic bases which serve the aggression against the southern part of our country are all established in the coastal regions of Central and Southern Trungbo°.

Because of the fact that they have to come from thousands of kilometres to undertake their aggression and wage a war dependent on an enormous quantity of supplies coming from their own country (they have no industrial rear at the approaches to our country as formerly they had the Japanese springboard in their aggression against Korea), the American imperialists have found it necessary to establish a whole network of military and supply bases on the spot. The strategic value of their bases in South Vietnam is therefore essentially that of logistics. As they include also airfields the latter are so often attacked that the Pentagon thinks that it may be necessary in the future to count mainly on floating airfields, for greater security.

As the main value of these bases derives from their role in logistics, they have the capital defect that they cannot be properly defended, despite the presence of 34,000 troops stationed to protect Danang, 10,000 more at Chulai, etc. Confronted with such a resourceful, courageous, mobile and ever-present enemy as the South Vietnamese Liberation armed forces, the military and logistic bases will never be able to be guaranteed security.

If therefore these bases regularly suffer heavy losses, to the point where they can no longer satisfy the needs of an ever-growing number of American troops, nor supply the hundreds of thousands of puppets, deprived of local supplies, seeing that the roads needed to transport equipment and other supplies from the coastal bases to the interior are almost all cut, nobody can estimate the difficulties of the enemy's logistics system in the future. Nobody can believe, given these conditions, that the affirmation of the American imperialists, according to which they are capable of fighting on for decades in South Vietnam with a battle corps of 500,000—700,000 or a million troops, is a well founded opinion.

To sum up, in examining the fundamental reasons of our certain

°Central Vietnam.

victory and the inevitable defeat of the enemy, and in examining closely the arms and services of the American and puppet forces, we see still more clearly the solid basis which enables us to march ahead towards complete victory.

Our Entire People Are United to Overcome All Difficulties in View of Greater Victories

We are aware of the American imperialists' and their stooges' intention and capacities in South Vietnam. We have assessed their war efforts as well as the concrete strong and weak points of their arms and services. At the same time we have clearly seen the capacities and factors of success of the army and people in both parts of our country. *It is obvious that the prospect of great successes and of the final victory are widely opened up before us.*

However, the American imperialists will step up war efforts to cling to the South and pursue sabotage activities in the North. Now that they lavishly produce feats of skill to make people believe in their "good will" and "peace efforts", they are actually preparing to increase the 1966 budget for the war in Vietnam to over 13 billion dollars, that is, more than three times that of last year and nearly half of the total expenditure for the three-year war in Korea. They are dispatching more brigades to South Vietnam, spraying toxic chemicals and using poison gases there on an unprecedented scale. They are continuing to bomb and strafe North Vietnam, even more frenziedly than before. Our people in both zones supported by the socialist camp and the peace- and justice-loving people the world over, will unswervingly carry on their sacred resistance to defeat the aggressors and the traitors. Therefore, *the war will be fiercer in both zones.*

If the American imperialists double or treble their war efforts, we must multiply ours tenfold in the South as well as in the North. Realizing clearly the enemy's nature and intention we should not harbour any illusion about him.

We are determined to defend and build the North at all costs, ensure communications and transport, and see to the increase of production in whatever situation. On the other hand, we strive to rely mainly on our own strength while winning over greater support from the socialist camp and the world people to strengthen the defence potential of the North to the highest degree possible.

We are ready to endure all hardships and sacrifices and calmly face any measure of destruction that the enemy may cause to us.

We are ready unstintedly to support our Southern compatriots' heroic struggle with a view to defeating the American aggressors and their stooges, liberating the South, defending the North, advancing towards the reunification of our country. U.S. and satellite troops have invaded South Vietnam and are massacring our compatriots there. In the North, U.S. Air Force is sowing devastation and death by bombing and strafing. Many American citizens have committed self-burning in protest against the war of aggression and support our just struggle. Many of our friends abroad have volunteered to fight on our side. The sacred duty of us all, Vietnamese patriots, is not to recoil before any sacrifice to drive out the aggressors, save our homes and our fellow-countrymen.

In the new situation, our urgent task demands of us a revolutionary spirit, utmost combativeness, a very high sense of organization and discipline and a style of work suitable to the war conditions. Each of us must give the full measure of his energy, his strength and his abilities to defeating the U.S. aggressor. Each of us must fully apply President Ho Chi Minh's words: "fulfil whatever task, overcome whatever difficulty and defeat whatever enemy".

We are waging a great patriotic war. Our revolution is the condensed picture of the world revolution at present: national liberation, building and defence of socialism, contribution to the safeguard of world peace and the speeding up of the revolutionary struggle of the world people. We are fighting with arms in hands against a most cruel enemy of mankind—U.S. imperialism.

Glory belongs to our people. Final victory will be ours. From North to South, shoulder to shoulder, our entire people and army are determined to do their utmost to defeat the U.S. aggressors.

NOTES AND SOURCES

NOTES—CHAPTER TWO

[1] Zbigniew Brzezinski, "The Soviet Political System—Transformation or Degeneration?" *Problems of Communism* (January–February, 1966).

[2] Giorgio Galli, "Bureaucracy Under Fire," *Problems of Communism*, (September–October, 1966).

[3] Robert Conquest, "Immobilism and Decay," *Problems of Communism* (September–October, 1966).

[4] New China News Agency *(NCNA)*, August 15, 1963.

[5] Bernard B. Fall, "Tribulations of a Party Line: The French Communists and Indo-China," *Foreign Affairs* (April, 1955), p. 499.

[6] Ellen Hammer, *The Struggle for Indochina* (Stanford, California: The Stanford University Press, 1954), pp. 297–298.

[7] Ho, however, did not seek diplomatic recognition until late in the anti-French War. On the contrary, aware of the great distance separating Vietnam from the Soviet Union and of Soviet reluctance to become embroiled there, he vainly sought American recognition and a United Nations seat.

[8] Harold Isaacs, *No Peace for Asia* (New York: The Macmillan Company, 1947), pp. 173–177.

[9] Hammer, *op. cit.*, p. 201.

[10] Isaacs, *op. cit.*, p. 174.

[11] Marshall Shulman, *Stalin's Foreign Policy Reappraised* (Cambridge, Massachusetts: Harvard University Press, 1963), pp. 13–17.

[12] Even then, there was apparently no military aid to speak of. Bernard Fall notes that if the Soviet Union over the past decade had given North Vietnam the kind of modern military equipment it supplied to East Europe, this would have greatly helped to protect North Vietnam from United States bombing. See Bernard B. Fall, "North Vietnam: A Profile," *Problems of Communism* (July–August, 1965), p. 24.

[13] See Donald Lancaster, *The Emancipation of French Indochina* (New York: Oxford University Press, 1961), pp. 336–37.

[14] Philippe Devillers and Jean Lacouture, *La fin d'une guerre*, cited in Bernard B. Fall, *Viet-nam Witness: 1953–1966* (New York: Frederick A. Praeger, 1966), p. 75.

[15] See Douglas Pike, *Viet Cong* (Cambridge, Massachusetts: The Massachusetts Institute of Technology Press, 1966), especially p. 52.

[16] See P. J. Honey, *Communism in North Vietnam* (Cambridge, Massachusetts: The Massachusetts Institute of Technology Press, 1963), p. 49. Soviet economic aid to North Vietnam totaled about 350 million dollars in the decade following Geneva—most of it after 1957. Chinese aid amounted to approximately 450 million dollars in this period—the great bulk of it in the years immediately after the Geneva conference. See Albert Parry, "Soviet Aid to Vietnam," *The Reporter* (January 12, 1967), p. 32. During the 1954–1964 decade, about 2,300 Soviet technical experts worked in North Vietnam.

[17] Arthur Dommen, *Conflict in Laos: The Politics of Neutralization* (New York: Frederick A. Praeger, 1964), p. 178.

[18] *Pravda* (July 7, 1964).

[19] Warning of the dangers of an enlarged war, *Pravda* noted that ". . . the aggressive actions of the USA in the Gulf of Tonkin . . . led to a dangerous intensification of the already tense situation in Southeast Asia. . . ." *Pravda* (August 8, 1964).

[20] Hanoi has consistently shied away from United Nations intervention in the war.

[21] *Peking Review* (September 18, 1964), p. 17. See also *Ibid.* (September 4, 1964), p. 7.

[22] See *The New York Times* (December 6, 1966), and Mario Rossi, "U Thant and Vietnam: The Untold Story," *New York Review of Books* (November 17, 1966), pp. 8–13. Washington maintained that a secret meeting would harm the morale of the Saigon government.

[23] The other members of the delegation were I. V. Andropov, Central Committee Secretary; Ye. P. Loginov, Minister of Civil Aviation, and I. S. Scherbakov, Soviet Ambassador to North Vietnam.

[24] *Pravda* (February 11, 1965).

[25] Jean Lacouture, *Vietnam Between Two Truces* (New York: Random House, 1966).

[26] Lacouture, *op. cit.*, p. 233.

[27] See, for example, *Nhan Dan* (January 27, 1965): ". . . as the Vietnamese saying goes, the dike will break if heavily pressed by the flood. The greater the pressure, the bigger the explosion." Also, the day before Pleiku, Pham Van Dong told a reception for Kosygin that "U.S. imperialists, under repeated attacks from many directions, continue to

weaken" and seek hopelessly to "prolong their last days." Thus, it is "all the more imperative" to step up the revolutionary struggle.

[28] Soviet caution was reflected in the difference between Russian and Chinese reaction to the United States bombing. Moscow said it was "compelled to adopt . . . new measures to . . . strengthen the defensive capacity of the DRV. Nobody should doubt that . . . the Soviet people will fulfill their internationalist duty. . . ." Peking, on the other hand, said "Aggression by the United States against the DRV means aggression against China. The 650 million Chinese people will definitely not stand idly by. . . ." Although the *people* rather than the *Party* or *Government* were mentioned in this context, the Chinese statement was still much stronger than the Soviet.

[29] See *Pravda* (February 9, 1965).

[30] *Vietnamese News Agency (VNA)* (February 11, 1965).

[31] Speech to Hanoi rally. See *VNA* and *TASS* (February 7, 1965).

[32] *New York Herald Tribune* (February 12, 1965).

[33] Such efforts were noted by several correspondents in Paris.

[34] *Peking Review* (November 12, 1965). See especially pp. 15–17.

[35] *Newsweek* (April 5, 1965), p. 36.

[36] For text of communiqué, see *Pravda* and *Izvestia* (March 10, 1965).

[37] *Washington Post* (April 20, 1965).

[38] See London *Observer* (November 14, 1965).

[39] For full text of Soviet-North Vietnamese communiqué, see *Pravda* (April 18, 1965).

[40] *New York Times* (April 1, 1966).

[41] See analysis by Ermath, *Radio Free Europe (RFE)* (January 21, 1966).

[42] See "Vietnamese Maintain Pragmatic Attitude," *RFE* (July 19, 1965).

[43] See *Pravda* and *Izvestia* (August 28, 1965).

[44] *New Times* (September 8, 1965).

[45] *New York Times* (May 12, 1966).

[46] *Asian Notes* (September 5, 1966).

[47] For these figures, taken from the Soviet foreign trade journal, *Vneshnyaya Torgovlya, USSR*, see "Soviet Trade With the Communist Countries of Asia: 1965," *RFE* (October 10, 1966).

[48] *New York Times* (January 9, 1966).

[49] *Zeri i Popullit* (December 30, 1965).

[50] *Washington Post* (April 1, 1966).

[51] *Pravda* (January 10, 1966).

[52] *Ibid.* (January 12, 1966).

[53] See especially speech on January 9th by Tran Duy Hung, Mayor of Hanoi, quoted in *VNA* (January 10, 1966).

[54] *VNA* (January 10, 1966).

[55] *New Times* (February 9, 1966), pp. 13–14. The Chinese were quick to seize on this statement as new evidence of Soviet "betrayal" of the NLF.

[56] *Red Star* (January 12, 1966).

[57] *Peking Review* (May 6, 1966) pp. 25–26. Reproduced in Appendix.

[58] *Ibid.*

[59] *Ibid.* In fact, the Soviet Union has been sending more and more supplies via the 7,500-mile sea lanes from East Europe to Vietnam because of Chinese obstruction of overland and air routes. China itself participates in the sea traffic to North Vietnam but not nearly to the extent that Russia does.

[60] *New York Times* (July 12, 1966).

[61] *Ibid.* (July 2, 1966).

[62] *Izvestia* (June 23, 1966).

[63] *New York Times* (July 10, 1966).

[64] *Pravda* (July 19, 1966).

[65] *New York Times* (July 17, 1966).

[66] Nicholas Turner, "The Soviet Stake in Vietnam," *Far Eastern Economic Review* (October 20, 1966), p. 182.

[67] *Pravda* (August 4, 1966).

[68] *Pravda* and *Izvestia* (August 4, 1966).

[69] *Ibid.*

[70] *New York Times* (October 28, 1966).

[71] *VNA* (October 30, 1966).

[72] *Radio Moscow* (October 28, 1966).

[73] *Agence France-Presse* from Karachi (November 3, 1966).

[74] *New York Times* (October 30, 1966).

[75] Significantly, while the first press release on the speech quoted Zhivkov as saying conditions were "ripe" for an international conference, subsequent releases reported him as saying conditions were "becoming ripe."

[76] *New York Times* (November 20, 1966).

[77] *Pravda* (November 14, 1966).

[78] *New York Times* (November 15, 1966).

[79] In mid-December Western intelligence raised its unofficial estimate of the number of MIG's in Vietnam to 180 or possibly 200 (see Albert Parry, "Soviet Aid to Vietnam," *The Reporter* [January 12, 1967], p. 31). North Vietnamese aid cadets receive training at the Soviet Air Force school of Bataisk near Rostov-on-Don.

NOTES—CHAPTER THREE

[1] For a perceptive analysis of these issues, see A. Doak Barnett, *China After Mao* (Princeton, New Jersey: Princeton University Press, 1967).

[2] *Peking Review* (August 5, 1966), pp. 8–10.

[3] Peng has been in disgrace ever since.

[4] According to secret exchanges between Moscow and Peking subsequently revealed by Edward Crankshaw in *The Observer* on November 14, 1965, never denied by either party, and publicized by several European Communist parties, the Russians asked Peking to grant them an air corridor and the use of airfields in southern China to help Hanoi. Peking reportedly rejected the proposal; see *L'Humanité* (November 16, 1965), *L'Unità* (November 17, 1965), and *Neues Deutschland* editorial (November 20, 1965), cited in Kevin Devlin, *Problems of Communism*, "Which Side Are You On?" (January–February, 1967). Several times in 1965 and 1966, Moscow called for summit meetings and international committees to help coordinate aid to Vietnam, but Peking rejected them all. See, for example, *Trybuna Ludu* editorial (December 3, 1965), which reveals that one united action proposal rejected by Peking advocated a meeting of party and government leaders of Communist states. The Chinese even rejected a compromise proposal for united action that was sponsored by the Japanese Communists and the North Koreans, with the apparent approval of North Vietnam itself.

[5] *Peking Review* (August 5, 1966), pp. 8–10.

[6] The two articles are included in Appendix IV.

[7] See "Refutation of the New Leaders of the CPSU on 'United Action,' " *Peking Review* (November 12, 1965).

[8] *Ibid.*

[9] *Peking Review* (August 6, 1965), pp. 6–16.

[10] *Ibid.* (August 13, 1965), p. 8.

[11] *Ibid.* (August 6, 1965), p. 5.

[12] See, for example, the testimony of Professor John K. Fairbanks before the Senate Foreign Relations Committee, *U.S. Policy With Respect to Mainland China* (U.S. Government Printing Office, 1965), especially pp. 147–150.

[13] Such a view has been stated on several occasions by Secretary of State Dean Rusk.

[14] See the excellent article by Professor Benjamin Schwartz on the inadequacy of "deep" cultural and historical explanations of the Sino-Soviet dispute in "Communist China and the Soviet Bloc" in *The Annals* of the American Academy of Political and Social Science (September, 1963), edited by D. Zagoria, pp. 38–49.

[15] For a recent perceptive analysis of Chinese foreign policy, see Harold Hinton, *Communist China in World Politics* (New York: Houghton Mifflin Company, 1966).

[16] See their RAND analysis, *Lin Piao on "People's War: China Takes a Second Look at Vietnam,"* (RM–4814–PR, November 1965, The RAND Corporation, Santa Monica, California).

[17] For a full text of Lin Piao, see *Long Live the Victory of People's War* (Peking Foreign Languages Press, 1966).

[18] *Ibid.*

[19] *Ibid.*

[20] *Ibid.*

[21] *Ibid.*

[22] Victor Zorza first pinpointed their significance in *The Manchester Guardian* (September 1 and 2, 1966). Zorza was also the first journalist to have recognized the Sino-Soviet split in its infancy.

[23] *Hoc Tap* (July, 1966).

[24] *Long Live the Victory of People's War.*

[25] *Ibid.*

[26] *Ibid.*

[27] *Ibid.*

[28] *Peking Review* (September 3, 1965), p. 3.

[29] *Ibid.* (August 5, 1966), p. 9.

[30] See "Challenge and Control," by Daniel Tretiak in *Far Eastern Economic Review* (October 27, 1966), p. 216–221.

[31] *Peking Review* (October 8, 1965), p. 14.

[32] *People's Daily* (January 1, 1966), p. 8.

[33] *Ibid.* (April 8, 1966), p. 8.

[34] *Peking Review* (May 13, 1966), p. 5.

[35] *Ibid.* (June 11, 1965), pp. 10–20.

[36] *Ibid.* (July 30, 1965), pp. 8–10.

[37] *Ibid.*

[38] See *Ibid.* (May 27, 1966), pp. 5–18.

[39] See *Ibid.* (June 17, 1966), pp. 7–13.

[40] See their article "New Tensions in Army-Party Relations in China, 1965–1966," in *The China Quarterly* (April–June, 1966).

[41] *Liberation Army Daily* (May 25, 1965).

[42] These remarks were cited by the Polish party newspaper *Trybuna Ludu*. See *Information Bulletin Number 83*, p. 60, issued by *World Marxist Review*.

[43] *Ibid.*

[44] *New York Times* (November 28, 1966), p. 1.

[45] *Ibid.*

NOTES—CHAPTER FOUR

[1] For the details of the North Vietnamese land-reform campaign, see Hoang Van Chi, *From Colonialism to Communism* (New York: Frederick A. Praeger, 1964).

[2] I was told this by an Indian diplomat who was at the time a member of the ICC.

[3] See Philippe Devillers, "The Struggle for the Unification of Vietnam," *China Quarterly*, (Jan.–Mar. 1962), p. 9.

[4] *Ibid.*

[5] For the details of Voroshilov's trip to Hanoi and Ho's tour of Eastern Europe in 1957, as well as the increase in Soviet aid to Hanoi in that year, see P. J. Honey, *Communism in North Vietnam* (Cambridge, Massachusetts, Massachusetts Institute of Technology Press, 1963), Chapter III.

[6] There is agreement among those specialists who follow North Vietnamese developments that, of the eleven members of the Hanoi Politburo, Truong Chinh, Nguyen Chi Thanh, Le Duc Tho, and Nguyen Duy Trinh have tended to be more militant and to lean more toward China, while Vo Nguyen Giap, Pham Van Dong, and Pham Hung have been more moderate and leaned more toward Russia. There is some dispute on the positions of Le Duan, Le Thanh Nghi, and Hoang Van Hoan. Duan, to this observer, seems to be a centrist. If one assumes that Ho Chi Minh himself seeks to balance the two tendencies, it would seem that there is a fairly even balance between "hawks" and "doves" in Hanoi. As indicated, however, these positions change in accord with changing circumstances. For more detailed information on factionalism, see Joseph Kun, "Factionalism in North Vietnam," *RFE* (March 14, 1966), and P. J. Honey, "Understanding Hanoi," *China News Analysis (CNA)*, (January 14, 1966).

[7] "On the Socialist Revolution in Vietnam," Volume I (Hanoi: Foreign Languages Publishing House *(FLPH)*, 1965).

[8]*Third National Congress of the Vietnam Workers' Party*, Documents, Volume 1, (Hanoi: FLPH, undated) pp. 23–215.

[9]*Ibid.*, Documents, Volume 3, p. 77.

[10]*Ibid.*, p. 54.

[11]*Ibid.*, p. 52.

[12]The Polish delegate to the ICC indicated this to me in a conversation in Saigon in October 1963.

[13]See speech of Le Duan, March, 1963, "Hold High the Revolutionary Banner of Creative Marxism, Lead our Revolution to Complete Victory," reprinted by Peking: *FLPH*, 1964.

[14]Speech by Liu Shao-Chi at the Higher Party School in Hanoi on May 15, 1963. See *Joint Statement of Chairman Liu Shao Chi and President Ho Chi Minh* (Peking: FLPH, 1963), p. 33.

[15]Nguyen Chi Thanh, "Who Will Win in South Vietnam?" (Peking: *FLPH*, 1963), p. 9.

[16]*Ibid.*

[17]See "Peace or Violence," *Hoc Tap* (September, 1963), republished by Peking: *FLPH*, 1963.

[18]Le Duan, "Some Questions Concerning the International Tasks of Our Party," (Peking: *FLPH*, 1964).

[19]*VNA*, April 25, 1966.

[20]For evidence that the PRP is the southern branch of the Lao Dong Party in the North, see Department of State, *Aggression From the North*, February, 1965, particularly the captured document in Appendix G on page 57. See also *The Communist Party of South Vietnam*, United States Mission in Vietnam (March, 1966); Douglas Pike, *Vietcong* (Cambridge, Massachusetts: Massachusetts Institute of Technology Press, 1966), pp. 136–145; *Studies on Vietnam*, Information Handbook, Number 1 of 1965, Department of External Affairs, Canberra, Australia, August, 1965.

[21]For stimulating my thoughts on the differences between Northern and Southern communism, I am indebted to Professor I. Milton Sachs of Brandeis University, who lectured on this question at Columbia University in the winter of 1966–1967. Professor Sachs is at work on a history of the Vietnamese nationalist movement which will undoubtedly shed much light on this question. His essay, "Marxism in Vietnam" in *Marxism in Southeast Asia* (Stanford, California: Stanford University Press, 1959), edited by Frank Trager, is indispensable for the background of Vietnamese communism.

[22]Pike, *op. cit.*, p. 48.

[23]*Ibid.*

[24]For biographies of the NLF leaders, see *Ibid.*, Appendix D.

[25]On Tran Nam Trung, see *Ibid.*, p. 433.

[26]See Pike, "How Strong IS the NLF?" *The Reporter* (February 24, 1966), p. 21.

[27]*Ibid.*

[28]*The Communist Party of South Vietnam.*

[29]For more on COSVN, see Pike, *op. cit.*, p. 137n.

[30]Vinh has written a number of articles in the past two years indicating important shifts in the line or explicating the North Vietnamese position on the war. See, for example, his important article in *Vietnam Courier* (September 27, 1965) in which he outlined Hanoi's position on negotiations. He also wrote one of the first authoritative articles assessing the effect of the entry of American ground troops on the war; see *Hoc Tap* (February, 1966). The article was titled "The Vietnamese People on the Road to Victory" and was published in English by the Hanoi FLPH in 1966.

[31]For an interesting explanation of the reasons the PRP was set up in 1962, see Joseph Starobin, "An Alternative for Vietnam," *New Leader* (July 18, 1966).

[32]For differences between Hanoi and the NLF on a series of tactical questions, see Pike, *Viet Cong*. Also see the interesting account of Hanoi-NLF differences by Lee Lockwood, a recent visitor to North Vietnam, in the April 7, 1967, issue of *Life*. See also the account of Lockwood's reportage in the *New York Times*, April 4, 1967.

[33]See Phat's statement of January 20, 1967. I am indebted to John McDermott, editor of *Viet Report*, for calling this to my attention.

[34]*VNA* (April 13, 1965).

[35]Ho Chi Minh, *VNA* (July 19, 1965).

[36]Ho Chi Minh in a letter to Linus Pauling, *VNA* (November 20, 1965).

[37]See, for example, Ho Chi Minh's interview with the able French writer Philippe Devillers, *VNA* (August 15, 1965).

[38]Cited in Franz Schurmann *et al.*, *The Politics of Escalation* (New York: Fawcett Publications, 1966), p. 98.

[39]Article by Nguyen Van Vinh, *Vietnam Courier* (September 27, 1965).

[40]*New York Times* (January 4, 1967).

[41]Vinh, *Vietnam Courier* (September 27, 1965).

[42]See DRV Foreign Ministry statement, September 23, 1965.

[43]*Nhan Dan* (August 23, 1965).

[44]Vinh, *Vietnam Courier* (September 27, 1965).

NOTES—CHAPTER FIVE

[1]See, for example, the article by General Vinh, "The Vietnamese People on the Road to Victory," in the February issue of *Hoc Tap*.

[2]April 1967.

[3]*Hoc Tap*, February 1966.

POETS CHAPTER FIVE

INDEX